MR & MRS R. S. SHORTELL
CHAPEL COTTAGE
MELLIS ROAD
YAXLEY, EYE
SUFFOLK IP23 8DB
Telephone: 0379-783612

GRAINGER'S
Worcester Porcelain

HENRY SANDON
British Pottery and Porcelain
Worcester Porcelain 1751–1793
Royal Worcester Porcelain
Coffee Pots and Teapots
Flight and Barr Worcester Porcelain

JOHN SANDON
English Porcelain of the 18th and 19th Centuries

JOHN SANDON, LAWRENCE BRANYAN AND
NEAL FRENCH
Worcester Blue and White Porcelain

HENRY, JOHN, AND DAVID SANDON
Sandon Guide to Royal Worcester Figures

GRAINGER'S
Worcester Porcelain

HENRY AND JOHN SANDON

BARRIE & JENKINS
LONDON

First published in Great Britain in 1989 by
Barrie & Jenkins Ltd
289 Westbourne Grove, London W11 2QA

British Library Cataloguing in Publication Data
Sandon, Henry
    Grainger's Worcester porcelain.
    1. Worcester porcelain. Grainger, 1807-1902
    I. Title II. Sandon, John
    738.2'7

    ISBN 0-7126-2052-4

Designed by Carol McCleeve
Typeset by SX Composing
Printed and bound in Portugal by Printer Portuguesa

CONTENTS

Dedicated to
GEOFFREY GODDEN

INTRODUCTION

During the twenty-five years that we have been researching into the Grainger factory two facts have become obvious. The first is that so much of the previously published information was very inaccurate. When one considers that the factory is relatively recent, it is staggering to find that it has taken until 1988 and the publication of Geoffrey Godden's *Encyclopaedia of British Porcelain Manufacturers* to correct these errors briefly. The second fact is that so much Grainger porcelain was of very high quality. Although positive ascription has always been very difficult, as so few of the early wares were marked, there is a growing awareness that, at their best, Grainger should be placed among the top manufactories of the nineteenth century.

A full and accurate history of this fine factory has proven to be a very difficult task, bedevilled by previously published inaccuracies and a relative dearth of records. Certain indispensable documents have survived to make an almost impossible task somewhat easier. First among these are the records that still survive at the Worcester Royal Porcelain Company, such primary materials as most of the pattern books, a quantity of copper printing plates, and a wage book. We are most grateful for the kindness of the Company directors in allowing us access to these, for permission to give a list of these patterns and illustrations of some, also for the assistance and skill of Edward Taylor, the foreman engraver, in discovering and making pulls of the coppers. These records must have been brought from the Grainger factory, before it was finally sold in 1902, by someone with the foresightedness of R. W. Binns or Eli and John Haywood. Our thanks to their memories.

The second most important source of records are the family wills and factory documents that have been made freely available by members of the family and the present owners of the leases of the factory site. Our grateful thanks for this invaluable assistance, and it is comforting to know that the Grainger descendants still take such an interest in the firm's history.

Third, as important as the other two sources, is the work that we have been able to do on the factory site when developments have taken place. In 1967, Heenan & Froude, the Worcester engineering company who own half of Grainger's old factory and now use it as a training centre, dug a deep trench across the site and we were allowed to follow this, clean up the trench, and collect the wasters. Wasters are unfinished broken sherds, proof positive that those pieces were made at the factory and of great importance in identifying finished shapes and patterns by comparison. These wasters are deposited at the Dyson Perrins Museum, and though not great in number were sufficiently interesting for us to hope for another and greater chance of excavation. Perhaps the most illuminating aspect of the first trench was the finding of an early kiln base, measured and drawn for us by Peter Ewence, designer at the Worcester Royal Porcelain Company, suggesting that the earliest period of production was centred on the Pheasant Street corner of St Martin's Gate.

Then in 1987–8 a major road development was carried out by Worcester Corporation, rebuilding and enlarging Pheasant Street and constructing a roundabout in St Martin's Gate, just outside the old factory, to provide a relief link between Lowesmoor and the City Walls Road. This involved a corner of Grainger's site being removed and a new wall construction undertaken, so a good deal of digging was needed and we were able to recover a great quantity of wasters, including a most important group from the earliest periods of the factory. Great help in this was provided by our families, by Ian and Margaret McMillan, and by the staff of the Worcester City Museum Service. Our thanks to them all.

Many others have helped with information and research. Henry Sandon's predecessor as Curator of the Dyson Perrins Museum, Cyril Shingler, was the first to point out the importance of Grainger and he recorded every bit of information that turned up. We are most grateful to the Trustees of the Perrins Museum and the present Curator, Harry Frost, for permission to photograph pieces from their important and growing collection of Grainger. Jack Collins drew our attention to some interesting notes in the James Ross diaries and notebooks in Birmingham Reference Library. We wish to give thanks to Phillip Miller for his help in tracking down elusive Grainger teapots and similarly to Michael Berthoud for assistance in researching the teawares. Collectors, auctioneers, museum officials, and antique dealers without number have passed on details and information as well as many key illustrations and have frequently pressed our noses back to the grindstone to ensure that this book was completed. Other photographs have been specially taken for us over the years by John and Joan Beckerley in Worcester and Chris Halton in London. We thank them for their patience and good work.

A special word of thanks to Henry Sandon's wife Barbara, who, as well as typing so much of the manuscript, has washed hundredweights of wasters and then had them all over the house. As a sideline on the problems of coping with these wasters, one morning a new dustman by mistake took two large boxfuls of wasters that had been cleaned and sorted and temporarily stored in the porch. There followed a scene worthy of the Keystone Cops as we followed the dustcart to the infill site at Lower Moor and, helped by the very concerned dustmen, managed to rescue most of the wasters from their covering of rubbish. We tell this, partly to show that research has its lighter moments, if only in retrospect, but also to explain to archaeologists of hundreds of years hence why Grainger wasters should be found ten miles away from the manufactory. To make this a truly family production we have had a great amount of help from John Sandon's wife Kristin, who took time off from being a Mum to help with the research and typing.

Finally, we would like to dedicate this book to Geoffrey Godden. He has not only taught us all the value and importance of ceramic research and in making the results available to everyone, but he even dedicated his splendid book on Chamberlain's Worcester to Henry Sandon. So it is only right to dedicate our present book to him, in gratitude, admiration, and friendship.

Henry Sandon and John Sandon

CHAPTER ONE

HISTORY OF THE
GRAINGER FACTORY AND FAMILY

George Grainger was apprenticed in August 1767 to Samuel Bradley, one of the partners of the Worcester Porcelain Company, which had been founded by Dr John Wall and his fourteen partners in 1751. As a painter presumably he worked alongside Robert Chamberlain, who later became an independent decorator and then started his own rival manufactory in the Diglis area of Worcester, on the other side of the Cathedral from Dr Wall's Warmstry House factory, in about 1786.

George Grainger married Robert Chamberlain's daughter Sarah on 30 March 1777 in the church of St Peter the Great, close to where Chamberlain was to have his decorating establishment and later to found his factory. Although one might have expected this union to foster a business relationship between two ceramic painting talents, it does not seem as though George was ever considered as a partner in the new venture.

Five children were born to George Grainger and Sarah Chamberlain, although the first two died within a year or two of birth, not a particularly remarkable figure in those days of high infant mortality. Nor was it unusual to reassign a favoured family Christian name to a subsequent child, as when their third child, born in 1781, was given the same name as little Sarah who had died the previous year. After all, Sarah was the name of her mother and she is likely to have been one of the favourite grandchildren of Robert Chamberlain, along with her younger brother Thomas. Although Robert Chamberlain had some seventeen or eighteen grandchildren when he died in 1798, it is interesting that he left bequests to only two of them, young Sarah and Thomas Grainger. We are grateful to Dr Sonia Parkinson for providing and commenting on the relevant details of Robert Chamberlain's will, which he signed and sealed on 13 July 1798, with a codicil of 8 December 1798: 'I give and bequeath to my Two Grandchildren Sarah Grainger and Thomas Grainger Ten Guineas a piece to be paid to them and each of them within Six Months after the decease of my said wife, and if either of them shall happen to die before she or he shall have attained the age of twenty one years it is my will that the legacy of her or him so dying shall be paid to the survivor. . .'

There are a number of reasons why these two grandchildren should have been thus singled out. Robert may just have liked them better than the others , but it is more likely that as their father had died in 1797 and their mother had remarried Benjamin Crane between then and Robert's death, he felt that they needed some special treatment. It is certain that young Thomas Grainger was apprenticed to Robert Chamberlain Senior, Robert Chamberlain Junior, and Humphrey Chamberlain in 1798 and his name appears in the accounts books in 1803 going on business journeys for his uncle. He must have been regarded highly by this time and on 9 September 1805 was admitted Freeman and Citizen of Worcester, indicating that he must have completed his apprenticeship. The granting of the rights of a Freeman and Citizen of the city gave parliamentary voting rights, which was of great use to the owner of a factory with a large number of employees, who would be more than likely to vote the way of their master, since the ballot was not secret at that time.

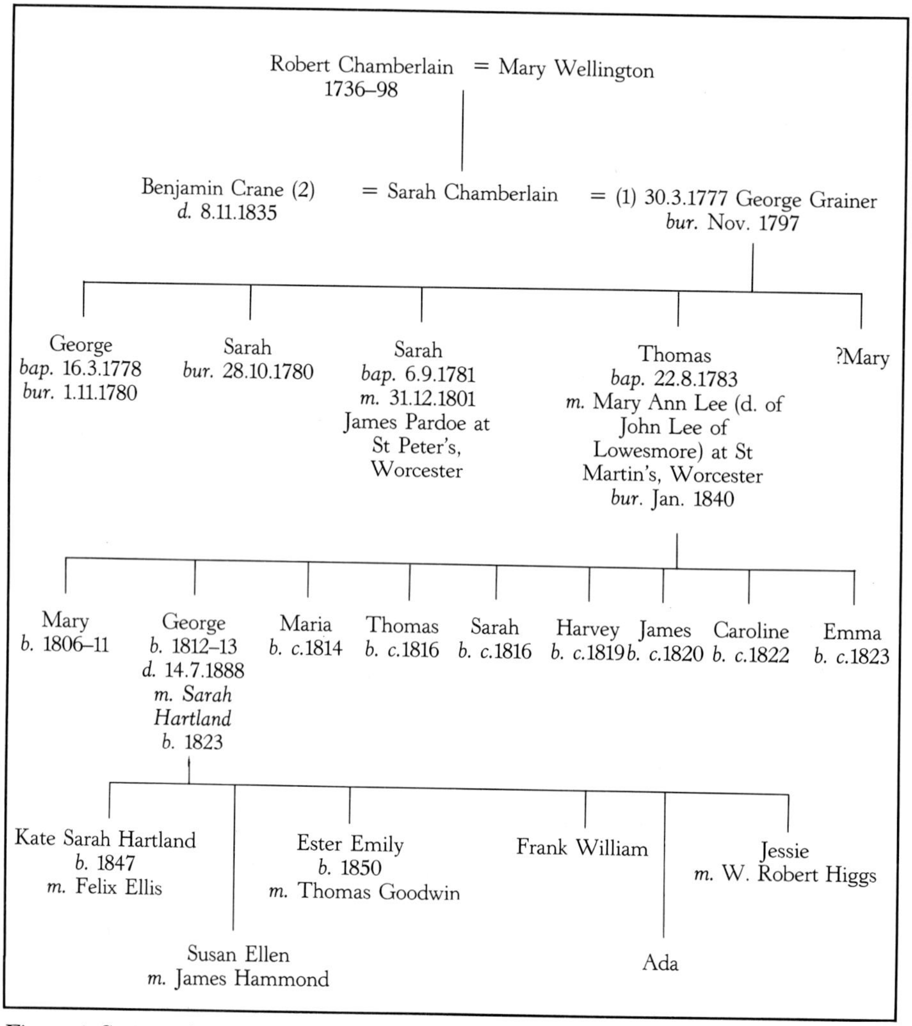

Figure 1. *Grainger family tree covering the main ceramic-working members of the family. (We are grateful to Mrs Caroline Sherlock, a descendant of Robert Chamberlain, for the production of this tree.)*

12

A complication arises in that there was another Thomas Grainger active in Worcester at that period, the son of yet another Thomas Grainger, who is referred to as a Drawing Master in a listing in 1759. In 1790 he was living in New Street (Grundy's Directory) and in 1794 in Fish Street (Worcester Index) and James Ross notes that 'on Tuesday August 4th 1812 Died Mr. Thomas Grainger Drawing Master of Worcester aged 69', which would make his year of birth 1742/3. During the years 1788 to 1804 a Thomas Grainger, sometimes referred to as Thomas Grainger Senior, is noted as buying wares from Chamberlain, perhaps to redecorate and sell, and on 29 March 1790 a Thomas Grainger, first-born son of Thomas Grainger, was admitted Freeman of Worcester. He was undoubtedly the son of the Thomas Grainger, drawing master, and not 'our' Thomas Grainger, who would not have been old enough to be a Freeman at that date. These Thomas Graingers, father and son, have caused complications in sorting out the history of the Grainger porcelain factory, but we hope to have now put the record straight.

Returning to 'our' Thomas Grainger, we have to consider the date when he started up his own porcelain factory, in the Blockhouse area of Worcester. It has long been held that the factory was formed in 1801, and this date was proudly incorporated in the factory mark from the 1890s, but this was probably a date conjured out of the air. There is no surviving record of the firm before 1808, when it is listed in the *History of Worcester* as Grainger, Wood & Wilkins in Lowesmore. R. W. Binns, the respected historian and art director of the Worcester Royal Porcelain Company, gave that year as the founding of the factory. The firm could not have been established while Thomas Grainger was an apprentice at Chamberlain and certainly not until he became a Freeman of the City in September 1805. Recently a most important mug has turned up, marked under the base 'Grainger & Co. Worcester, Sepr. 26. 1807' (Colour Plate I) and if this can be taken as the date the piece was made, which from the style and quality seems correct, then we have the latest date that the firm could have started. So somewhere between September 1805 and September 1807 the firm was founded.

Thomas Grainger's two original partners were John Wood and Stephen Wilkins. Wood had been a highly-paid painter at Chamberlain and presumably left at the same time as Thomas Grainger with the intention of setting up their own porcelain works. Stephen Wilkins was not a potter, but a vinegar merchant who owned land in Lowesmore and St Martin's Gate. Vinegar-making was an important Worcester industry in the nineteenth and twentieth centuries and a huge vinegar works was established along Pheasant Street, between St Martin's Gate and Lowesmore. To explain the relationship between Lowesmore and St Martin's Gate we have given a sketch in Fig. 2.

It has been suggested that John Wood remained on at the factory as a painter after he ceased to be a partner in 1811, for a J. Wood is mentioned several times in the pattern books and the foreman painter in the 1820s, according to William Evans, was 'The Late Mr. John Wood' (see p. 20). This painter's speciality was flowers, yet we know that at Chamberlain, the original John Wood was a landscape artist. We therefore very much doubt that the John Wood of the pattern books is the same as the original partner in the factory. We have proof that the original partner was in fact the John Wood later listed as a drawing master in Worcester. He died 7 March 1851 and his interest in the Grainger land leases was finally signed over to George Grainger in 1852.

An early reference to the factory site is contained in a lease dated 20 May 1807 which reads:

All that piece of ground called or known by the name of Pheasant Meadow formerly in the tenure or occupation of Thomas Huxley but now and for some time past of the said Stephen Wilkins containing by admeasurement exclusive of all the fences six acres and two perches . . . Sold by Stephen Wilkins of St. Martins, Vinegar Merchant and William Morton of Worcester, Malster; to John Rayment of the City of Worcester, Apothecary.

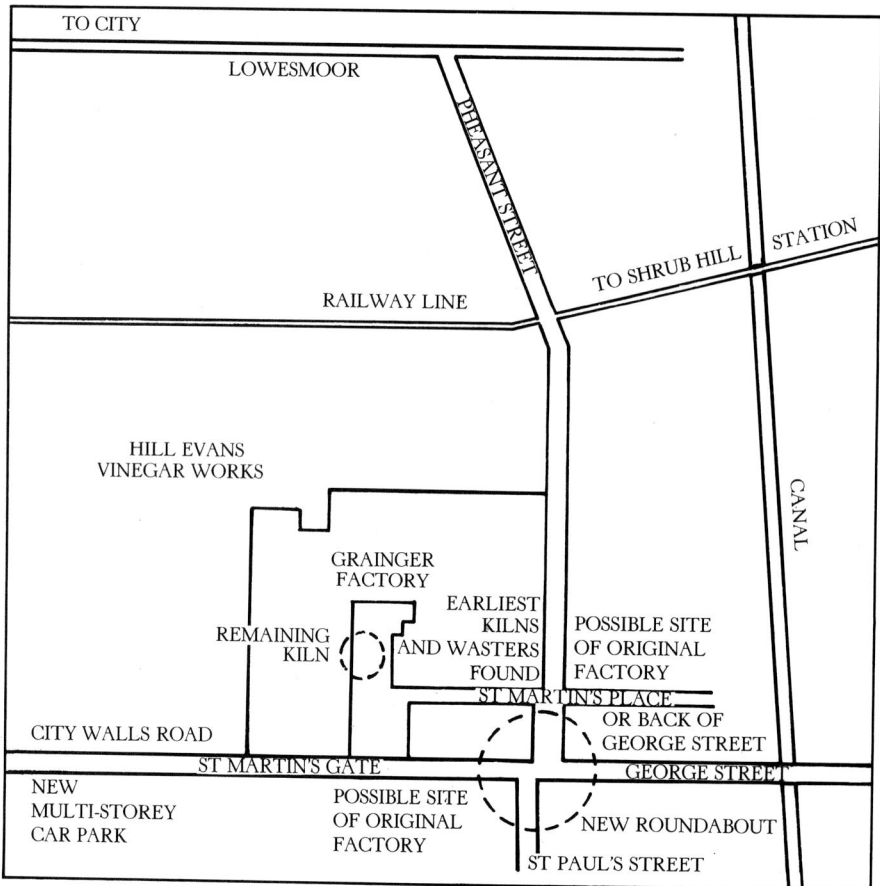

Figure 2. *A map showing the probable location of the original factory site in relation to the existing buildings (not to scale).*

Since the Grainger factory was to occupy only about one acre, it is likely that Stephen Wilkins owned the whole block of land between Lowesmore and St Martin's Gate. This lay outside and to the east of the old town walls, in an area that was being rapidly developed for industrial purposes and the driving through of the Birmingham Worcester canal in the 1810s made it even more desirable. In Victorian times major factories were producing carriages and trains there.

Grainger's first factory seems to have concentrated on teawares of a type of body and shape very similar to Coalport and Chamberlain Worcester. Geoffrey Godden, in his *Encyclopaedia of British Porcelain Manufacturers*, makes a strong case for the earliest production being decoration of blanks bought from Coalport. Coalport specialized in providing white wares to independent decorators at the beginning of the nineteenth century. Godden illustrates a tea service in the United States, marked inside the cover of the teapot 'Grainger & Co. Worcester, no. 135'. This would be of a hybrid hard paste and is of the 'Old Oval' shape which looks very like Coalport and could well be so, but neither Godden nor we have been able to see the actual pieces. We did not find any wasters of the Old Oval shape on the factory site, but considerable quantities of biscuit wasters of 'New Oval' shape and spiral fluted wares were found and it seems likely that these were the earliest productions.

Certainly, by September 1807 when the first dated Grainger mug was produced, the firm was able to make wares of quality and competence, decorated with great skill. Perhaps some of this decoration was done by the two ceramic-trained partners, Thomas Grainger and John Wood, or else they had trained others or enticed skilled craftsmen away from Flight and Chamberlain. All must have looked rosy, when a disastrous fire destroyed the factory on 25 April 1809. As the *Worcester Herald* reported on 29 April:

FIRE AT THE GRAINGER WORKS

On Wednesday evening last, about 11 o'clock, a fire broke out in the China Manufactory of Messrs. Grainger Wood & Co. situate in Losemore in this City. In a very short time assistance was zealously rendered by the inhabitants, and the 36th Regiment assembled to protect the property. Engines arrived at the spot without delay, and no means were left untried to subdue the element; but all efforts unhappily proved insufficient, and at one o'clock, these spacious premises became a heap of ruins. The most strenuous endeavours of the neighbours to preserve any part of the valuable effects were likewise abortive; and they had the regret and mortification to witness the entire destruction of every article connected with the manufactory. The property was insured in the Birmingham Fire Office, but we are sorry to find, by no means equal to the amount of the loss sustained. One of the firemen belonging to the Worcester Fire Office had his leg broken, owing to the fall of part of the roof and was immediately taken to the infirmary. We have not heard of any other accident.

A disaster such as this might well have destroyed Thomas Grainger's hopes but, phoenix-like, he rose quickly from the ashes with the insurance money and a loan of nearly £1,000 from local businessmen. In June 1809 Grainger and Wood leased new land in St Martin's Gate and built a new works.

Part of the lease is here quoted:

Lease of land and Tenements 23rd June 1809 between John Tymbs, printer and stationer; and Thomas Grainger china painter and John Wood china painter; and Robert Vellers, silk mercer [assignee of Ambrose St John for the Corporation of the City of Worcester] . . . to let to John Tymbs all those tenements and a stable, two gardens and a piece of pasture land late a garden on which had lately been erected 16 new tenements and other buildings and lately used as a vinegar yard situate and being at a place called Clapgate in parish of St. Martins in Worcester which said pasture ground is encompassed round about by a great ditch and which said premises have the said piece of pasture ground on the east a garden in the possession of the late John Batty on the west a late bowling green called Morris's bowling green on the north and the road leading from Clapgate to Tallow Hill on the south parts thereof . . . On the south west corner of said premises had been lately erected by Miss Elizabeth Stephens the owner of acttefsuage on the west side thereof part of the said messuage then formerly occupied by Edward Tipton and were then in the tenure of occupation of the said John Tymbs, further leased to Grainger and Wood for 40 years at cost of £945. Thomas Grainger and John Wood not being able to pay the whole of the said purchase money have applied to Robert Vellers to advance and lend them the £940.

What all this means is not very clear, and what Wilkins's role in the enterprise was, or when he left it, are matters that we have been unable to resolve. In June 1818 Charles Tearn was admitted Freeman of Worcester after apprenticeship to 'Thomas Grainger, John Wood and James Wilkins'. Either this is an error for Stephen, or James, probably a relation, was another partner in 1811/12.

A lot of white ware must have survived the fire and we found a fine jug some years ago (Plate 75) inscribed and dated 'Manufactured by Messrs. Grainger and Co. Worcester, May 1809', only a month after the fire, perhaps decorated as a present for one of the new financial backers, or even for the injured fireman. It is possible that some part of the old factory could be used to decorate wares until the new factory was opened. This we cannot know, but a fair amount of early tewares must have been produced in the hybrid hard-paste body, the teapots and sugar boxes normally being marked in script, inside the covers 'Grainger Wood and Co Worcester', or 'Grainger and Co Worcester'. In addition, the word 'Warranted' was sometimes added under the teapot cover, denoting, as Chamberlain had done, that the ware was warranted not to crack by the use of hot liquids. The Grainger body was well fired and evenly glazed, with a slightly glossy appearance, but in all other respects indistinguishable from the wares of Coalport and very similar to Chamberlain and other makers.

James Ross in his diary mentions the next happening of interest: 'October 13th 1810: Grainger's China Factory Bell put up'. From this note you can almost hear the bell clanging across the St Martin's Gate area, calling the workers into the newly-opened factory. The year before, in August 1809, Thomas Grainger had married Mary Anne Lee, daughter of John Lee, a glove manufacturer. The firm continued as Grainger Wood & Co. until the partnership was dissolved on 7 March 1811, when John Wood withdrew. Geoffrey Godden quotes the notice from the *London Gazette* of 12 March 1811 in his *Encyclopaedia of British Porcelain Manufacturers*:

Notice is hereby given that the Partnership between Thomas Grainger, John Wood, Benjamin Crane and James Pardoe of the City of Worcester, China Manufacturers, trading under the firm of Grainger Wood and Co. is this day dissolved by mutual consent, the said John Wood having withdrawn himself from said Copartnership concern, the same will in future be carried on by us Thomas Grainger, John Lee, Benjamin Crane and James Pardoe under the firm of Thomas Grainger & Co.

As witness our hands this 7th day of March 1811. Thomas Grainger, John Wood, John Lee, Thomas Pardoe, Benjamin Crane.

It is somewhat difficult to be sure of the sequence of factory marks used during the years up to March 1811. Both 'Grainger Wood and Co' and 'Grainger and Co' seem to be used and we have not so far found any piece marked Grainger Wood and Wilkins – perhaps this seemed too much of a mouthful. One teapot is known with an incised script G under the base. The position is not helped by a section in Laird's *Worcestershire*, published in 1810 which describes the three porcelain factories in Worcester, but there are so many confusing references that not a lot can be taken on face value. For instance, he calls the main factory 'Flight, Barr and Flight', when that combination of names had never been used and they should have been termed Barr, Flight and Barr between 1804 and 1813. Referring to the other two factories, Laird says that the retail shop of Chamberlain 'is at No 59 High Street, the property of Messrs Grainger Wood & Wilkins'. We have not been able to clear up these problems and if any readers can throw light upon them we would be most grateful.

So the firm traded as 'Thomas Grainger & Co.' or 'Grainger & Co.' between March 1811 and October 1814 and marks on pieces should coincide. In October 1814 the firm officially became Grainger Lee & Co. and this mark is used in script form under the cover of teapots, and often under plates and on the growing number of ornamental pieces such as vases. As the *London Gazette* states:

Notice is hereby given that the Partnership lately subsisting between Thomas Grainger, John Lee, James Pardoe and Benjamin Crane of the City of Worcester, China Manufacturers, trading under the firm of Grainger & Co. was this day dissolved by mutual consent as far as related to the said James Pardoe and Benjamin Crane and John Lee. The Business will in future be carried out in all its branches by the said Thomas Grainger and James Lee, son of the said John Lee . . .

As witness our hands the 10th day of October 1814. Thomas Grainger, John Lee, James Pardoe, Benjamin Crane, James Lee.

James Lee was a financial backer not a potter. He has sometimes been confused with his father, but the sequence of events has been made clear by Geoffrey Godden's researches.

During the period between 1811 and 1814 an important new change took place in the porcelain body used at Grainger. Just as New Hall and Coalport succeeded to a bone china recipe in about 1814 and by 1820 respectively, Grainger changed over to a completely different formula. The change, sadly, was not one for the better. Presumably the supply of raw materials for the hybrid body dried up, and while a larger factory could prepare for such a change and perfect a suitable alternative, Grainger seems to have been thrown into the position of having to make a rapid substitution.

The teaware shape which spanned the turn-over was the 'London' shape which is generally accepted as having become popular from 1812. Grainger made fine London-shaped teawares in the hybrid body and so it must have remained in production until then. A scallop-rimmed version printed with the Broseley pattern is illustrated in Plate 14 and is marked Grainger & Co. Worcester, indicating a date before October 1814. This is in a bone china body and, as no marked pieces of Grainger Lee & Co. are known in the hybrid body, the change to bone china must have taken place between 1812 and 1814.

The situation is further complicated by the fact that Grainger apparently used two different pattern number sequences in this period. In the introduction to the pattern lists in Appendix 7, we explain our reasons for thinking that the early pattern numbers were duplicated in different pattern books. This can make dating according to pattern numbers very tricky indeed.

The quality of potting evident from the fine handles of hybrid-paste London-shaped cups clearly could not be maintained in the inferior china. The examples we have seen are thick, with particularly clumsy handles, and the heavy glaze tends to be uneven, masking much of the modelling. There was little real improvement until the 1820s, and while some early examples can be well-glazed and remain white without crazing, the poorer pieces must have been a considerable embarrassment to the factory.

A further change has been discovered by Geoffrey Godden in the pages of the *London Gazette* regarding the partnership:

Notice is hereby given that the Partnership subsisting between Thomas Grainger, James Lee and Joseph Gillam in the City of Worcester Porcelain Manufacturers trading under the firm of Thomas Grainger & Co. was dissolved by mutual consent so far as respects the said Joseph Gillam on the 1st day of January 1817.

As witness the hands of the Parties the 26th day of April 1817. Thomas Grainger, Jos. Gillam, James Lee.

Joseph Gillam was, presumably, of the Gillam family who were closely involved with the Flight and Barr families of the main Worcester Porcelain manufactory and in Henry Sandon's *Flight and Barr Worcester Porcelain* are many references to the Gillams, and marriages between the Gillams and the Flights. It is interesting to find this constant linking between the three Worcester porcelain manufactories of Flight and Barr, Chamberlain, and Grainger, but competition between them must have been intense and family blood almost certainly spilt. Grainger were not averse to copying shapes and patterns of the other factories, and Geoffrey Godden has pointed out that Chamberlain was copying Grainger patterns, as listed in the full Chamberlain pattern list in *Chamberlains-Worcester Porcelain*:

636 Grainger's 302 enamelled gold edge and ring £3: 3: 0:
638 Grainger's 972, green leaf border etc. coloured (not gilt) edge £1: 14: 6:
640 Grainger's 930, enamelled & gold boss border of purple red etc. £5: 5: 0:

A year lease was drawn up on 20 May 1818 between John Rayment, Apothecary and Stephen Wilkins, merchant on one part and Thomas Grainger and James Lee, china manufacturers and co-partners. The lease was 'for all that parcel of land being part of a certain meadow, called the Pheasant Meadow in the possession of Grainger & Lee'. On 1 October 1818 a mortgage bond for £1,000 was drawn by Grainger Lee to Hannah Moore of St John's, Worcester, widow, connected with an agreement of the same date to purchase land drawn up between Thomas Grainger and James Lee and an extended group of Hannah Moore, John Rayment, apothecary, Stephen Wilkins, merchant, Samuel Wall (a trustee), Anthony Lechmere, William Wall, and Elias Isaac, bankers, Edwin Lee, glover, and William Welles (a trustee).

On 9 September 1828 there was a transfer from George Woakes as executor of the late Hannah Haynes, widow, formerly Hannah Moore, widow of Joseph Moore, by direction of Thomas Grainger and James Lee, China Manufacturers to William Nevill Vincett. On 29 December 1829 the mortgage was transferred from William Vincett by direction of Messrs Grainger and Lee to Messrs Yapp and Barnesley, trustees of E. Knife and George Hope.

It appears that the Grainger factory was still known as Grainger & Co. for some trading purposes after Grainger Lee & Co. had become the official title, as Geoffrey Godden notes references in the Chamberlain account book, the 'Journal Wholesale and Retail', from 2 March 1824 to 30 June 1826.

10 March 1824 Grainger & Co.
16 March 1825 Grainger Lee & Co.
23 January 1826 Thomas Grainger & Co.
21 April 1826 Grainger & Co.
1 May 1826 Grainger Lee & Co.

Of course, in a town as small as Worcester, the title of a firm for book entry purposes would not be very important. Much more important was the paying of the account and there would naturally be a fair amount of business done between the firms. If someone orders an odd piece of a shape you do not have, it makes sense to buy it from the rival manufactory rather than go to the expense and time of making a one-off yourself. We think it likely that after 1814 the usual mark on Grainger porcelain is 'Grainger Lee & Co. Worcester', but a lot of Grainger was not being name-marked and pattern numbers are often the only way of sure ascription. Grainger & Co. does not appear to have been used as a mark after 1814, until it was revived in the 1850s.

It is worth stressing at this point that two factory marks which are often thought to be Grainger are not. One class of wares dating from the 1820s is marked in script, 'New China Works, Worcester', and another group of porcelains in the style of the early 1830s is often seen marked with just the script word 'Worcester' and a pattern number. None of these agree with definite Grainger shapes and pattern numbers, and it is likely that they are the work of outside decorators in Worcester, perhaps someone such as Conningsby Norris (see p. 175).

The wares of the Grainger Lee & Co. period from 1814 to 1837 are generally of good quality, even though the bone china body often produced a fair amount of sugary crazing and staining. Gilding and painting continued to be of fine quality and the gilding tended to have a reddish tinge, which gave a rich effect. Thomas Grainger seems to have kept a very personal control on the production and the Dyson Perrins Museum possesses an interesting plaster model for a relief-moulded saucer which is incised 'Engraved by Thomas Grainger, March 10th 1818'.

The important acquisition of David Evans, the fine floral artist, from Swansea in about 1819 led to a growing quality of production as his influence was felt by the other painters. The pattern books mention a number of patterns specifically intended to be painted by David Evans himself and his work must have been greatly admired by his colleagues. Many years later an interesting account of the factory was published in the *Pottery Gazette* of February 1887, written by William Evans, David Evans's son. This was reprinted in the *Worcestershire Advertiser* on 19 February 1887:

OLD TIMES AT WORCESTER PORCELAIN WORKS

The Pottery Gazette contains the following which will be of interest to Worcester: When I was a boy, there were three first-class potteries in the ancient city of Worcester – Flight, Barr and Barr's, Chamberlain's and Grainger and Lee's, at the latter of which I served my apprenticeship as a decorator and gilder. I well remember the Japan pattern placed in my hands to commence my novitiate and the shades, used in red. The principal decorating room of the works would accommodate from 20 to 30 hands, over which presided, as foreman, the late Mr. John Wood, a most intelligent and painstaking flower painter, and overlooker of the apprentice workers and journeymen, having under him another flower painter, his brother, Mr. Stanley Wood. A more intelligent body of enamel artists, to be found in one room, it has not been my good fortune to meet with through a long life of

1. A corner of the Grainger factory site today showing the only remaining portion of a bottle kiln left in Worcester. A large number of wasters were found nearby. See also the outline diagram in Figure 2.

labour. They were all intelligent, and worked in harmony together. They were all studious men, and united reading in their general employ, it being their practice to decide upon a book of some interest, and for each to read aloud for a quarter of an hour in the course of the day, or to work for a substitute in the allotted time specified. Joshua Williams was a bird painter; John Daniel, a most excellent gilder; Christopher Walker and George Morgan, landscape painters; Daniel [David] Evans, the finest wild-flower painter in the trade; and the others equally good in their several departments, and all more or less musicians. Amongst these they had a most excellent band, fostered by their young employer, Mr. George Grainger, who took his part on the flute, Mr. Joshua Williams arranging and composing the parts. This band would have its periodical trips to the surrounding villages of the ancient city, and play their instrument from the works to the place of appointment, either up the river or down the river Severn, to "The Ketch", or to "Portobello", with their bowling-greens, the band beating up around the village for a dance on the village-green, putting life and amusement into the whole surrounding neighbourhood, and returning in the evening to the city, and concluding the day's amusement by playing "The Fine Old English Gentleman" opposite the residence and show-rooms of their employer, at the Cross in High-street. Masters and men were always in harmony; and what are now known as lock-outs and turn-outs were seldom or never heard of. Then, as now, the city was famous for its porcelain, the principal London trader being Mr. Mortlock, who had his name on his purchases as the manufacturer of the same. I well recollect the red-letter days when word went round the works "Mortlock is coming" and then the cleaning and the bustle to have all things in order. Those were happy times; and work-men and masters pulled together as one family.

The partnership between Grainger and Lee was dissolved in 1837 when James Lee and his wife Rachel moved away from Worcester. James Lee had probably had little to do with the day to day running of the factory, although he maintained a business interest. In 1852 he lived in Brampton, moving to Pangbourne in Berkshire in 1853. Thomas Grainger continued the business on his own until his death on 28 December 1839. During the two years from 1837 until then the mark Thomas Grainger & Co. was used but as the shapes by this time were very Victorian, the mark should not be confused with the earlier period. In view of Lee's less important role prior to 1837 and the large number of pieces bearing Thomas Grainger's name, we feel it likely that the Thomas Grainger & Co. Worcester mark was used during the latter part of the Grainger Lee & Co. partnership.

After the death of Thomas Grainger the factory was run by his widow Mary Ann and his son George. On 30 March 1843, George bought out his mother's interest and was solely in charge, although some sleeping partners remained. The most important financial backers were Richard Yapp, a Worcester grocer, and Alexander Turner, Esq., of Douglas, Isle of Man. Turner's share was bought by James Penn in 1856 and Penn sold this to George Grainger in April 1877 for £900. A final important partner was George Pearce, a farmer, who seems to have advanced money in 1867. Under George Grainger, the factory moved into a different gear and some interesting innovations are to be seen. The factory introduced parian in 1845 and a vitrified earthenware body which was termed 'semi-porcelain' or 'chemical porcelain' in 1848. This semi-porcelain was opaque but had an attractive porcelain glaze and was reported on in the November 1848 issue of the *Art Journal* in the following words:

... for cleaness and beauty it is nearly equal to porcelain ... it is vitrified throughout and has a sharp, clear fracture when broken, equal to that more expensive ware. It combines the beauty of china with the economy of ordinary earthenware, as its price is little beyond the cost of the latter ... we can confidently recommend this new and beautiful fabric.

A lot of semi-porcelain or chemical porcelain was made for dinner and dessert ware and decorated with expensive patterns, which surprises collectors who expect the mark of 'Chemical Porcelain' under the plate to be associated with cheap patterns. The same body was used for items made for the growing laboratory, chemical, and photographic businesses and Dr Frankland, FRS, commented most favourably on it.

Grainger's semi or chemical porcelain is decidedly the purest and best of English manufacture that has ever come under my observation; to the excellence of which I can bear personal testimony, having used their chemical vessels for a considerable length of time in my own laboratory.

Another testimonial was written by William Herepath, and reproduced on plaques of the semi-porcelain body to be hung in shops (Plate 152), dated 'Bristol Dec. 1st 1849'. It reads:

Sir, – I have now worked for some months with your Semi Porcelain Ware in my Analytical Laboratory, subjecting it not only to the ordinary usage of the place, but to very severe trials, with the view of learning the extent of its qualities, and I feel pleasure in certifying that, for Chemical purposes, it is superior to every article of English Manufacture I have hitherto had in use.

By far the larger amount of these fascinating laboratory and homoeopathic wares were not marked but they are well worth while looking for. The same body was used for pot lids to cover containers of Muroma, a fragrant pomade for the hair, sold through the various shops of Lea & Perrins, the Worcester and Malvern chemists who were later to turn to making Worcestershire sauce. At least one sauce bottle was produced, printed with a view of Cheltenham College and named 'Cheltenham College Sauce'. This strangely-shaped bottle was proven to be Grainger by the existence of the original copper plate among the factory coppers. George Grainger seemed to delight in bringing forward unusual ceramic inventions, including the 'Schlesinger's Patent Hydraulic Ink' with metal fitments; a

'New Improved Bedroom Vase', which guaranteed no smell, no noise, no damp; and the 'Patent Drawing Room Flower Pot'. The latter comprised two cases, the outer one of glazed porcelain could be ornamented to correspond with the dinner or dessert service, the inner case composed of a porous white clay. George Grainger's enquiring mind interestingly went together with musical ability and many of the Grainger workmen were musically inclined as well, able to form their own band to serenade George outside this shop. In his shop he sold Bohemian and French glass, gooseberry bottles and pickling jars, and his own biscuit china figures of girls with ceramic lace, in the German style.

From the 1840s Grainger porcelain tends to be marked much more commonly than before, either with the full name of George Grainger or the impressed letters G G W for George Grainger Worcester and the addition of S P for the semi-porcelain body. However, a lot of teawares still went through unmarked except for the pattern number. Some wares just bear the mark of retailers, such as Mortlock of London, and also found are addresses of the 28 Princess Street, Manchester shop and the Worcester shop and showroom, the address of which was 19 The Foregate. An interesting early photograph exists showing George standing in the doorway of his shop, the front of which is covered with a great frieze of wall tiles, one of the specialities of the factory (see back of jacket).

George Grainger was in the forefront of Worcester civic life. He was a town councillor and later a magistrate and seems to have instilled this sense of responsibility in his family and workmen. Many of the senior employees of the porcelain factory signed a petition to the local board of health asking them to adopt the Public Health Act of 1846. They were headed by Henry Grainger of Chestnut Walk and their addresses are briefly noted, so it may be of use to list them.

Thomas White – Factory Walk	Stanley Wood – York Place
Joseph Brock – Lowesmore	Henry Copson – St John's
John Jones – Park Place	John Hawker – St Paul's Street
William Taylor – London Road	Richard Bowker – Pheasant Row
Henry Taylor – London Road	James Plant – Portland Place
John Partridge – High Timber Street	Walter Bevington – Bath Road
Alfred Plant – Portland Place	Robert Mills – Sidbury
Edwin Baker – Henwick Hill	Thomas Stephenson – Park Place
John Scarratt – Diglis Street	Henry Gummery – Clement Street
Henry Spencer – New Street	William Manison – Park Place

Many of these are famous Worcester porcelain names, showing the thin line that divided potters of Flight, Chamberlain, and Grainger. In the 1840s George Grainger produced three fine services to mark the Mayoralty of William Lewis. These were presented by the citizens of Worcester in gratitude for his successful fight in getting the railway to come through Worcester, which was in danger of being bypassed. Through the efforts of Mayor Lewis, Worcester reaped the benefit of the O W & W, commonly known as the Old Worse and Worse, but in reality the Oxford, Worcester & Wolverhampton Railway. The services are all beautiful and one is of outstanding quality, shown in Colour Plate X, depicting scenes in and around Worcester. The main pedestal comport has a superbly-painted scene of Worcester Guildhall; the tall comports depict Worcester from Diglis, Edgar Tower, Claines Church, and Malvern Abbey; the low comports depict the County Courts, Worcester Cathedral, St Nicholas Church, Worcester Bridge and river, Westwood Park (seat of T. S. Packington), Astley Hall (seat of T. S. Lea), Holt Castle (seat of J. Pickernill), Yew Tree House (seat of F. Rufford); and two comports depict the residence of William Lewis at The Mount, Rainbow Hill, Worcester. The bases are marked 'G. Grainger. Royal Porcelain Works. Worcester'.

It is interesting that George Grainger should have used the Royal title on the Lewis service, and this title appears again in the later Victorian period when Grainger's factory entitled itself the Royal China Works, no doubt to differentiate it from the main Worcester Royal Porcelain Company. As far as we have been able to trace, Grainger never had a Royal Warrant, so perhaps it was just wishful thinking. At the 1851 Great Exhibition, Grainger had an interesting display of parian china and semi-porcelain, particularly concentrating on vessels in the forms of leaves, flowers, and plants. The critic in the *Art-Journal Illustrated Catalogue*, where some jugs and a tea set are illustrated, wrote a review of the Grainger exhibits. The report, reproduced on p. 127, is surprisingly complimentary although production seems to have been rather small.

George Grainger followed up his showing at the 1851 Great Exhibition with a strong display at the International Exhibition of 1862. He presented a fine selection of the splendid pierced parian produced under the supervision of the chief reticulator Alfred Barry and it was described as

perforated with very elegant patterns, and of a very pleasing tint. The design is cut out with a knife when the clay body is about half dry, the outlines of the pieces are very well composed and the general effect is very agreeable and novel, having almost the appearance of pierced embroidery. The material of which it is composed is a modified parian.

In addition, the factory showed

china, chemical porcelain, dinner and dessert services and busts. Specimens are exhibited of Worcester china tea services; the pure chemical porcelain (unequalled for economy and durability) for dinner and dessert services, chemical apparatus, telegraph insulators etc. etc. The exhibitors are also manufacturers of parian busts, perforated vases, toilets and every other variety of ornaments.

In the 1861 Worcester Census the Grainger factory is recorded as being 30 to 40 men and boys and 10 to 12 women and girls. Although a relatively small factory,

2. The site of the Grainger factory photographed in 1988 before a new roundabout was built at the junction of Pheasant Street (right) and St Martin's Gate. Many of the original factory buildings are still standing although the kilns have all gone.

they had been able to capture and hold some of the great names in Worcester ceramics, such as the painters John Stinton senior, his sons John and James Stinton, George Cole, and Edward Locke and his children. A great amount of their late nineteenth-century wares are of fine quality and if we may mention some of our favourites they would include the *pâte-sur-pâte* decoration of Kate Locke, the landscape and bird painting of John and James Stinton, and the perforated wares of Alfred Barry. While Barry's work does not display such complete mastery as that of George Owen of the Worcester Royal Porcelain Company, it is still of very great beauty and skill.

George Grainger died on 14 July 1888 and his passing was sincerely mourned in the City of Worcester. The local paper gave a long tribute and we quote it in full, as it shows the many things that had endeared him to the populace.

THE LATE MR. GEORGE GRAINGER

We regret to state that Mr. George Grainger died on Saturday at his residence, the Foregate. He was 76 years of age, and had been in failing health for a long time. He was the oldest master potter in the country. During all his life his name had been connected with the porcelain manufactory of which he was the head, and in the conduct of which he succeeded his father, Mr. Thomas Grainger. The business was established in the second year of the century, and the deceased gentleman applied himself to it with constant assiduity and worthy pride. Such relaxation as he allowed himself was somewhat notable in middle age, when he gratified the love of sport which is common to most Englishmen by a keen interest in coursing. He was one of the principal supporters of the defunct Worcester Coursing Society, and for some time its president. He kept greyhounds himself, and at one time was fairly successful with his entries. As age advanced, this pursuit gave place to a taste for horticulture, and Mr Grainger became a well-known exhibitor at local shows. In 1856 he entered the Town Council as a representative of Claines Ward, and held his seat until 1864. After two years absence from the Council he was elected for St. Nicholas Ward in 1866, and finally retired in 1873. In 1878 he was placed upon the roll of magistrates for the city, and continued to serve the public in that capacity until illness prevented his further attendance at the Court.

At the City Police Court, on Monday, Ald. Barnett, in referring to the loss the Bench had sustained in the death of Mr. G. Grainger, said: He was an aged man, but he had up to a short time ago led a very active life, not only as a public man, but in the business which he had conducted in the city. Mr. Grainger was well-known almost everywhere, and he was well respected by his fellow-citizens, but nowhere more so than among his employees. He had spent a great many years as head of a large manufactory; and the beautiful work on which he was engaged had much increased under his management. The many beautiful articles produced by his firm were produced mainly owing to the active energy of the late Mr. Grainger. Mr. Grainger was an old school-fellow of mine, and I believe that I am now the only one left out of a large school. Since that time we have been great friends. Up to the very last Mr. Grainger took every opportunity of attending to his magisterial duties, and whenever he attended, his judgement was combined with great soundness, and he always looked to the merciful side. Mr. Grainger had a true and noble heart, and his fellow-magistrates will very much miss him. Alderman Barnett asked Mr. Halford to address a letter of condolence from the magistrates to the family of the deceased, conveying an expression of the loss which had fallen upon them. He was also sure that the legal gentlemen practising in that Court would miss a good heart. Mr. Grainger had been a magistrate for upwards of ten years, and on two or three occasions he had been a member of the Corporation. But for his retiring disposition he would have been elected to a higher office, and he possessed that retiring disposition to the last. The Mayor had expressed his regret to him at being unable to be present.

Mr. Tree, on behalf of the legal profession, heartily concurred in the remarks which had fallen from the Chairman. He was certain that nothing but illness prevented Mr. Grainger from attending so frequently of late. He himself was always very much struck with one trait in his character – his extreme leniency to all offenders that were brought before him, and he could say that he treated every one with the greatest respect.

At the City Police Court, today, a letter was read by Mr. Halford, deputy Magistrates' Clerk, from Mr. F. W. Grainger, acknowledging the references made by Ald. Barnett to the death of his father, also the many expressions of sympathy from his brother magistrates and other citizens.

The year before he died, George Grainger had taken his son Frank William Grainger into full partnership, on 20 August 1887. George Grainger's will was proved at Worcester on 22 September 1888 by Sarah, his widow, Frank William Grainger, his son, and Walter Robert Higgs. It showed a gross amount of personal estate of £3,235 17s (net £1,662 2s 6d) and virtually everything was left to his family, the remaining shares in the business going to Frank William Grainger. Frank does not seem to have had his heart in the business and the following year he sold it to the Worcester Porcelain Company. In the conveyance from Frank

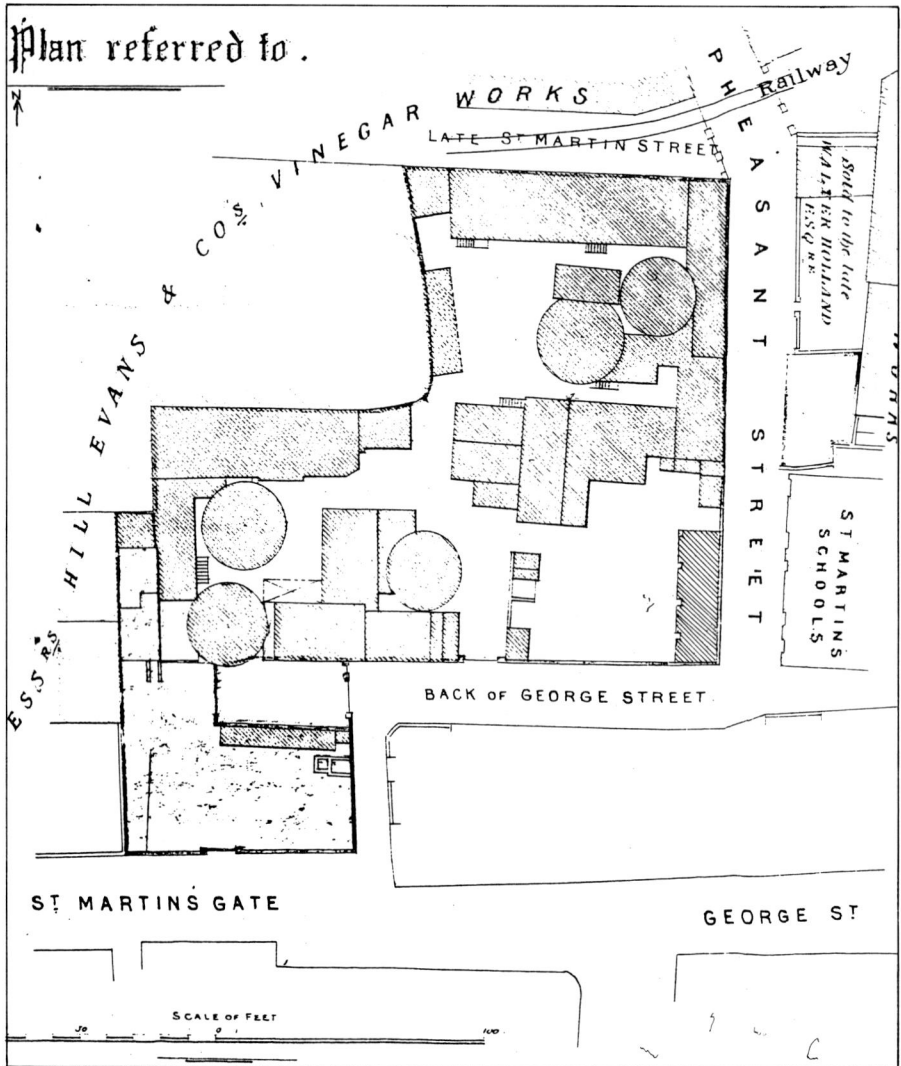

Figure 3. *A plan of the Grainger Porcelain Works prepared for a conveyance dated 20 March 1889, transferring ownership to The Worcester Royal Porcelain Works.*

William Grainger to the Worcester Royal Porcelain Company of 20 March 1889 the factory is described as a 'parcel of land formerly part of a meadow called The Pheasant Meadow and containing two thousand seven hundred and eighty six square yards and all the Factory China Works warehouses workshops hovels and other buildings erected on the said land and situate lying and being in or near Lowesmoor in the parish of St. Martins.' A number of the family went to Canada where they founded a township called Grainger.

Although owned by Royal Worcester, the Grainger works were allowed to keep their own identity and operated completely separately from the parent factory. Wares from 1889 were marked with a shield, inside of which were 'G. Grainger & Co. established 1801' and three black pears (the black pear is an old Worcester City emblem). Around the outside of the shield were the words 'Royal China Works Worcester' and from 1891, the word 'England'. Below the word England appears a date code, starting with the letter A for 1891 and reaching L in 1902.

In 1902 the factory was sold in two parcels. Many old factory buildings still survive, most in subdivided tenancies, and include the last surviving part bottle oven kiln in Worcester. Mr Tim Bridges of the City Museum Archaeological Section has made a complete survey of the buildings and the plans may be inspected at The Commandery in Worcester.

In 1967, a major archaeological investigation of the site occurred when pipes were laid across the yard of the present premises. Large numbers of fragments from all the periods of the Grainger factory were uncovered and these are now in the Dyson Perrins Museum. During 1987 and 1988 extensive development in the Blockhouse area of Worcester involved the resurfacing of Pheasant Street and the construction of a new roundabout adjoining the south-east corner of the site. Rescue work, often in appalling weather conditions and under pressure from construction deadlines, enabled us to uncover a most remarkable quantity of factory wasters, including numerous pieces of moulds, trials and one of the original millstones used for crushing raw materials. Processing these finds delayed completion of this book, but in view of the wealth of new information the wasters had brought to light, it was a most justified postponement.

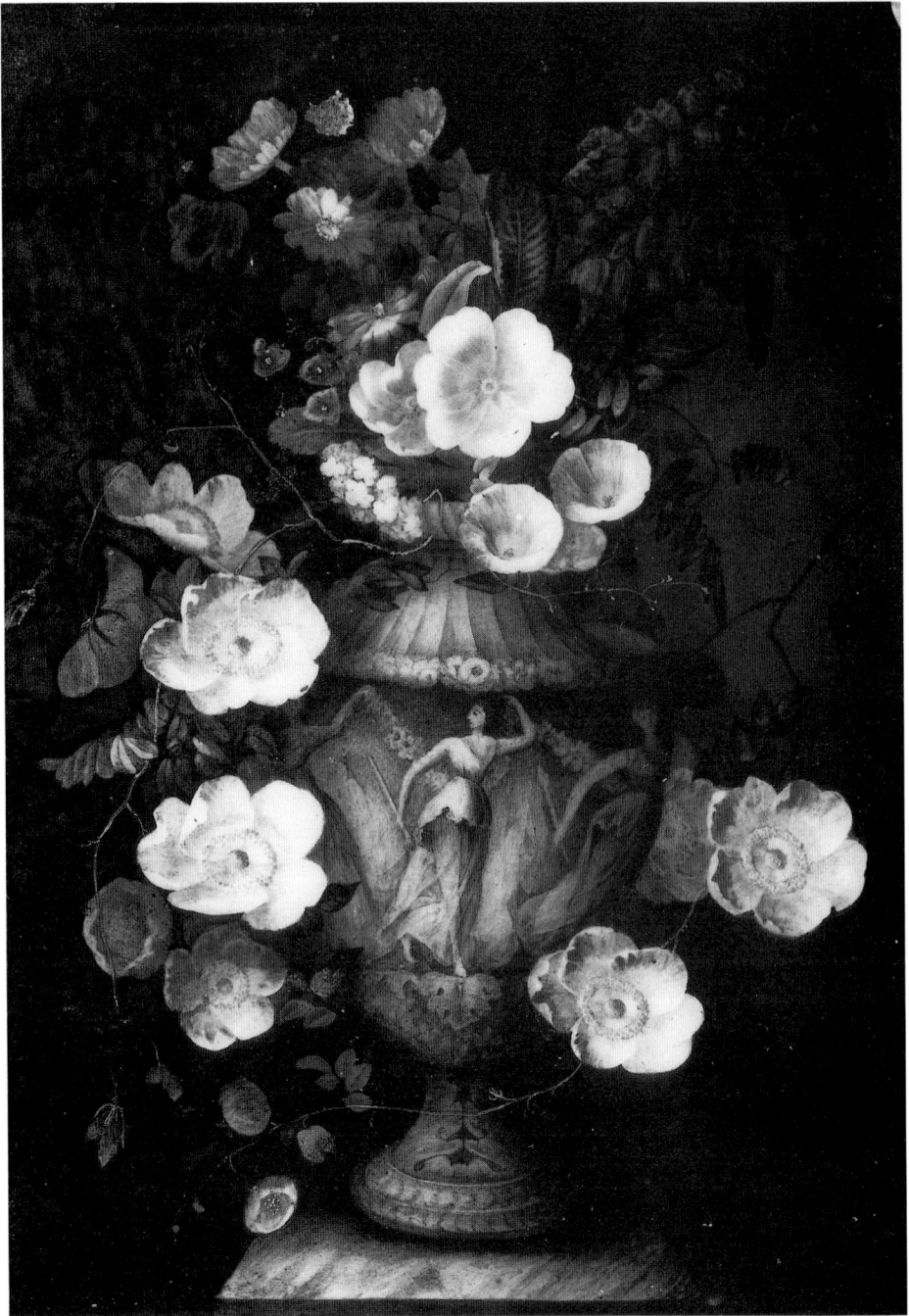

Figure 4. A page from the Art-Journal Illustrated Catalogue of the Crystal Palace Exhibition, 1851. Grainger's ornamental jugs were greatly admired, although the public failed to share the judges' enthusiasm and examples are extremely rare.

CHAPTER TWO

THE FACTORY WORKFORCE

Records relating to the Grainger workforce are virtually non-existent. The only surviving wage records cover the years 1846–51, commencing 21 March 1846. There are occasional references to painters and gilders in the pattern and shape books, and a number of apprenticeship indentures survive as well. Aside from these sources, there is little else to work with from the factory archives. Census, rates, and parish records from the St Paul's Blockhouse area in Worcester have provided invaluable information, as have lists of the Freemen of Worcester. As well as the scarcity of records, the prolific nature of the ceramic industry in Worcester has been a problem. Parish records list many china painters, for example, but never indicate for which factory they worked.

Bearing these difficulties in mind, we have tried to record the names of as many as possible of the Grainger workforce. We hope that new information will eventually come to light to help complete this list.

ASHCROFT: appears in Wages Book, first entry 21 March 1846, last entry 1 April 1848. An Aschcroft painted for Chamberlain *c.*1830–2.

BAKER, EDWIN: signatory to the 1846 Health Board application.

BAINES, HENRY: apprentice indentured 10 January 1872 as a china potter.

BARRY, ALFRED: main reticulator with Grainger, transferring to the Worcester Royal Porcelain Company in 1902, where he worked until 1907 when he was presented with some busts which he had modelled. He lived in Cole Hill and then 35 Stanley Road. His daughter gave a photograph of him to the Dyson Perrins Museum where a great deal of pierced work produced under his direction can be seen (see Plates 179–82).

BEARD: in Wages Book, first entry 21 March 1846, last 24 April 1846. In St Paul's Blockhouse birth records appear John Beard, Tallow Hill, Potter (14 years old in 1846) and George Beard, potter (13 years). A John Beard was at the Coalport factory but is not connected.

BEVINGTON, WALTER: signatory to the 1846 Health Board application.

BIRCH: in Wages Book 7 March 1848 until 20 May 1848.

BLY (or *BLIGH*): some of the Bly family may have worked at Grainger as a number of them lived in the Blockhouse area, for example John Bly and wife Sarah in Carden Street and a son named Jabez. A plaque with a scene of Worcester in a style similar to paintings on Grainger wares has been seen ascribed to Jabez. The Bly family originally came to Worcester from Lowestoft and John Bly senior was a painter at Flight's factory, working on the William IV coronation service.

BODEN, HENRY: in Wages Book, first entry 30 November 1850, appears in the 1851 census living in Tallow Hill, described as a potter, born 1838.

BODEN, HENRY: another Henry Boden was apprenticed to the factory, 18 December 1871.

BODEN, JAMES: apprenticed as a potter at Grainger, 7 September 1840.

BODEN (senior): in Wages Book, first entry 21 March 1848.

BONE (also appears as *BONES*): in Wages Book, first entry 29 May 1847.

BOWKER, RICHARD: signatory to the 1846 Health Board application.

BROCK, JOHN: painter, first entry in Wages Book 28 August 1847, wage between 10/- and 14/-.

BROCK, JOSEPH: painter, first entry in Wages Book 12 June 1847 appearing as Joe Brock. Pattern 2/129 states 'large and small sprig in each compartment, larger sprig centre of saucer and inside cup by Brock', but it is not clear which Brock this is. Geoffrey Godden lists Joseph Brock senior and junior in his *Chamberlains-Worcester*. When Grainger was acquired by the Worcester Royal Porcelain Co. Brock was foreman with the high wage of 44/- per week.

BROWN: in Wages Book 21 March 1846 to 15 August 1846.

BRUNDRETH, A. (also spelt *BRUNDISH*): painter in Wages Book 20 June 1848. 'Ran Away' appears against his name 10 July 1847, the same day as two other apprentices, Wood and Coombs.

BULLOCK, J.: a decorator, pattern 100x has 'fine line by J. Bullock'.

BURY: in Wages Book 21 March 1846 until 14 December 1847.

CALE, FREDERICK: painter, in Wages Book 21 March 1848, admitted Freeman of Worcester 8 June 1830, described as a china painter in the 1851 census living in Pheasant Street.

CASELEY, JOHN: apprenticed as a clerk in the Wholesale Department, date not recorded.

COLE, GEORGE: born 5 February 1863, a fine painter of roses and other flowers on later Grainger wares, transferring to the Worcester Royal Porcelain Co. in 1902. He died in 1912.

COOMBS (or COOMBES): in Wages Book 21 March 1846. 'Ran Away' appears against his name on 10 July 1847, same date as Brundreth and Wood.

COPSON, HENRY: painter, first mentioned in Wages Book 28 December 1847. An Octar H. Copson was a fine painter at the Worcester Royal Porcelain Co. and may have been a son of the Grainger painter.

COPSON, JAMES: painter, first mentioned in the Wages Book 11 November 1848. A James Copson was made a Freeman of Worcester 5 July 1845.

DALLOW: painter, mentioned in the Wages Book 21 March 1846 to 7 November 1846.

DANIEL, CHARLES: painter, first entry in the Wages Book 19 May 1849.

DANIEL, JOHN: in the list of Worcester Freemen in 1834 described as a china painter, apprentice to Thomas Grainger and James Lee. In the 1851 Directory a John Daniel is described as a dealer in china and glass. William Evans refers to him as a most excellent gilder (see p. 22). Patterns 1368 and 99x are ascribed to him. In the Ornamental Shape Book an Albert-shaped basket is described as 'Group of painted flowers in bottom, as dessert ware plants Mr. Daniel, November 27 1840'. Probably refers to John Daniel, rather than William.

DANIEL, WILLIAM: pattern 1431 says 'Wm Daniel done the set'. He was probably the gilder. A mug in the Dyson Perrins Museum, believed to be Grainger, has the gilt inscription 'Harriet Ann Gosling. A birth day gift from her Affectionate Uncle Wm. Daniel'.

DAVIES, ROBERT: apprenticed to Grainger as a painter, 18 July 1836. Admitted Freeman of Worcester 1844, described as a china painter, in Wages Book earning between 10/- and 20/- per week.

DAVIS: mentioned in the Wages Book from 21 March 1846 to 24 October 1846.

DAVIS, THOMAS: apprenticed to Grainger as a painter, 23 January 1860.

DELLY, JAMES: first entry in Wages Book 7 July 1849.

DOVEY, HOWARD: in the list of Freemen of Worcester admitted 24 July 1846, described as a china painter. In the Wages Book from 21 March 1846, left 7 September 1850, 'left work not done' appearing against his name.

DOVEY, THOMAS: admitted Freeman of Worcester in June 1845, in the Wages Book from 21 March 1846. Pattern numbers 1752x, 2/233 and 2/242 are ascribed to T. Dovey.

DOVEY, WILLIAM: painter, first mentioned in the Wages Book 21 March 1846.

EMERY, LILIAN: paintress, appears in a list of paintresses from the Royal China

Works in the apprentices Exhibition of 1892, aged 13, when she had served one third of her time.

EVANS, ALEXANDER: admitted Freeman of Worcester 14 July 1834, he was apparently both a painter and a gilder.

EVANS, DAVID: a superb painter of wild flowers, he worked at the Swansea porcelain works from 1815 until it closed in 1819. He came to Worcester at the same time as Thomas Baxter, but while Baxter joined Chamberlain, David Evans elected to become the most accomplished artist Grainger could have employed. His speciality was wild flowers, and the vase shown in Colour Plate XV is typical of his delicate style. Many patterns are assigned to him (see Plate 165) and three signed plaques, probably on Grainger porcelain, help us to recognize more elaborate groups of flowers in vases which can now be attributed to David Evans.

William Evans, whom we believe to be David's son, writing in 1887 called him 'the finest wild-flower painter in the trade', with certain justification. David Evans later joined Copeland as a painter.

EVANS, GEORGE: apprenticed to George Grainger as a painter, 16 April 1853.

EVANS, JOHN: patterns 1650 and 1772 both list flowers 'by Jno Evans'.

EVANS, WILLIAM: believed to be the son of David Evans, William wrote an interesting account of his early days at the Grainger factory, reproduced in full pp. 20–2. He recalled his earliest work was painting Japan patterns, and pattern 148x is listed as 'Japan Bird by W. Evans'.

FORD: pattern 1573 is called 'Ford's printed pattern'.

FRANCIS: in Wages Book from 21 March 1846.

FRANCIS, GEORGE: in Wages Book from 1 May 1848 until 14 September 1850.

FRANCIS, WILLIAM: in Wages Book from 1 May 1847, probably father of Francis junior.

FRANCIS (junior): in Wages Book from 22 August 1846.

FREEMAN, THOMAS: several patterns are ascribed to Freeman, some painted with flowers, others gilded. Pattern 47x says '1 set done by Thomas Freeman'. It is possible that there was more than one decorator called Freeman at the factory.

GALE (senior): factory thrower when Grainger bought out by Worcester Royal Porcelain Co. in 1889, receiving 47/- per week.

GEORGE: in Wages Book from 10 June 1848.

GIBBS: in Wages Book from 12 September 1846 to 7 April 1849. A George Gibbs was elected as a Freeman of Worcester.

3. A dessert service of the earlier Brunswick shape, reissued with roses painted by George Cole against a shaded ivory ground, the plates 8¾ inches wide, shield marks with date codes for 1894. (Private Collection)

GOODMAN, EDWARD: apprenticed to the factory as a Warehouseman, date not recorded.

GRAINGER, FRANK WILLIAM: owner of the factory at the time of the amalgamation with the Worcester Royal Porcelain Co. in 1889 but does not seem to have been involved in the artistic side.

GRAINGER, GEORGE: son of Thomas, took control of the factory in 1839. Admitted Freeman 14 July 1834. He appears to have done some flower painting as pattern 1601 has 'panels of roses, rose centre, brown leaves by George Grainger'. We have seen a plate fitting this description and if it is by George Grainger he was a competent amateur rather than a skilled china painter.

GRAINGER, THOMAS: founder of the factory and also did some painting and designing. He probably painted for Chamberlain before establishing his own works where he must have played a significant part in overseeing the decoration. His skill may have been as a modeller rather than a painter, as a trial mould preserved at the factory is inscribed 'Engraved by Thos. Grainger Senr November 10 1818'. His son Thomas had been born in about 1816, hence the title senior.

GREEN, (Mrs): pattern 556x is ascribed to Mrs Green.

GREEN, H. J. (junior): painter, in Wages Book from 21 March 1846, probably son of Samuel Green.

GREEN, SAMUEL: painter, listed in the Wages Book from 21 March 1846.

GUMMERY, HENRY: signatory to the 1846 Health Board application.

HANDY: in Wages Book from 7 July 1849.

HARRIS, MARY: apprenticed to Grainger 23 May 1817. Pattern 1449 is ascribed to her; see also pattern 1411.

HATHAWAY, C.: a gilder, see pattern 1543.

HAWKER, JOHN: signatory to the 1846 Health Board application.

HEMMING, WILLIAM: in Wages Book from 21 March 1846; in 1851 census described as a potter living in Clapgate.

HEWITT, MARY: apprenticed to Grainger as a paintress, 15 February 1820.

HEWITT, (Mrs): pattern 1439 mentions bronze sprig done by Mrs Hewitt and patterns 1432–3 lists Mrs Hewitt's flowers. See also pattern 1709. Possibly mother of Mary Hewitt. Godden, in *Chamberlains-Worcester Porcelain*, mentions a Mrs Hewitt as head of the female burnishers, and several other members of the Hewitt family were employed at Chamberlain.

HICK: named in patterns 243x and 245x, possibly connected with printing.

HILL, GEORGE W.: in Wages Book from 21 September 1850.

HODGES: in Wages Book from 21 March 1846; does not appear for three weeks in August 1846 and last entry is 18 May 1850. In parish records, a Samuel Hodges living in Tallow Hill is described as a china manufacturer.

JOHNSON, HENRY E.: in list of painters in Apprenticeship Exhibiton in 1892, aged 16.

JONES: in Wages Book from 21 March 1846. 'To be left out' appears by his name on 9 June 1847, which is his last entry.

JONES, (Mrs): pattern 1494 is neat purple sprigs done by Mrs Jones.

JONES, HENRY: apprenticed as a china potter, 8 July 1852.

JONES, JAMES: in Wages Book from 21 March 1846. Pattern 2/166 is ascribed to Jones.

LANGFORD, SAMUEL: in Wages Book from 28 September 1847; in the 1851 census he is described as a painter living in St Martin's Street.

LEE, JAMES: partner of Thomas Grainger; in list of Freemen described as living in Pheasant Street in 1818. He was probably not a practical potter, although one tea and dessert shape is referred to as 'Mr. Lee's shape', becoming 'Lee's Embossed'. He may well have designed the shapes. For more information see Chapter 1.

LEWIS, MICHAEL: in list of Freemen described as the apprentice of Thomas Grainger and John Lee, 15 June 1818.

LLOYD, JOHN: a John Lloyd is included in a list of Freemen admitted 10 August 1829, where he is described as apprentice to Thomas Grainger and James Lee, now of Coalport, Shropshire. Several patterns are ascribed to a gilder named John Lloyd, such as patterns 717, 1426, 1654, and 1689, gilded 'by Jn. Lloyd'. He seems to have been a senior decorator.

LOCKE, EDWARD (senior): in Wages Book 21 March 1846; last entry 2 April 1847, 'left' appears by his name. Is in list of Freemen 13 July 1835 as a china painter.

LOCKE, EDWARD: (1829–1909) son of above, a fine floral and bird artist; left to form his own factory in 1895, taking his family and Arthur and Walter Stinton with him. In 1889 he is listed as earning £160 per annum but that possibly includes money for his family; was in the Wages Book from 21st March 1846.

LOCKE, KATE: daughter of above and a specialist in the painting of *pâte-sur-pâte*, examples of her work are in the Dyson Perrins Museum (see Plate 173).

LUCAS, JOHN: admitted Freeman 14 July 1834, came about the same time as John Daniel and Alex Evans. He was probably a gilder, see pattern 229x.

LULMAN (various spellings): a number of patterns are ascribed in the 1810s and 1820s, for instance 1366 which is called 'Lulman's pattern'.

MANISON, WILLIAM: signatory to the 1846 Health Board application. Chaffers lists a William Manason as a painter at Flight, Barr & Barr. The census returns of 1841 and 1851 list the same as a china painter.

MAY, WILLIAM: a number of patterns are ascribed to him, for instance 1497/98, 1675 and 1682 which has birds in landscapes (see Plate 28). Patterns 1882 and 1884 are 'ground by W. May'.

McCLAY, GEORGE: in Wages Book from 21 March 1846; on 7 August he appears as MacClay.

MEIGH, JAMES: in Wages Book from 19 October 1850; there was at least one other James Meigh at the Chamberlain factory and perhaps the Grainger painter was related. One is recorded as living in Tallow Hill, not far from Grainger's factory in 1835. Pattern 1356 is ascribed to him and Norris.

MILLS, ROBERT: signatory to the 1846 Health Board application. A Robert Mills senior and junior are recorded in the Chamberlain wage records, and pattern books up until the 1840s. One was listed in the Worcester census returns for 1851 as a 'china painter', with a son, Thomas, also a china painter.

MORGAN: in Wages Book from 2 March 1846, leaving on 31 October 1846.

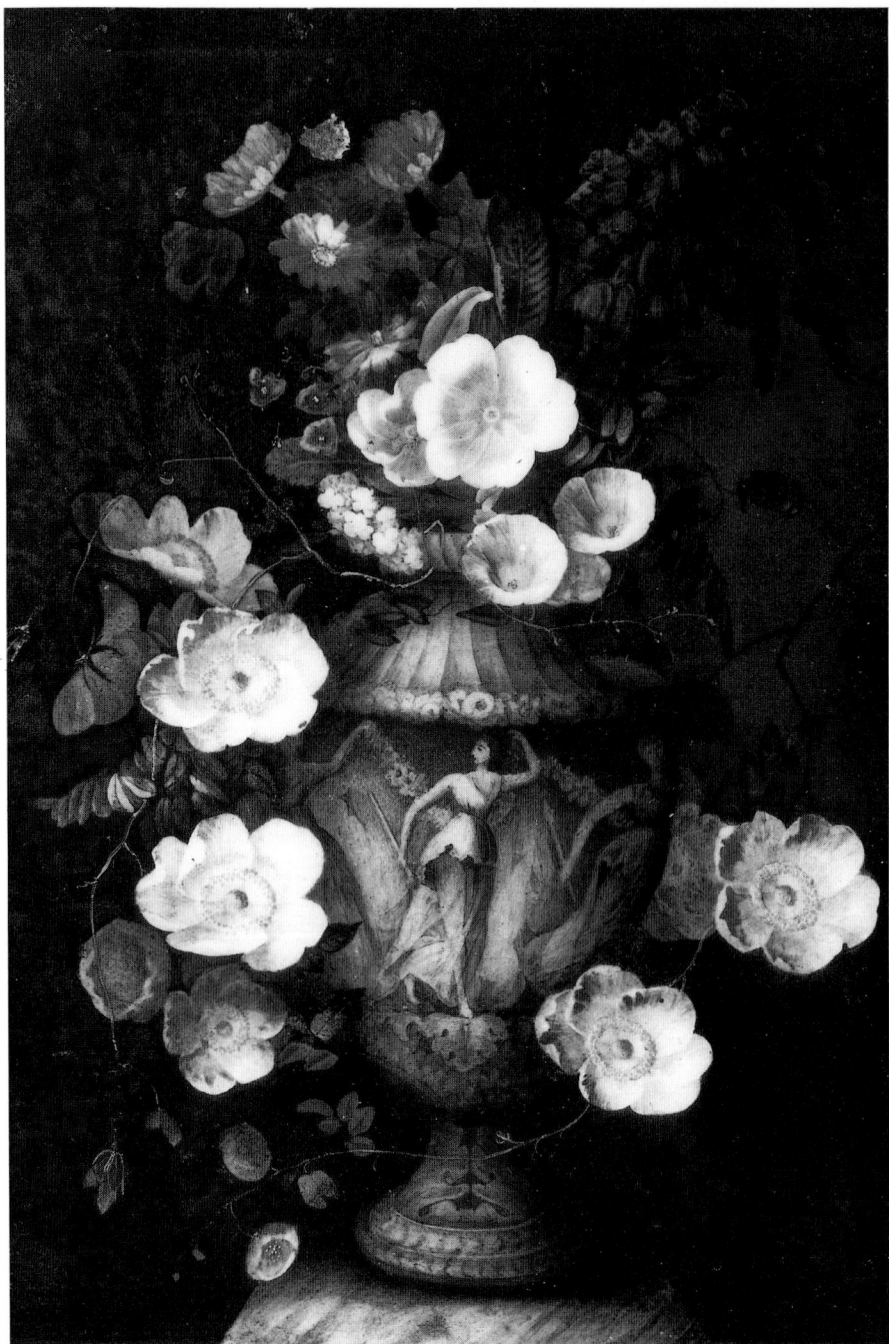

4. A fine plaque painted and signed by David Evans while at Worcester and almost certainly on Grainger Porcelain, 9¾ inches high. (Private Collection). For another example of his work see Colour Plate XV.

MORGAN, GEORGE: a landscape painter, mentioned in William Evans's article.

NORRIS, CONNINGSBY: apprenticed to Grainger Lee & Co. in 1826, a good landscape painter who frequently worked free-lance. In Pigot's 1841 Directory he is listed under china, glass and earthenware as a dealer at 55 Tything and in Lascelles & Co.'s 1851 Directory and Gazetteer he had an advertisement: 'C. Norris, 55 Tything, Worcester. Manufacturer of Burnished Gold China Tea and Breakfast Sets, Desserts, Ornaments etc. Matchings executed on the Premises, at the shortest notice.' He married Mary Grainger, daughter of Joseph Grainger. Pattern 1356 is ascribed to Norris and Meigh.

NORRIS, FRED: a painter at the factory in the 1890s, holding a violin in Plate 5.

OSBORNE, CHARLES: in Wages Book from 11 to 25 April 1846.

OSBORNE, JOHN: a painter who began his career at Grainger, moving to Royal Worcester in 1902. He appears in the group photograph, Plate 5.

OSWELL, JAMES: in Wages Book from 21 March 1846.

PARKER, THOMAS: apprenticed as a clerk in the Wholesale Department, 9 January 1868.

PARRY, T.: in Wages Book in 1840s, see patterns 1710x and 1761x, noted as flowers by Parry.

PARTRIDGE, JOHN: signatory to 1846 Health Board application.

PEACOCKE, SAMUEL: in Wages Book 10 April 1847 for one week only.

PLANT, ALFRED: signatory to the 1846 Health Board application.

PLANT, JAMES: signatory to the 1846 Health Board application. A James Plant was at Chamberlain's factory.

POPE, MARY ANNE: apprenticed in the 'process of china painting called transferring', 7 October 1862.

POTTER, ERNEST T.: appears under painters for the Royal China Works in the 1892 Apprentices Exhibition, aged 19, having served 4½ years of his apprenticeship.

PRICE, THOMAS: in Wages Book from 21 March 1848, crossed out 9 June 1849 but returns 17 November 1849. He seems to have been a gilder.

PROSSER: in Wages Book 2 May 1846 until 8 August 1846. In the 1851 census a Henry Prosser, china dipper, was living in Pheasant Street.

RABY, ENOS: apprenticed to George Grainger as a potter, 15 June 1840. Appears in Wages Book from 21 March 1846 until he left, 19 June 1847. Geoffrey Godden notes an Enos Raby as a ground layer and gilder at Thomas Martin Randall's decorating establishment at Madeley prior to 1840. This Raby is listed in the 1851 census returns as still living in Shropshire, so he cannot have been the same as the Grainger Raby. Raby is a famous ceramic name in both Bristol and Worcester.

RABY, H. J.: in Wages Book from 21 March 1846.

RABY (or *REABY*), *JAMES:* pattern 1739 is so ascribed.

RABY, SETH: in Wages Book from 21 March 1846. In the 1851 census Seth Raby was living in Tallow Hill and was described as a potter.

RICHARDS, C.: referred to in pattern 982x.

RICKETTS, BENJAMIN: apprenticed to George Grainger as a potter, 15 June 1840. In Wages Book from 21 March 1846. In the 1851 census he was living in Tallow Hill and is described as a potter.

RICKHUSS, J.: the name (various spellings, including Rickus) occurs frequently in the records and it appears that he was a very important figure within the Grainger factory. A number of patterns include his name, although it seems to be in connection with the colours rather than implying that he decorated the pattern. Patterns 1607–10 are listed as 'In Ruckus's book', while 1344 is 'Pattern done by Boys in Rickhusses room'. Shape 19 in the Ornamental Shape Book is a vase and pencilled against it is 'Rickhuss's China'. Shape 67 is 'Rickus's violet basket'. Geoffrey Godden, in his *Encyclopaedia of British Porcelain Manufacturers*, records that the 1861 census returns list 'John Rickhuss, aged 59, master china and parian manufacturer, born Madeley.' Earlier partnerships in Hanley (Staffordshire) comprised Rickhuss, Wilkinson & Toft of Broad St (c.1855), and then Wilkinson & Rickhuss (1856–62).

RIDER, JOHN: in Wages Book from 21 March 1846. The 1841 Worcester census lists him as a 'china painter'.

ROBINSON: first entry in Wages Book, 9 November 1846.

RODEN, MARGARET: apprenticed to Grainger as a paintress, 15 February 1820. A flower painter. Patterns 1465 and 1500 are ascribed to her. Pattern 1615 is by Mr Roden, possibly a mistake.

ROGERS, HENRY: a painter apprenticed to Grainger & Lee, 18 July 1836.

SCARRATT, JOHN: signatory to the 1846 Health Board application. A John Scarratt painted earlier at Chamberlain and Geoffrey Godden records the 1851 census return where he is listed as a china painter born at Hanley, aged 70.

SCRAGG, JOSEPH: in Wages Book from 21 March 1846. A presentation bowl given to him as a mark of respect by the potters in January 1860 is now in Australia and was probably a leaving gift (see Plate 93).

SKINNER: in Wages Book from 21 March 1846 until 17 June 1846, when 'Run away to BM' (Birmingham?) appears by his name. An Edward Skinner was apprenticed to George Grainger as a potter, the date not recorded.

SKINNER, WALTER: apprenticed to Grainger as a china potter, 6 July 1857.

5. The Grainger workforce on a factory outing in about 1895. They include George Cole (standing at the back); James Stinton (back row, far left); John Stinton junior (back row, centre); John Stinton senior (front row second from left with white beard); John Osbourne (third from left); a kiln man named Brown (front row, far right); and Fred Norris (holding the violin).

SPARKES: see patterns 1993 and 1996, probably a reference to Sparks's china shop.

SPENCER, HENRY: signatory to the 1846 Health Board application.

STANAWAY, JOHN (also *STANWAY* and *STAN, J.*): in Wages Book from 21 March 1846. In the 1851 census, John Stanaway, described as a potter, was living in Victoria Place.

STEPHENS, JOHN: in *Berrows Worcester Journal*, November 1813 there is a notice: 'An inquest was on Thursday taken at the Curriers Arms, Angel Street in this City by the coroner on the body of John Stephens, a china painter, who was seized by an apopletic fit and instantly expired. Verdict. Died by the Visitation of God.' There is no trace of a John Stephens at the Flight or Chamberlain factories so it is possible that he was an early Grainger painter.

STEPHENS, JOSEPH: in Wages Book from 21 March 1846. In the 1851 census he was living in Tallow Hill, described as a painter. He may also have been a modeller. See patterns 924x, 925x.

STEPHENS, JOSEPH: in Wages Book from 1 June 1850.

STEPHENSON, THOMAS: signatory to 1846 Health Board application. The 1841 Worcester census returns list a Thomas Stevenson as a 'china painter'.

STINTON, ANNIE: (1882–1964), second daughter of John Stinton junior, paintress at Grainger and then at the Worcester Royal Porcelain Co.

STINTON, ARTHUR: (1878–30 December 1970), eldest son of John Stinton junior. Was articled to Grainger's factory doing flower painting and colouring-in. Not as skilled as his more talented brother Harry. He left Grainger and went to Locke's factory, and later to the Brierley Hill glass firm as a decorator.

STINTON, HARRY: (1883–1968), fourth child of John Stinton junior, started at Grainger in 1896, moving over to Royal Worcester in 1902. A pupil of his father and did the same type of Highland cattle studies. Also a very fine water-colourist.

STINTON, JAMES: (1870–1961), youngest son of John Stinton, senior, specialized in game birds on the ground or flying, with misty woodland backgrounds. At Grainger first, moving to Royal Worcester in 1902. Did a great amount of fine water-colours. Rarely signed his work at Grainger. See Plate 178.

STINTON, JOHN (senior): born 1829, employed at Grainger from about 1840 to 1895, specializing in landscapes and figures. From the 1850s, one of the senior and finest of the factory painters. See Plates 176 and 178.

STINTON, JOHN (junior): (1854–1956), eldest son of John Stinton senior and a superb painter, whose work is now highly collectable. Specialized in ordinary English cattle-watering scenes at Grainger, although these are generally not signed. Moved across to Worcester Royal Porcelain Co. in 1902, where he produced his famous Highland cattle scenes.

STINTON, KATE: (1880-1955), daughter of John Stinton, junior, at Grainger before moving to Royal Worcester in 1902.

STINTON, WALTER: (d. 1950), fourth son of John Stinton, senior, painted first at Grainger, then moved to Locke, specializing in landscapes. Left Locke to work for 'Pumpy' Thomas's hydraulic windmill firm in Droitwich.

STRETCH, ALEXANDER: apprenticed to George Grainger as a painter, 12 April 1856.

TAYLOR JAMES: in Wages Book from 18 March 1848 to 28 July 1849. A James Taylor also worked at Chamberlain.

TEARN (or *TEARNE*), *CHARLES:* admitted Freeman of Worcester 19 June 1818 as apprentice of 'Thomas Grainger, John Wood and James Wilkins'.

TEIGUE, CHARLES: apprenticed to George Grainger 21 March 1845 as a painter. In Wages Book from 21 March 1846 to 21 August 1847.

THOMAS, WILLIAM: apprenticed to Grainger as a painter, 8 July 1852.

TURNER, CHARLES: apprenticed to Grainger as a painter, 7 September 1840.

TURNER, JAMES: in Wages Book from 21 March 1846.

TURNER, WILLIAM: in Wages Book from 21 March 1846.

TYLER: in Wages Book from 1 December 1849. In St Paul's records, there is a Joseph Tyler living in Silver Street, described as a painter.

UNDERHILL, SARAH MARIA: apprenticed to Grainger & Lee as a paintress, 27 May 1824.

VAUGHAN: first entry in Wages Book 2 November 1850. Godden records a Samuel Vaughan as a 'china painter' in the 1851 census returns, born in 1785 and originally employed at Chamberlain.

WALKER, CHRISTOPHER: a landscape painter, mentioned in William Evans's article.

WHITE, MARY ANN: apprenticed to Grainger & Lee as a paintress, 27 May 1824.

WHITE, THOMAS: in Wages Book from 21 March 1846. In the 1851 census Thomas White lived in Factory Walk, described as a painter. See pattern 1053.

WHITE, (Mrs): a painter of flower sprigs and moss roses, see patterns 1377–9 etc.

WILKINS, STEPHEN: business partner of Grainger and Wood.

WILLIAMS, ELIZABETH: apprenticed to Grainger & Lee as a paintress, 27 May 1824.

WILLIAMS, JAMES: apprenticed to George Grainger as a potter, 8 November 1853.

WILLIAMS, JOSHUA: a bird painter at the factory, mentioned by William Evans.

WOOD, ALBERTA: in list of paintresses at the Royal China Works at the Apprentices Exhibition of 1892, aged 15.

WOOD, ARON: in Wages Book from 21 March 1846 until 15 August 1846, wage below average, under 10/-.

WOOD, A.: in Wages Book 28 August 1847 until 18 December 1847, wage about 12/- to 15/-. Probably not Aron Wood.

WOOD, HENRY: in Wages Book from 21 March 1846 until 10 July 1848, when 'Runaway' appears by his name, same day as Coombs and Brundreth.

WOOD, JOHN: Partner in the original firm of Grainger, Wood & Wilkins. Came from Chamberlain where he was a highly paid painter, leaving at the same time as Thomas Grainger to establish their own factory. Probably painted at Grainger (see Colour Plate XIV). The partnership was dissolved in 1811.

WOOD, JOHN: probably different to the above, he was overlooker of the apprentices and journeymen, and a fine flower painter and teacher, for example pattern 1664, 'Group of flowers by Jno. Wood'.

WOOD, STANLEY: brother of above, fine flower painter, lived in York Place. A number of flower patterns are ascribed to him, for example 1520 and 1812x.

YARWOOD: pattern 767x is ascribed 'gilded by Yarwood'.

CHAPTER THREE

TEAWARES

Over the years our search for the Grainger teaware shapes has been tantalizing. We have been haunted by some of the names which appear in the factory pattern books, such as 'Wellington Embossed', 'Nantgarw', or 'New Gadroon', listed alongside some of the pattern illustrations but rarely drawn. Some are sketched lightly in outline as a guide to the painter or gilder but with little detail to assist in matching the shape with a finished cup or teapot.

A few teawares are marked, under the lid of early teapots or printed in blue on some cups where blue printing features in the pattern. These are important starting points and, assisted by patterns which match their pattern number in the books, we have now been able to identify positively the majority of the Grainger teaware shapes. A great many are illustrated here but there are also several gaps. We know approximately what some of the others look like, and where we have matching wasters, the exact form is known. We hope, by publishing these details here, that some of the shapes will not remain unknown for long.

Important links can be made by studying the products of other contemporary factories, as each followed changes in taste and fashion which were exactly copied by other rival manufacturers. Grainger's shapes are closely linked to Chamberlain in Worcester and Coalport in Shropshire and the factory clearly copied other makers as well as designing some of their own apparently unique shapes. More important in providing positive identification is the material excavated from the Grainger factory site. Our rescue work has yielded examples of most of the early teaware shapes and in several instances we have been able to identify certain pieces as Grainger only through finding matching wasters.

As discussed in Chapter One, the earliest marked Grainger tea service is probably on Coalport porcelain. This set, illustrated by Geoffrey Godden in his *Encyclopaedia of British Porcelain Manufacturers*, is of the standard 'Old Oval' shape identical to know Coalport wares. Such shapes were available to many independent decorators in the first decade of the nineteenth century.

By 1807, when we know for certain that Grainger were making their own porcelain, the popular shape in English porcelain had changed to what is now known as the 'New Oval' teapot, the ovoid body with rounded rather than straight sides. Grainger made the same basic shape in three distinct versions: plain, spiral-fluted, and with straight vertical flutes. No shape or pattern records survive for this early period and so we do not know the original factory names for these shapes. Certain names seem to have been in fairly wide use in England at the time, however, and so we will take the liberty of using these accepted names here.

Plate 6 illustrates the main shapes from a tea service of the plain 'New Oval' shape. The teapot and jug handles have a single spur which points upwards at about forty-five degrees to the vertical, while on the sugar box the spurs on the handles point upwards almost twice as sharply. Many factories made New Oval shape with their own minor differences, and the Grainger version is closer to Chamberlain than to any other factory. Inside the teapot is a D-shaped opening and a plain pierced strainer at the base of the spout as opposed to the domed strainer used at some factories. The finial is the most distinctive feature which indicates, above all else, a Grainger origin. Domed, with a nipple on top, it is the tallest and fattest finial recorded on any factory's New Oval pots.

The cup handles most often used with the New Oval shape are plain ring or figure '9' types and these are, once again, a significant clue to a Grainger origin. The ring is a perfect circle with a tapering shaft, again similar to Chamberlain but generally more thickly made. This is a characteristic which is apparent in many Grainger cup handle shapes, a tendency to be much thicker and generally clumsier than their contemporaries. The examples illustrated here show a range in thickness which confuses the situation considerably. It is hard to believe sometimes that such extremes all came from the same factory.

The other handle shape used occasionally on the plain or 'Bute'-shaped tea cups and coffee cans is a plain loop with an inward spur near the bottom. We illustrate it here on several wasters of different shapes (Plate 43) and it is evident that the thickness and size of the loop also vary here. Michael Berthoud, in his *Anthology of British Cups*, shows a Bute cup, and it has been noted on a single cup of straight vertical fluted shape. Normally, however, these shapes have ring handles. Archaeological evidence suggests that this plain loop handle with inward spur was the only handle used on the 'shanked' or spiral-fluted shape. Popular in the 1780s and 1790s in particular, shanked forms were going out of favour by 1807 and Grainger probably only produced this shape for a short time. The only finished example known to us is the teapot shown by Phillip Miller and Michael Berthoud, in their *Anthology of British Teapots*, item 1181, and we have been unable to trace any cups, although a great many wasters littered the factory site. Grainger spiral-fluted teawares must be somewhere, probably masquerading as Coalport, and we would love to hear of any examples. Wasters from the site include a miniature coffee can with spiral flutes (Plate 12), and part of a jug which shows that the main shapes follow the plain New Oval without the flutes. The teapot mentioned has double stringing to the flutes or, in other words, each flute has two close peaks. Much less pronounced than Chamberlain, we found only one double-stringed waster.

Large numbers of wasters found at the factory site suggest that the spiral-fluted version of the New Oval shape was as popular as straight-fluted or plain, but

6. *An early tea service with Grainger's version of the 'New Oval' shape, decorated in a most splendid Japan style. The pattern was popular at many factories but seems to be particularly suited to the Grainger hybrid body, the underglaze blue exhibiting a particular richness set off by the colours and gold. The cover is marked Grainger & Co Worcester Warranted No. 140. c.1807–10. (Geoffrey Godden, Chinaman)*

surviving examples seem to contradict this. Grainger clearly made two distinct versions of the shanked or spiral-fluted tewares, yet they remain elusive.

A clue to the identification of these wares lies in the cup shape illustrated from the wasters. Very similar to Coalport, the handle is more rounded and thicker and ought to be distinctive. Oddly, none of the wasters has a ring handle on the spiral-fluted shape, just the loop with inward spur. Now that we know what to look for, it will probably be only a matter of time before some completed shanked tewares are identified.

Straight vertical flutes on New Oval and Bute shapes were referred to by several manufacturers as 'Hamilton' or 'Hambleton' Flute, probably after Sir William Hamilton rather than the luckless Emma Hamilton. Examples illustrated here (Plates 7 and 8) show that the handle and finial shapes exactly match the plain New Oval tewares, and while the ring handle is usual, the loop with inward spur has also been recorded occasionally.

The plain ring handle has been found on two other cup shapes, illustrated here in Plate 22. One is the so-called 'Porringer' shape which is squat with almost straight sides and sharply rounded base. Our example exactly matches a waster from the factory site and is painted with ruins in a landscape, predominantly in green and brown, a distinctive painting style seen on other early Grainger tewares. Porringer cups were probably supplied with conventional New Oval teapots.

A shape apparently unique to Grainger has a moulded angle around the cup below a plain straight border. The section is clearly seen by the matching waster (Plate 22) and the cup appears unusually shallow, with a reasonably thin ring handle. No other factory seems to have made such a shallow cup of this type and examples in Grainger are very rare, suggesting that it was very unpopular. A part service has been seen painted with a single flower and includes a rectangular teapot stand, which suggests a teapot of 'London' or oblong shape rather than New Oval.

Two other shapes seem to fall into this early Grainger Wood & Co. period before 1811. One is represented here by a waster of the handle, found alongside shanked shapes and plain ring handles. Closely copying Chamberlain, the ring handle meets inside with two scrolls, and has been seen on two finished examples which are a little more rounded than the waster which is possibly a little misshapen. One of the finished cups, which is uncomfortably thick in its potting, has a pattern number which matches the Grainger pattern books. The other has a marked saucer.

Probably introduced around 1810 and initially issued with the same loop and inward spur handle, a cup with light half flutes seems to have been as popular at Grainger as at many other factories, especially for blue and white printed patterns. Our waster (Plate 22, top left), matches a cup with a different plain handle, with a slight kick at the base, probably replacing the more uncomfortable original handle shape seen on the coffee can. This bears the blue portion of a pattern called 'Old India', which we will discuss later. It is marked 'Grainger Lee & Co., Worcester' in an underglaze blue print, a mark often used on this type of teware with blue decoration. It is clear that Grainger called this shape 'Broseley' after the village near

7. Grainger's standard New Oval shape teapot of straight fluted form known at several factories as Hamilton Flute, decorated in underglaze blue and gold, 5½ inches high, marked under the cover Grainger & Co Worcester, in gold, c.1807–10. (Geoffrey Godden, Chinaman)

8. An early sugar box of fluted New Oval shape, together with a Bute-shaped cup, the cover marked Grainger Wood & Co. Worcester, c.1807–10. (Dyson Perrins Museum)

9. *A New Oval shaped teapot bat-printed in black, the signpost on the right of the picture inscribed 'To Worcester'; marked under the cover Grainger Wood & Co Worcester, c.1808–10. (Dyson Perrins Museum)*

10. *The reverse of the teapot shown in Plate 9.*

11. *An oblong teapot and cover printed with the same subject as Plate 9, but without any inscription. Possibly Grainger. (Sold at Phillips in 1978)*

Coalport, and it is apparently copied from a very similar Coalport model.

The cup with the 'Blue Dragon' pattern (Plate 22) is also marked Grainger Lee & Co., Worcester, although others just have Grainger & Co., Worcester. The name of the shape should not be confused with the pattern also known as 'Broseley' at the time. This pattern was a chinoiserie riverscape printed in underglaze blue and was made by many factories. Broseley pattern was used by Grainger on their Broseley shape, as well as on a version of the London shape (Plate 14).

The shape popularly known as 'London', seems to have been introduced at Grainger in about 1812 or 1813. It is very confusing as the factory produced several totally different versions, one usually in the earlier porcelain, the others in the much inferior bone china. Miller and Berthoud illustrate the earlier version of the teapot, plate 1507. The pot has a low foot and the same finial as used on New Oval shapes. The cups which accompanied the teapot were of plain Bute shape, indicating clearly that it is a transition, before the London shape was established at Grainger. Another service which included a New Oval teapot marked 'Grainger & Co., Warranted' had London shaped cups in hybrid porcelain, an example of which is shown in Plate 22, bottom right. It is thinly potted with straight sides typical of the earlier Grainger London shapes, although the handle is much more finely potted, certainly as fine as any other maker's London shape handles. Exactly matching wasters were found on the factory site, but sadly this quality seems to have been short-lived. When the body was changed to the inferior china, the London shape was adapted to three altogether new shapes.

The first, shown on a marked Grainger & Co. cup (Plate 14) has straight sides and a scalloped rim. The handle is weak and only found on this version, the spur at the top hardly pronounced at all. All examples we have seen have been printed in blue underglaze with the Broseley pattern, and one service with a gold rim bears the painted pattern number 705.

The version called by the factory 'Old Embossed' has been of great interest to us. It was first discovered twenty years ago on fragments found on the factory site and no finished example was known. A drawing was made by Neal French from some of these fragments, predicting what the shape would look like, but it was some years before the first finished piece was discovered. The cup shapes and a sugar box are shown in Plate 16, with a deep underglaze blue ground and bright gilding picking out the modelling. The decoration is high quality, let down by the body which has crazed and stained. The finial on the cover has become a conventional London shape and is seen clearly on the waster in Plate 12, top right. Old Embossed, occurring in pattern numbers in the high 500s, is also found on dessert wares and a most interesting mould survives at the Dyson Perrins Museum. Carved with an unfinished portion of the pattern, it is inscribed 'Engraved by Thomas Grainger Senr. November 10th 1818'. Why it should have been made is completely baffling, but it does give a useful date to this shape and shows that Thomas Grainger was very skilled as a practical craftsman.

12. A group of wasters from early Grainger teaware, including spiral fluted cups (top and left), New Oval and London finials, a Royal Flute jug handle, an unidentified ring handle from a tureen, a new Gadroon teapot handle, and New Embossed teawares with modelled flowers.

Four apparently unrelated fragments discovered in the most recent excavation on the site led us to a major discovery, thanks to a photograph in Michael Berthoud's *Anthology of British Cups*. The border around the base of the moulded London-shape cup (Plate 18) corresponded exactly with part of a bowl and three pieces of flower moulding also linked up (Plate 12). What we had discovered were pieces of teaware called by the factory 'New Embossed', and the wasters themselves give a strong clue as to why they should be so rare. The unglazed biscuit flower moulding is beautifully sharp and crisp, while under the thick glaze, most of the detail is destroyed. It could not have been worth the cost in time of producing fine modelling only for it to be hidden by the glaze so the factory probably decided to concentrate on plainer shapes.

By about 1820, London-shaped wares were a principal product of many factories and Grainger made a large amount, again in differing qualities. The cup in the foreground of Plate 22 has a very thick, crude handle, while those with the tea service of 'Old India' pattern (Plate 19 or Colour Plate VII) are much more delicate. The cups have flared rims unlike the earlier Grainger London shapes, and the teapot has a more pronounced foot. Instead of the rather oversized handles on the sugar box in Plate 16, those here have become small scrolls and the shape is more successful.

Alongside the London shape, Grainger produced many shapes which seem to be unique to the factory, as well as others copied from rival firms. Most have been traced and we are pleased to be able to illustrate a fair selection here. A few still elude us, even though from the pattern books we have a good idea of what they must look like.

Just as Old Embossed and New Embossed were used on both teawares and dessert wares, so too was 'Wellington Embossed', a name suggesting an introduction around 1815. A drawing in the pattern book shows the approximate outline of the moulded panel, based on a Paris porcelain design with scrolling panels flanked by sprays of what appear to be cornflowers. It could be that this was used on London shape, but this is only guesswork. Pattern numbers fall into the range 429 to 549.

At the same time, a popular shape seems to have been 'Nantgarrow' (*sic*), named after the Welsh factory, and exactly copying a shape used at the Nantgarw works. The cups have a high loop handle with a heart or kidney-shaped ring, and one part service has been recorded combining these cups with a conventional Grainger teapot. This set, described to us by Michael Berthoud, was of high quality, the cups easily as fine as Coalport's version of the shape and much finer than known Derby examples.

The name Nantgarrow is first mentioned in the pattern books for numbers 468, 469, and 470, but the term 'Nantgarrows pattern' is used. Pattern 470 has been seen on a very different gadroon shape and so we feel that in these cases only the pattern derives from South Wales. The Nantgarrow shape at Grainger occurs mostly in the pattern range 1297–1373.

13. *A coffee can of Broseley shape with moulded half flutes and a characteristic Grainger handle. The popular Old India pattern has been left uncoloured. Marked Grainger Lee & Co Worcester, c.1815. (Private Collection)*

14. *An early form of London-shape cup with a scalloped rim, printed in blue with the Broseley pattern, marked Grainger & Co Worcester, pattern 705, c.1812–14. (Private Collection)*

15. *A drawing by Neal French based on wasters from the factory site of an Old Embossed coffee cup and saucer; the moulding is unique to the Grainger factory.*

Another shape copied from Welsh porcelain is 'Paris Flute', a form used at Swansea and taken directly from Paris porcelain. It occurs between pattern numbers 750 and 787, and again for shape 1394, but as yet no specimen has come to our notice and no wasters were discovered. The cups are shallow with fine vertical corrugation stopping just short of the rim. The plain curved handle rises over the top of the cup rim and is very thick at the base. It is possible that examples of Grainger's Paris Flute and Nantgarrow shapes are at present in collections masquerading as genuine Welsh porcelain.

At this point it is worth mentioning a number of cup and teapot shapes drawn on three pages of the pattern book between patterns 576 and 577. Most are shown here (Plate 20) and are curious as they are given a number and two of the cups are further identified by initials. Cup No. 1, with a serpent handle, has 'S & Co' inside it, possibly referring to Spode, who produced this exact shape. Cup No. 3 similarly is marked 'R & Co' and the shape is close to one made by John Rose's factory at Coalport. These drawings remained for a long time a complete mystery, as none linked up to Grainger wasters or any finished pieces. Recently, however, we have been fortunate to locate two tea services which matched some of these drawings and correspond with the patterns books as well.

16. Old Embossed teawares decorated with the rich blue ground which Grainger controlled so well at this period, the modelling picked out in gold. Unmarked, but definitely Grainger, c.1815–18. (Authors' Collections)

17. *A plaster mould for an Old Embossed saucer, left unfinished and inscribed 'Engraved by Thomas Grainger Senr. March 10 1818'. (Dyson Perrins Museum)*

18. *A coffee cup of New Embossed shape, identified from matching wasters found in 1988. The thick handle is characteristic of Grainger at this period, c.1815–18. (Berthoud Collection)*

Colour Plate VI shows a very rich tea service sold at Phillips in 1987. The cups are of No. 1 shape and this is how they are referred to in the pattern book entries. The teapot, however, is No. 2 shape, with sugar box and jug to match. The handles have spreading leaf-moulded terminals and the finials resemble pinecones. The saucers are very flat, unlike the Spode examples they are copying. The slop bowl is in keeping with the cups but does not live happily with the other main pieces. The decoration on this service is exceptional, the finest rich Japan pattern in the wonderful warm gold which Grainger did so well. At present, no other examples of any of these shapes are known to us, although a fairly similar design was made by Davenport.

Examples of the drawings of cup No. 2 and teapot No. 1 are still unknown, but a service of shape No. 3 is in a private collection in Kent (Plate 21). The shape does not appear to have been given another name at the factory, although the closely matching shape made at Coalport has been called the 'Empire' shape. The flanges on the rims of the Grainger cups are even more pronounced than at Coalport, making drinking difficult, and the jug is a very uncomfortable shape to use. The drawing of teapot No. 3 in the pattern book exactly matches the other shapes shown here, but sadly is missing from the surviving service. The finial is the same as on the sucrier, and the handle rests on a tapering shoulder. The shape must be very peculiar and is understandably rare. One other teacup, again with corresponding pattern number, is shown in Plate 41, top left.

Having traced four out of the six drawings, it is clear that cup No. 2, with its strange bird-head handle, and teapot No. 1, with a raised ridge around its circumference, must also have been made and still lies undiscovered. Cup drawing No. 4 seems to be a teacup to match coffee cup No. 2, but this drawing has been crossed out.

The next shape seemingly introduced at Grainger was 'New Gadroon', which has several different spellings, including 'New Gaderoone'. We have been fortunate enough to trace two complete tea services, one in the popular Old India print, the other with a design of large convolvulus flowers (Plate 23). The former was marked Grainger, Lee & Co., Worcester, in underglaze blue. A further example of the teapot shape is illustrated by Miller and Berthoud, plate 1868. The gadroon rim on the cups and saucers is reasonably plain, while the main pieces have a moulded flower head design breaking up the gadroons. The finials are the same as those used on shape No. 3, referred to previously.

Wasters of a teapot handle and numerous cup handles have been found on the Grainger site and are illustrated here (Plates 12 and 41), leaving no doubt about the origin of what appear to be the first successful shapes attempted by the factory without directly copying a rival. In Grainger tradition, the handles on the sugar box appear overlarge, but otherwise the shapes are well balanced and practical.

The next shape referred to in the pattern books against pattern 1418 is 'New L shape', although it is not drawn. Pattern 1432 is 'New fluted shape', and pattern 1463 has a drawing of the shape which links up with the service of pattern 1423 illustrated here (Plate 26). We believe these are the same shape, but before the factory had worked out a name for it. By pattern 1569 the name 'Royal Flute' seems to have become established for this popular shape made by most factories in the 1820s, sometimes now referred to as 'Old English'. The teapot we illustrate (Plate 25) is of pattern 1665, described as 'Royal flute, flowered by women', showing Grainger's version with a rose forming the finial. The cups have unusually large handles which match the waster (Plate 43, right). A complete service, sadly lacking its teapot, is in a collection in Kent and the main shapes are illustrated in Plate 26. The jug is a strange round shape with a thin scroll handle quite out of keeping with the rest of the set, but it matches a waster from the site shown in Plate 12. Grainger made many different patterns on the Royal Flute shape, but surprisingly few examples are known to us. The shape was clearly altered slightly, as pattern 1731 is called 'New shap'd Royal flute' with a drawing of the cup handle indicating that the top of the handle is longer and flatter than previously. We have not yet found an example.

Patterns 1574–87 include references to a 'New French flanshed' (flanged?) shape with a drawing of a complicated scroll handle. No example has yet turned up. It is possible that it will be something like the shape of the cups shown by Berthoud, items 611–15.

Pattern book 3 begins at pattern 1595 and is watermarked for the year 1835. It seems reasonable to conclude that the book was started in that year or very soon afterwards. It marks the beginning of an important new range of shapes which occur on patterns in the 1550–800 range, confusingly called by different names.

19. *A tea service of Old India pattern printed in underglaze blue, with added colours and gold; in this case, pattern 1418. These London-shape teawares have well-potted thin handles. Marked Grainger Lee & Co Worcester, c.1818. See Colour Plate VII. (Private Collection, USA)*

20. *A page of drawings included in the Grainger pattern book between pattern numbers 576 and 577. Examples of teapot No. 1 and cup No. 2 have yet to be identified. (WRPC)*

21. A tea service of shape 3 corresponding with drawings in the Grainger pattern book. The pattern number also links with the factory records. (Private Collection)

22. A selection of Grainger cups shown with matching wasters from the factory site. Top row from left: Broseley shape, c.1820; Porringer shape, c.1810; a later plain cup c.1845 marked G Grainger Worcester. Centre row: Plain and fluted coffee cans with ring handles; and a rare shallow cup with a central moulded angle, all c.1808–10. Bottom row: Old Embossed shape, c.1815; London shape with thick handle, c.1818; and with thin handle c.1812. (Authors' Collections)

23. New Gadroon shape introduced in about 1820, shown by a full service. A matching waster is shown in Plate 41. (Phillips)

24. A New Gadroon coffee cup decorated with a rich Imari pattern, the gold remaining incredibly bright, pattern 469 in red enamel. (David John Ceramics)

25. A teapot and trio of Royal Flute shape, c.1825. The teapot, pattern 1665, is an example of the flowers painted by the women. (Private Collection)

26. Other shapes from a Royal Flute shape tea service, of pattern 1423. The rose finial was also used on dessert tureens, and a waster matching the jug handle is shown in Plate 12, c.1825. (Private Collection)

The shape discussed previously, when it was called New Gadroon (Plate 23), has been changed to 'Old Gadroon' for pattern 1609. It was replaced by two new shapes. One is referred to variously as 'New Gadroon', 'New Gadroon, high handle', or just 'Gadroon High Handle'; the other is called 'Gadroon Low Handle'. The latter will be discussed later. The shape with a high handle was apparently not called 'New Gadroon' for long. It had been changed to 'Clarendon' shape by pattern 1690, and 1693 is called 'Clarendon shape (gadrooned)'. Pattern 1703 on Clarendon shape includes a drawing of the handle showing clearly that the name change has taken place. Subsequent references to gadroon shape could be what had become Old Gadroon or the gadroon with a low handle, or else the workmen entering the pattern forgot that New Gadroon had become Clarendon. It all sounds very complicated, and indeed it is. For the purpose of this work, we have decided to use the name Clarendon for the new shape with a high handle, and leave the earlier shape as New Gadroon.

Clarendon has a very similar cup handle to ones made by H. & R. Daniel, as well as Coalport, but the Grainger cups have higher feet. The teapot closely follows a Minton model known as 'Bath Embossed' and is raised on three large paw and scrollwork feet. An example from the Phillip Miller collection is illustrated here alongside a matching waster, and this design is particularly elegant. One of the most significant services of the shape was owned by Mercury Antiques who kindly allowed us to photograph a trio and one of the cake plates (Plate 27). The claret

27. Part of a presentation service of Clarendon shape, the plate inscribed on the reverse as a gift from James and Rachel Lee to Mr and Mrs Bilton, in 1830. The ground is rich claret and the quality is superb. (Mercury Antiques)

28. A teapot of Clarendon shape closely copying a Minton shape also called Clarendon. This example, shown with matching wasters, bears pattern 1681, c.1832–5. (Phillip Miller)

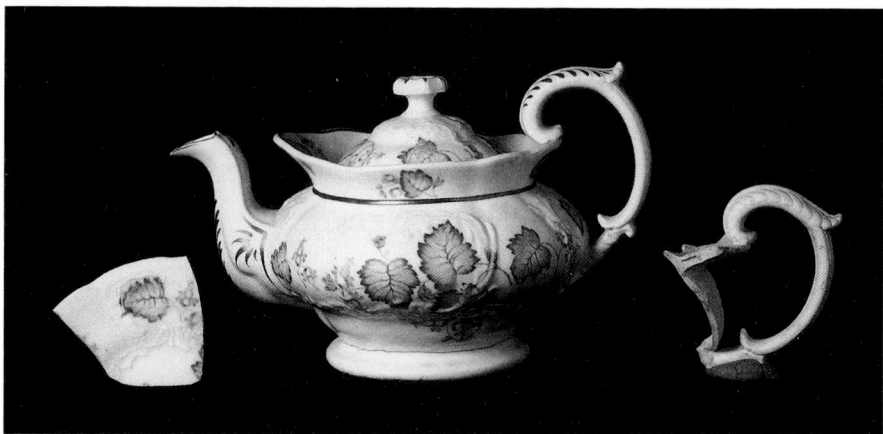

29. A teapot of Dresden Embossed shape with underglaze blue printed leaves, and matching wasters. Marked Grainger Lee & Co Worcester, c.1835. See also Plate 59. (Authors' Collections)

ground and dentil gilding are typical Grainger features and the gilded 'Union' sprays and initials are superbly done. Each piece is painted with the crest of a demi-lion/dragon, and the reverse of the plate bears the interesting inscription 'To Mr. and Mrs. Bilton, this small but sincere token of affectionate remembrance is offer'd by their friend, James and Rachel Lee, Worcester 1830 – Grainger Lee & Co. Manufacturers'. This confirms the date at which the shape was popular, and is evidence of the high standard of decoration capable at the factory at that time.

Pattern 1662 marks the introduction of a new shape using the same teapot handle as the Clarendon shape. 'Dresden Embossed' is copied from a Meissen model used at the end of the eighteenth century, although shapes are much more French. Wasters were found in remarkable quantities, and while finished examples are rarely seen, we do know of two very sizeable services indeed, for breakfast, dinner, and dessert. One is illustrated here, with panels of cornflower sprays in the French manner, while the other has an underglaze blue floral print. Both are plain, without gold rims, relying on the subtle rococo scroll moulding to speak for itself. More elaborate patterns were done on this shape, such as 1682, with a bird in a landscape in each panel, framed in gold with gilt grapes between each, the birds by William May. Generally, though, the Dresden Embossed shape was one of the cheaper ranges produced at the factory. The teapot shape (Plate 29) uses the same basic shape and handle as Clarendon but without the paw feet. The finial is once again copied from Minton. In this case, the transfer-printed leaves bear little relationship to the moulded panels and were clearly not engraved specially for the shape. This pot is marked Grainger, Lee & Co. Worcester.

A very different teapot is shown in Plate 31. This example, recently discovered by Phillip Miller, is painted with the popular 'Blue Ball Japan' pattern frequently

30. A trio of finely-moulded Lee's Embossed shape, c.1835. The subtle detail is lost below the thick glaze and rose pink ground colour, although the effect is very delicate. (Authors' Collections)

31. Blue Ball Japan pattern used on a teapot, c.1825–30. The handle links with the Royal Flute service shown in Plate 26, while the finial was used with Clarendon and Dresden Embossed shapes of slightly later date. (Phillip Miller)

32. A full tea service of Gloster shape, including the rarely seen teapot shape, with characteristic Grainger decoration. Pattern 1855, c.1835–40. (Geoffrey Godden, Chinaman)

seen on dessert wares. This is the first time the design has been noted on teawares. We do not know what shape of cup would have accompanied this teapot.

The cup handle on Dresden Embossed shape was used on one other shape popular at the same time. This is shown in Plate 40, top right, alongside an almost complete waster which exactly matches. The pattern books indicate that the factory name for this shape was 'Gadroon, Low Handle', probably to differentiate it from Clarendon with its high handle, as the rim is hardly gadrooned at all. We have not traced the matching teapot shape.

33. A Leaf Edge tea service of c.1840. The cups use the same handles as the earlier Gloster shape, and the plate and teapot stand issued with this service have the Gloster moulded rim overpainted to match the Leaf Edge saucers; pattern 476x. (Christie's)

34. A tea service of pattern number 500x using cups and a bowl of a shape similar to Gloster but known as 'Shell Edge', the other wares gilded to match but without the shell moulding. c.1842. The teapot spout and finial in this example have unfortunately been replaced incorrectly. (Private Collection)

35. A teapot closely related to the shape in Plate 34, probably representing an earlier version, c.1842. (Private Collection)

36. The sugar box matching Plate 35. Note the inward curving handles in contrast to the usual version, Plate 38. (Private Collection)

37. A part of a tea service of c.1845, the conventional teapot matched with a rare cup shape called Gloster Plain. (Private Collection)

38. A Grainger teapot, sugar box and jug of a standard shape, here combined with cups and a bowl of 'Kent Fluted' shape, c.1845. The popular pattern known as Leaf Ground is printed in bright blue and used to cover the entire service as an inexpensive 'sheet' pattern; printed marks with pattern name and initials G. W. (Private collection)

This difficulty of shapes being entered into the factory pattern books before a name had been decided is evident once again in relation to Grainger's most important shape of the 1830s. Patterns 1791–6 are called 'New Shape', while 1797 is 'New Gloster shape'. It remains as New Shape until pattern 1809, when it is clear 'Gloster' is to be the factory's name. Nowhere is it spelled Gloucester and therefore we will continue to refer to the shape by Grainger's unorthodox spelling.

A full service of Gloster shape is shown in Plate 32, courtesy of Geoffrey Godden. The rim is moulded with fine beading broken by a group of two flowerheads between scrolls. Versions of this moulding were made by a number of factories including Derby, Davenport, and Copeland & Garrett. Grainger made the shape over a long period and the handle form and quality of moulding can vary considerably, as is evident from the two wasters in Plate 43, bottom centre. The cup handle itself was used by Grainger on four different shapes, and for this reason discussing the progression of Grainger shapes becomes difficult from this point onwards.

Pattern 2011 is the first evidence that the border known as 'Leaf Edge' had been introduced using the Gloster handle. This version is shown in Plate 33 on a service of pattern 476x, with pink ground and colourful painted flowers. This has a moulded rim with stylized leaves instead of beading and here it is accompanied by a new sort of teapot, sugar box, and jug. These shapes are squat, fluted, and raised on four shell feet. One interesting feature of this service is that there was clearly a shortage of matching plates. The large cake plate as well as the stand for the teapot on the left and right of the illustration are of the conventional Gloster shape, decorated with a white leaf rim to match the cups, but with moulded beading underneath.

39. A full service of Malvern shape combined with conventional teapot, jug and sugar box. The pattern number is 1847x, c.1845 (Geoffrey Godden, Chinaman)

40. Grainger's most popular pattern in the 1840s and 1850s was Moss Fibre, a printed version of the gold 'Twigging' which the factory decorators favoured so much. Here the conventional teapot and sugar box are combined with a cup, bowl and plates with slightly moulded rims called, we believe, Queen's shape. Printed marks and initials G W, pattern number 2/420, c.1850. (Private Collection)

During the later 1830s and 1840s Grainger seems to have been very inconsistent in the combination of cup shapes with teapots and other parts of services. There are three basic forms of teapot with matching sugar boxes and jugs. These are represented here in Plates 33, 35, and 39. It seems any one of these could be combined with eight principal cup shapes of which we have records, and there was no consistency whatsoever. The same pattern could be used on more than one shape, leaving it difficult to interpret the shape names given in the pattern books. We feel it is likely that when a pattern entry lists a shape, this refers to the cup shape rather than that of the teapot. The slop bowl and cake plates in these services tend to be moulded to match the cups, whereas the teapots, jugs, and sugar boxes only match a service through painted and gilded decoration.

We cannot put a shape name to any of the three teapot shapes, but it is likely the following names relate to the cups illustrated.

Gloster:
The ring handle has a moulded florette in the centre. The rim is alternately divided into a line of beading and two flowerheads flanked by scrolls (Plate 32).

Gloster variant, probably called Leaf Edge:
Similar handle and fluted body, the rim lightly moulded with a leaf-like scroll and hanging leaf sprigs (Plate 33).

Gloster variant, probably called Shell Edge:
Again same basic shape and handle as Gloster, rim lightly moulded with feathery scrollwork and a slight shell motif repeated 3 or 4 times (Plate 34).

Gloster Plain:
A similarly shaped cup with Gloster handle, plain rim with no moulding (Plate 37).

Kent Fluted:
A lightly fluted ogee cup, the double twisted handle with feathery terminals (Plate 38).

Malvern:
The handle has a kidney-shaped ring with a high single spur pointing over the rim of the cup. The border is lightly moulded with foliate scrolls (Plate 39).

Other names which appear in the pattern books are French, Squat, Queen, flang'd, and Plain Sussex. These will probably include the following, which have not been linked:

A plain cup with a lightly-moulded shell or featherlike rim, the handle with a graduated crest on top and featherlike moulding below (Plate 40, possibly Queen shape).

A cup with a moulded foliate scroll rim, the handle with an inward pointing crest at the top (Plate 42).

In addition to the above, there are two further shapes produced in around 1830 which would have had their own matching teapots and cups. Pattern 287x is on 'Mr. Lee's shape' and this becomes 'Lee's Embossed' shape by 312x. The handle is the same as Dresden Embossed but the body is finely moulded with pleats and waves above a band of wavy lines around the foot. One tea service is known with a jug, cake plate, and bowl, all moulded to match, and several fragments were found on the factory site. We feel it is unlikely that James Lee actually modelled this set, but he may well have played some part in its design. The wasters are beautifully sharp, although the glaze covers a great deal of the detail in the finished examples (Plate 30).

41. A selection of distinctive Grainger cups shown with several exactly matching wasters. Top left: shape 3, c.1815–18; New Gadroon, c.1820; Gadroon, Low Handle, c.1828. Bottom left: name unknown, c.1840–5; Leaf Edge, with Gloster handle, c.1842–5; probably Queen's shape, c.1845–50; Clarendon, c.1830–5. (Authors' Collections)

42. A tea service combining a popular teapot, jug and sugar box with a cup, saucer and plate using very distinctive handles. We do not know the name of this shape, c.1845. (Phillips)

69

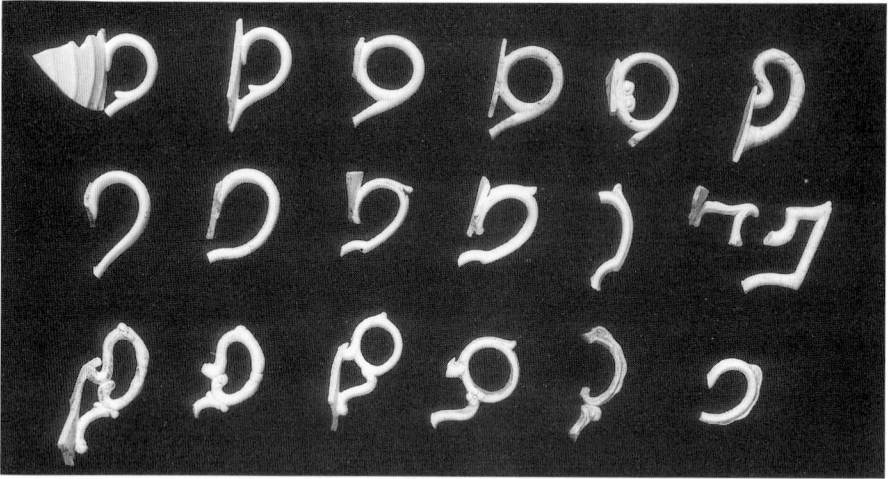

43. *A range of cup handles found during excavations on the factory site. Any finished cups exactly matching these handles must be of Grainger origin. Indeed, many are unique to the factory. The incomplete handles (numbers 5 and 6 in the centre row) have not been seen on any finished examples.*

44. *A tea service of Exhibition shape dating from c.1850. The quality of Grainger's gliding at this period is here seen at its best. Note the gold 'Twigging' on the teapot spout, marked G Grainger Manufacturers Worcester. (Private Collection)*

'Oxford Embossed', used on patterns 186x and 493x, amongst others has a distinctive handle in Meissen style. No finished example is known, although a waster of an incomplete handle is shown in Plate 43, centre row, second from right. A closely similar shape was made at Minton, called shape E, Dresden Embossed, and is shown by Michael Berthoud, plate 479. We assume the Grainger version had a similar panel moulded on each side, but no evidence survives.

During the 1840s several other shapes of teaware were introduced and are mentioned, usually over only a short range of pattern numbers, in the factory books. Probably short-lived, examples have proven fairly elusive. Those which can be roughly described are as follows:

A plain loop handle on a plain U-shaped cup, similar to the waster in Plate 43, centre left. Some examples seem to have a reinforced rim and narrow circular foot. Pattern 2/376 draws the shape and calls it 'T' shape.

A wide bell-shaped cup with a high spur handle, possibly notched all the way down, used on shape 1366x.

Witley Edge:
The moulded rim has groups of three 'C' scrolls linked by a short meander. The handle seems to be a long gentle 'S' shape. Wasters of the rim moulding were found on the site.

Windsor:
Described as a 'new shape' against pattern 1922. The cup is of a full double ogee lobed shape. The handle is long, angled inwards at the base, with a backward kick.

Imperial Shape:
A wide cup on a very narrow scroll-edged spreading foot. The handle loops above the rim. A very similar shape seems to have been made by Daniel. Patterns used range from 2/23 to 2/229.

Argyle:
Originally called mellon shape, a tall double ogee shape cup rather like the Windsor but with a thin double twisted handle with leaf terminals. Used on patterns between 2/180 and 2/259.

Exhibition:
Used from patterns 2/321 to 2/424, the name suggests a date around 1851 but it must have been introduced before 1845. The handle is pointed upwards and the bases are fluted. A full tea service is illustrated here (Plate 44).

Reform Club:
A specially commissioned shape decorated with pattern 2/367. The badge of the Reform Club is printed on the front. The cup is waisted with a ring handle set with a single spur at the top.

A plain cup with a squared letter 'C' handle. An example has been incorrectly included in Plate 22, top right, amongst much earlier cup shapes, but it is marked G. Grainger, Worcester dating it into the 1840s. It was used for pattern 2/454.

Various further shapes were made in the 1850s and 1860s and beyond. By this time, they are likely to be marked and so we have chosen not to include descriptions or details here. We are pleased to have been able to illustrate so many of the shapes from the first forty years of the factory, and look forward to hearing from collectors of any shapes which fill some of the gaps in our knowledge.

45. *A Chemical Porcelain service of c.1860. Simple sets like this were the factory's 'bread and butter', and far more were made like this than the rich ornamental wares sought by collectors today. Such services frequently bore an additional crest or badge. (Private Collection)*

CHAPTER FOUR

DESSERT
AND DINNER WARES

The problems in identifying Grainger dessert wares are somewhat greater than the teawares as almost no drawings exist in the pattern books. Early examples are very much rarer than the contemporary teawares and there is therefore much less opportunity to contrast marked examples. The range of different shapes does not seem to be that great, fortunately, and we are pleased with the results of our research, although the chronology is much more difficult than with the teawares, and it is likely that the order in which we have chosen to discuss the shapes differs from the actual order of introduction. Only one piece of early dessert ware in the hybrid porcelain body is known to us. This is the tureen shown in Plate 46 which is unmarked. The attribution is based on the finial which is unique to Grainger on teawares of New Oval shape. The pattern is truly magnificent and the piece is as fine as any factory's dessert wares of the period. The large soup tureen in the same photograph is marked in red 'Grainger & Co. Worcester' and must date from around 1812 to 1814. It is in the inferior bone china body and is somewhat stained, although the gilding remains as bright as ever. Both tureens have eccentric handles and are generally elegant.

A plate from the same service as the soup tureen is perfectly plain and would imply that early Grainger plates were just plain circular without notched rims or any moulding. It would seem likely that Grainger copied the shapes popular at Chamberlain and Coalport at this period, and it may well be that other early moulded forms survive unmarked and unrecognized. Gilding played an important part in Grainger dessert wares, and Plate 47 shows a plate with similar simple flower painting within a remarkable border. This is marked Grainger Lee & Co. Worcester.

Two shapes from the 1812–15 period have been identified purely as a result of the excavations. Plate 48 shows a 9″ dessert plate with an all over pattern of moulded daisy heads. Small nursery plates and jugs with daisy moulding were common in English pottery throughout the first half of the nineteenth century, but a porcelain plate is most unusual. The wasters are beautifully crisp but under the thick glaze the finished plate is disappointing. The style of painting is typical of a large number of Staffordshire factories and without the matching waster this plate could never have been identified.

Plate 49, right, shows another border moulding which is unique to Grainger and corresponds with an identical fragment found on the Grainger site. Repeated herringbone or arrow motifs encircle the rim but once again the thick glaze obliterates most of the detail. The centre is typically Grainger painting, inspired by Dr George Davis at Chamberlain. The gold remains refreshingly bright.

Pattern 399 is fully drawn out in the pattern books and is called 'New Embossed'. In Plate 18 we illustrate a cup and wasters of the teaware version of New Embossed. The dessert plate has flower sprays moulded all over in low relief, and these probably will match a waster from the site shown in Plate 12, bottom right. The modelling on this biscuit waster is remarkably sharp, and it is sad to think that when a finished example does turn up it will be a great disappointment under the thick glaze. This characteristic is emphasized by the plate with a moulded flower border shown in Plate 49, left. We recognized this, the only known example, only because the glaze felt so thick and crazed and the gold remained bright. On checking, we found the border sprays and painted decoration exactly matched pattern 435 in the Grainger pattern book. The quality of potting is very disappointing on Grainger wares of the period around 1815, and this plate is a poor specimen of English porcelain, although typically Grainger.

The teawares of Old Embossed pattern are shown in Plate 16. This most elaborate moulded design was also used for dessert wares, and we know of two dishes and a few plates with the moulded palmette and scrollwork seen on the cups

46. Two early Grainger tureens, the dessert tureen (left) in hybrid hard paste porcelain, c.1810, the soup tureen in bone china, marked Grainger & Co Worcester, c.1812–14. Both tureens have the eccentric handles that appear to have been popular at this time. (Left, Phillips; right, Jill Gosling Antiques)

47. A plate marked Grainger Lee & Co with distinctive painting; the fine gilding includes half-shaded bell flowers, a popular motif at Grainger's factory, c.1815–18. (Private Collection)

48. A dessert plate with delicate daisy head moulding, 9 inches, c.1815. Unmarked, but identified by exactly matching biscuit wasters. (Private Collection)

and saucers. The dishes use the same mould as a plate, with just a crude shell handle stuck on at one side. Lacking gold, badly crazed and crude, the quality leaves a great deal to be desired and these are in no way a credit to the factory.

The Old India pattern occurs on a great range of early Grainger Lee & Co. services and can be used to illustrate the different dessert service forms as well as the way the factory combined their basic shapes with different moulded borders. The plain circular shape without a rim design is seen on the tureen and stand in Plate 50. The finial is a flanged artichoke and there are classical loop handles on the side. The plates and dishes in this service have a gadrooned rim and are lobed in

49. Two poorly-potted dessert plates of early Grainger Lee & Co period, c.1814–18. Left, pattern 435; right, border matching factory wasters; unmarked. (Authors' Collections)

50. A dessert tureen in Old India pattern. Examples are known without handles and with other finials. Grainger Lee & Co Worcester, c.1815–18. (Private Collection)

51. A Gadroon-edged dessert dish from the same service as the tureen in Plate 50, pattern 391 in gold on the reverse. (Private Collection)

outline (Plate 51), the standard form of gadrooning occurring on many such sets, although a plain plate also went with similar dessert tureens. The round dessert tureen was made without handles, and on another version, instead of a circular foot, the tureen rises on the backs of three swans. In this case, an eagle forms the finial and a waster from an identical tureen is shown alongside in plate 52. The example on the left in Old India has a plain rim, while the richer tureen on the left has a very elaborate moulded rim called by the factory 'Full Gadroon'. We will return to this version later, but in the meantime there are a number of more unusual shapes which accompanied Grainger Lee & Co. services around 1815.

The leaf dish in Plate 53 is a shape from eighteenth-century English porcelain, revived by Grainger Lee & Co. here using pattern 1418, suggesting a date after 1820. Old India pattern has additional painted thorns and a feathered edge. We know of only a single example of this shape which is raised on three flat curving feet and is 7″ long.

The ice pail which accompanied the plain dessert wares is shown in Plate 54. Here the finials are clearly pineapples rather than artichokes and the handles are scallop shells. The base is raised on three bun feet and this example is marked 'Grainger Ice Box, Worcester', along with pattern 660. It stands 9″ high. Ice pails were in no way unique to Worcester and why Grainger should mark their own 'Ice Box' so proudly is a mystery.

52. Two different versions of a standard dessert tureen of c.1815–20, the bowls supported on three well-modelled swans. One has a plain rim, the other with 'full gadroon' moulding. A biscuit waster of the foot of a similar tureen was found on the factory site and has been photographed alongside. Left, marked Grainger Lee & Co. Worcester and decorated with the popular 'Old India' pattern. (Authors' collections and Phillips)

A much more splended ice pail shape which went with the Full Gadroon service is shown in Plate 56. Here the border is in deep blue and gold and the bases simulate marble. Gilded lions adorn the handles and the pineapple finials are the same as on the Grainger Ice Box. This fine pair is painted with named views in Devon and in Paris. The reverse decoration on both contains a gilt songbook, the notes of 'God Save the King' clearly discernible. Full Gadroon seems to have been reserved for the finest decoration of this period. The plate illustrated here in Colour Plate IV is a magnificent specimen only 8″ across, the painting attempting to rival Chamberlain or Barr, Flight & Barr. This example is marked Grainger Lee & Co. and represents their finest flower painting before the arrival of David Evans.

53. A large leaf-shaped dish raised on three curving feet, c.1820. This elaborate version of Old India pattern bears number 1418 in red, 7 inches long, marked Grainger Lee & Co Worcester. (Private Collection)

54. A large ice pail in Old India pattern, number 660; marked under the lid Grainger Ice Box, Worcester, 9 inches high, c.1815–20. (Private Collection)

55. *A full service of Blue Ball Japan patttern in two tones of underglaze blue, red enamel and gold. The gadroon edge is used on standard shapes of c.1825, pattern 1472. (Sotheby's)*

56. *Two splendid ice pails from a dessert service of Full Gadroon shape, c.1820. The views are titled underneath Lynmouth and Linton, Devonshire; and Rue Castiglione, 14½ inches high, marked Grainger Lee & Co Worcester. (Phillips)*

57. Copied from a Chamberlain shape, this elaborate ring finial was used on most Grainger dinner and dessert tureens in the 1820s, usually combined with large claw feet. The handles have female mask terminals, marked Grainger Lee & Co Worcester. (Christie's)

By 1820 the gadroon rim was widely used for dinner services and we show two extensive sets in contrasting styles of decoration. Colour Plate VIII shows part of a dinner service which comprised 117 pieces. The finials on the tureens are complicated rings copied apparently from Chamberlain. The large paw feet occur on all of the tureens and are very distinctive. For some reason it was usual for tureens to have a rectangular outline in these services while the dishes were basically oval. Plate 55 is a service of a pattern called by Grainger 'Blue Ball Japan', a single plate of which is shown in Plate 168 alongside matching wasters. In this service, the soup tureen is circular while the vegetable dishes and sauce tureens are the more conventional rectangular forms. This set was sold at Sotheby's in 1988 as Staffordshire, an understandable mistake as the decoration is much more suited to an ironstone service than the poor bone china. The shapes and pattern number 1472 link them conclusively to Grainger, however. Interestingly, the service also included a pierced drainer.

Grainger's gadroon edge is in itself fairly distinctive. The rim-moulding includes three fine lines betweeen each larger lobe, and while Grainger do not seem to have been unique in this, it is an easy way to distinguish them from Coalport, for example, who used a different form.

A variant of the small tureen shape is shown in Plate 57. The finial and feet are distinctive enough, although here the section is circular and the cover is heavily fluted with oak leaves modelled around the finial. This is from a marked Grainger Lee & Co. service and is shown with a deep soup plate or muffin dish.

58. *A plate of Essex Embossed shape, c.1822–5, copied from Staffordshire pottery of seventy years earlier. The wasters reveal how crisp the modelling is and the plate is shown with a waster of the rare Essex Plain shape; unmarked. (Authors' Collections)*

59. *A breakfast service of Dresden Embossed shape, c.1830. Large quantities of wasters of this shape were found on the factory site, suggesting production was substantial, although examples are rarely seen. The matching teapot is shown in Plate 29. (Private Collection)*

Reverting back to the pattern books, mention is made of other dessert wares, some of which have been traced. The first distinctive shape is Wellington Embossed, a lobed plate with moulded borders of three rococo scroll cartouches flanked by cornflower-type sprays. Copied directly from French porcelain, we have seen versions of this shape in English bone china but none which can be attributed to Grainger.

'Essex Embossed', first mentioned on pattern 1487 around 1822–5 is copied from early English pottery which in itself was copying silver shapes. The lobed plates with panels of embossed 'seed diaper' occur in saltglazed stoneware and Whieldon glazed pottery in the 1750s. Grainger seems to have been the only factory to have revived this fairly striking shape and the examples we have seen have all been sparsely decorated to emphasize the crispness of the modelling. The plate illustrated here alongside matching wasters (Plate 58) is painted in the manner of Welsh porcelain with wild roses and strawberries. Although David Evans had joined Worcester from Swansea, the quality of this plate lacks his delicacy and is possibly the work of a pupil.

We have photographed the Essex Embossed plate alongside a waster which is essentially the same except that the border has omitted the seed diaper panels. The factory name for this was understandably 'Essex Plain' and examples are surprisingly rare. We know of a single service only of pattern 1473, Dragon Japan, in the Kakiemon style inspired by Oriental porcelain. The shape is very English, however, and the handle of the shell-shaped dessert dish is a most remarkable affair in the form of a closed head of a thistle plant within pierced scrolls. Curiously, the shape was reintroduced around 1900 and a plate of Essex Embossed in the Dyson Perrins Museum has cattle painted on it by John Stinton.

60. *Hand-coloured transfer prints on a dinner service of pattern number 759x, c.1837–40. The simple lobed rim on the dinner plate was popular at many factories. (Private Collection)*

61. *Fine quality gadroon-edged dessert wares with a semi-matt blue ground. Each piece is painted with an English landscape, c.1825. Most are marked Grainger Lee & Co Worcester. (Sotheby's)*

62. *Three dishes from a further gadroon-edged service with distinctive pierced handles, all marked Grainger Lee & Co Worcester, with the title of the view, c.1825. Chamberlain made very similar shapes but with not quite such strong scroll modelling. (Private Collection)*

63. *Further pieces from the gadroon-edged service shown in Plate 62. The centrepiece is particularly elaborate, marked Grainger Lee & Co Worcester. (Private Collection)*

64. *A Grainger dessert centrepiece which again is very similar to a Chamberlain model, although in this case the Grainger version is slightly more flamboyant. This piece is unmarked, although marked examples have been noted; c.1825. (Private Collection)*

65. *A dessert service of New Dresden shape, c.1830–5. The flowers are painted over lightly-printed outlines and these are particularly fine examples of the rococo revival popular at this time. Pattern 203x. (Phillips)*

66. *Three dishes from a dessert service of Brunswick shape with different garden flowers treated in a botanical way. The largest dish is 11¾ inches; marked Thomas Grainger & Co Royal China Works Worcester, pattern 723x, c.1835–40. (Private Collection)*

67. *A dessert service with characteristic gold 'Twigging', the shape probably called Queen's or Queen's Embossed, marked Thomas Grainger & Co Royal China Works Worcester, c.1837–8.*

Dresden Embossed, discussed at length on pp. 62–3, was also used for breakfast and dinner services and some sizeable dishes and tureens were made. Plate 59 shows a small number of shapes showing that the modelling was consistent throughout the service. It was probably inspired by Minton, although Grainger could have introduced the shape first, copying Meissen of the same period.

The teaware shape called Broseley seems to have been used for dinnerware too, although in a more simplified form. The plate, a standard shape at Coalport and a great many other makers, has six pairs of notches lightly cut into the rim. The Blue Dragon pattern plate (Plate 169), marked Grainger Lee & Co., probably dates from before 1820, while the dinner service of pattern 759x (Plate 60) is from the late 1830s. This is decorated with a coloured-in transfer print popular at the time and the tureen shapes would have been given their own names, which we have not traced. These are part of a very extensive dinner service still used regularly by its owners in Surrey.

During the 1820s the gadroon edge was used with two principal shapes of dessert service. One is represented on a service (Plate 61) which was purchased in Ireland in 1972 and subsequently sold at Sotheby's. Every piece is painted with a named landscape view, mostly of country houses and listing the name of the owner and, in addition, most are marked Grainger Lee & Co. Worcester. The handles are rustic twigs with vine-leaf terminals and the tureen finial is a spray of grapes. We know of several services with the same inner tooled gold border and either blue or red grounds, and mostly these sets are unmarked. It has been suggested that the decoration was put on outside of the factory by Doe & Rogers or Sparks, both china painters in Worcester, but as one of the sets is marked Grainger Lee & Co. in full, this seems unlikely. One service has a matching ice pail of the same shape as that shown in Plate 56, using the earlier Full Gadroon border, presumably because there was no up-to-date ice pail model available.

The other standard gadroon-edged service is shown in plates 62 and 63. Here the ground colour is again blue and the named views are of exceptional quality. The rustic handles have been replaced with rococo scrollwork, while the tureen is raised

68. A dessert service of the same shape as the William Lewis presentation service shown in Colour Plate X. This distinctly Grainger style of flower painting continued into the 1840s. Marked Thomas Grainger & Co Worcester, c.1840–5. (Phillips)

on twig and leaf feet. The circular centrepiece is an unusually grand affair with a pierced rim, although an alternative shape is shown in Plate 64. Here the example is unmarked and probably outside decorated by an artist such as Conningsby Norris (see p. 175). Marked examples of this shape have been recorded and these are virtually identical to a Chamberlain model. Geoffrey Godden illustrates several pieces of this service in his Chamberlain book and these show just how close the two factories came. Great care has to be taken in attributing unmarked examples. Godden, in fact, illustrates a Grainger dish in plate 285 of his Chamberlain book, but the pattern number 1473 corresponds with 'Dragon Japan' in the Grainger pattern book, not the Chamberlain list. We do not believe Chamberlain made this twig and leaf handle.

'New Dresden' shape on dessert wares is shown in Plate 65 on a service sold by Phillips in 1988. The pattern number 203x links up with the pattern books and the date will be around 1830. The shapes are pleasing and without a coloured ground the effect is light and flowing. Rococo modelling was certainly used extensively at Meissen (Dresden) but we have not been able to trace an exact prototype for this Grainger service.

The botanical dessert service shown in Plate 66 is of a shape given two names in the pattern books. Originally called 'Plant Dessert', it appears to have been changed to 'Brunswick Embossed' or just 'Brunswick'. It was used on patterns in the 650x–750x range and the set illustrated, of pattern 723x, is marked Thomas

69. A dinner service with a strong border design contrasted with plain centres, a style popular c.1850. Note the distinctive diamond-shaped finials. Impressed mark G G W S P. (Private Collection)

70. A dessert service of a distinctive form, featuring one of the strong well-controlled ground colours used in the 1850s; marked G Grainger, Semi-porcelain Prize Ware. (Private Collection)

Grainger & Co., Royal China Works, Worcester. In this case, only part of the embossed border has been picked out in gilding to leave room for the painted flower specimens, while other patterns have much more elaborate borders. The shape was reintroduced in the 1890s. Brunswick shape used the same basic form of centrepiece as another dessert shape introduced at about the same time.

Queens shape is another rococo shape with an irregular shell edging used in the range 1000x–1200x. It is referred to in two different versions, 'Queens Embossed' and 'Queens Plain dessert' and we have been unable to determine the difference. We are convinced that the shapes shown in Plate 67 are of Queens shape, named after Queen Victoria, as this pattern range was used around 1837 or 1838. This service is again marked Thomas Grainger & Co., Worcester.

A very important dessert service is shown in Colour Plate X. Painted with views of the City of Worcester, each piece bears the civic crest and the initials of William Lewis. It was made for Lewis when he was Mayor of Worcester in the 1840s (see p. 24). This illustration shows clearly the high quality of which the factory was capable. Worcester Cathedral is faithfully reproduced on one comport, while the centrepiece shows the Guildhall in an elaborate painting with numerous coaches and figures in the foreground. The shapes used were popular around 1840 but we have not identified their factory name. In the case of the presentation service, the

71. *A dessert service of the standard shape used around 1870. Delicate painting such as this is usually attributed to John Stinton senior but clearly more than one painter worked on this service. The named scenes are mostly dated 1873, and the plate is 9½ inches; impressed shield marks. (Private Collection)*

72. *A plate with a named Scottish castle, from a dessert service with turquoise border and simulated pearl rim, 9½ inches, impressed shield mark, c.1870. (Bowes Museum, Barnard Castle)*

cups and saucers are of Malvern shape. More simple decoration, although just as fine in its own way, is on an earlier service of the same shape shown in Plate 68 and marked, once again, Thomas Grainger & Co., Worcester.

From the later 1840s until the 1860s the general quality of Grainger services declined. Flower or landscape painting tended to be replaced by plain centres or formal gilding, with the use of strong ground colours and gold in the borders. Two such services are illustrated here. Plate 69 shows the standard shapes of around 1850, the plates moulded with five sets of triple lobes. The diamond-shaped finials are distinctive also, and these wares will generally be marked G. Grainger, Royal Porcelain Works, Worcester, on every piece. The most popular border colour was a bright turquoise ground, lighter generally than the turquoise enamel popular at Coalport and Minton in this same period. It was used in conjunction with some magnificent armorial decoration, such as the set made for the Earl of Carnarvon, although these are exceptional and most centres were rather plain. The dessert service in Plate 70 again uses pentagonal symmetry for the plates, and will date from around 1850.

During the 1860s and 1870s a standard shape was used for almost all Grainger dessert services. The rim is embossed with 44 studs, left in brilliant white against a tinted ground with gold settings to imitate pearls. Turquoise or deep blue grounds

73. A late Grainger dessert service with distinctive lobed shapes and unusual flower painting in contrasting colours, shield marks, c.1880. (Private Collection)

90

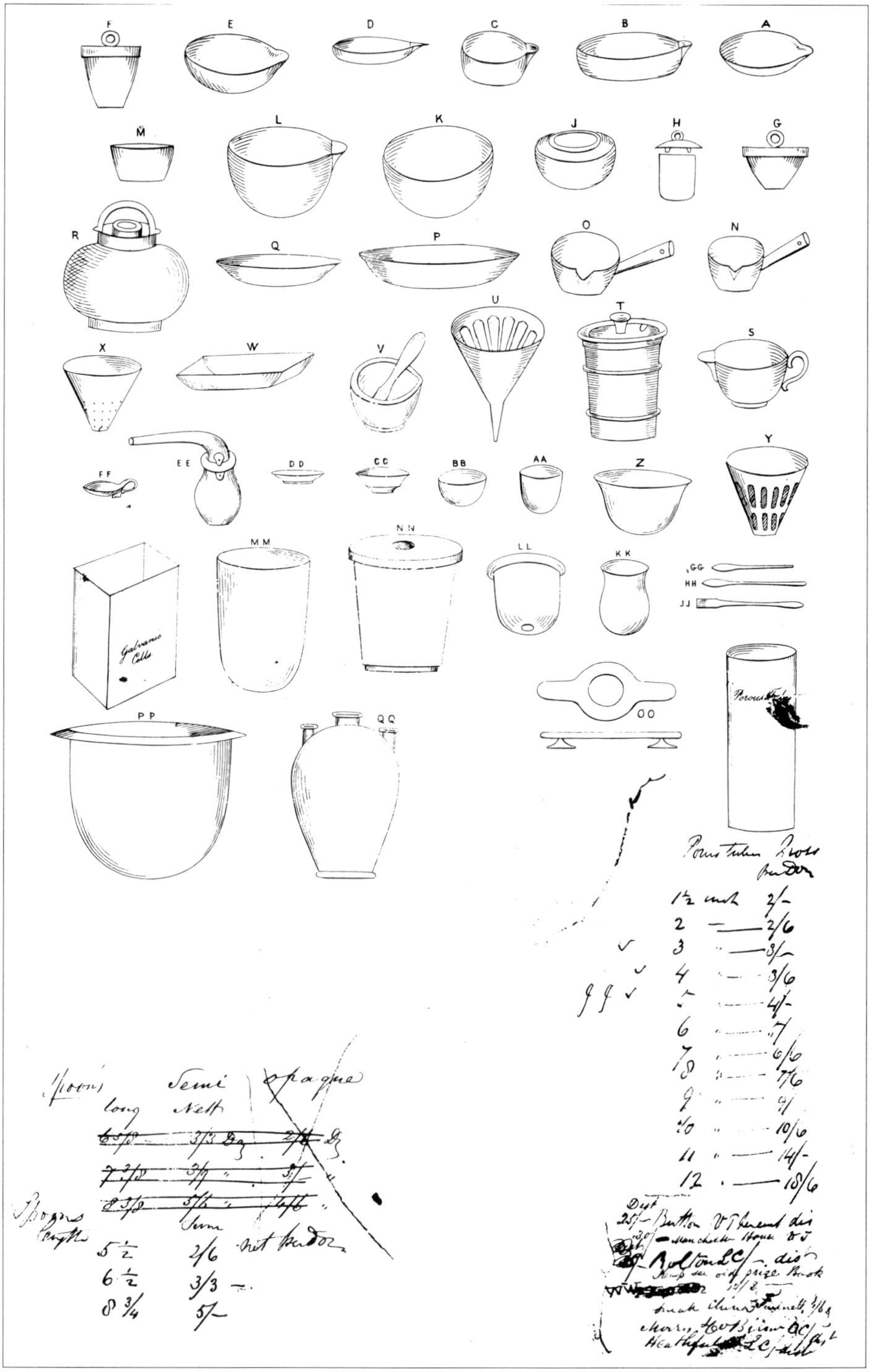

Figure 5. *Grainger's chemical porcelain shown in a factory catalogue sheet dated 1854. Most examples will have been unmarked and it is likely that very few will have survived.*

91

were favoured, with landscape centres usually delicately painted. Often unmarked, the comports and some of the plates can have the impressed shield mark to confirm a Grainger origin, and the comports will always have dolphin supports.

Finally, in the 1880s and into the early 1900s, the factory seems to have introduced few new dinner or dessert shapes. The only exceptions of which we know are the plain lobed shapes painted with sweeping plants, shown in Plate 73. Instead, they reused moulds from fifty or more years before, such as Essex Embossed or Brunswick. Plate 74 is a dish with the shield mark and date code for 1899, although the shape would date stylistically to the 1830s. We have not come across an earlier service of this shape, but illustrate the replacement in the hope that this will bring an original Grainger set to light.

74. A late Grainger dessert dish in flamboyant rococo shape, bearing the date code for 1899 but nevertheless probably using a mould which was made nearly seventy years earlier; shield mark. (Private Collection)

CHAPTER FIVE

MUGS, JUGS,
AND PRESENTATION PIECES

All porcelain manufacturers could afford to put more time and effort into special commissions than into their general range of tea and dinnerwares. Grainger were no exception and the range of presentation jugs and mugs produced in the early years of the factory represent some of their greatest achievements. It is, however, likely that a great many are unmarked and therefore very difficult to attribute to Grainger.

The first marked and dated piece (Colour Plate I) came as a great surprise when we discovered it in a job lot in a small auction in Malvern in 1987, sitting forlornly, its handle broken into several pieces placed inside the mug. Cleaned up and restuck, it is a stunning example of the Japan style and we are proud to own such an historic piece. We do not know Grainger's name for the pattern but Chamberlain called it Fine Old Japan. The two quail found in the Chamberlain and Coalport versions of this pattern have become herons in the panel on this Grainger mug and the gold is remarkably warm and bright. On the base is the mark 'Grainger & Co. Worcester Sepr 26 1807' in red. The piece stands 5″ high and the handle has the very slight hint of a spur on top.

It is clear from the various examples shown in this book that there was no consistency in the ways in which handles were formed. Some early mugs have only very slight spurs, while others are quite pronounced, and the shape of the handle is not evidence of a Grainger origin. Clues normally lie in the decoration and in particular the gilding, which was Grainger's greatest asset. We discovered the small jug in Plate 75 in Portobello Road antiques market early one Saturday morning and were delighted to read another important inscription on the base. Neatly around the footrim is the legend 'Manufactur'd by Mesrs. Grainger & Co. Worcester May, 1809'. The significance of the date dawned on us only later. Just one month earlier, the factory had been destroyed by fire, yet they were able to take a jug, probably salvaged from the ashes, and gild it superbly with a slight use of red enamel in the cypher on the front. Perhaps it was a gift to a local person who had advanced money following the disaster, the inscription proudly declaring Grainger was back in business.

This slight combination of red enamel and gold is seen on two further pieces and is clearly a Grainger characteristic. The small mug in Plate 77 is decorated with a border design seen on Grainger Wood & Co. teawares in red and gold, with the

75. *An important documentary jug gilt with a cypher J P, the base dated May 1809, one month after fire destroyed the works; 6½ inches. (Dyson Perrins Museum, Gift of John Sandon).*

76. *The underside of the jug illustrated in Plate 75, showing the elaborate documentary inscription in red.*

addition of a cypher and wreath flanked by sprigs. There is no doubt in our minds whatsoever that this unmarked mug is Grainger, but if it had been painted with coloured flowers or a landscape it would be called Coalport by most collectors and dealers. Simple mugs of this shape are not uncommon, and almost always a Coalport origin is put forward, although none are ever marked. Some of the mugs must surely be Grainger.

A wonderful presentation jug is in the Victoria and Albert Museum, with a cypher in gold and red and underglaze blue leaves and border picked out in rich gilding. We have chosen to illustrate the side view (Plate 78) because it is the quality of the gilding which makes this, in our view, such a remarkable piece. The front is painted with a subject of game and the jug is marked 'Grainger & Co. Worcester 1811'.

77. A simple presentation mug with a gilt initial on the front and with the characteristic Grainger sprigs in gold and red; the same border was also used on tewares. Unmarked but almost certainly Grainger, c.1808–10. (Authors' Collections)

78. The side view of an important presentation jug, the front with a painted panel of game, the rich underglaze blue ground finely gilded; marked Grainger & Co. Worcester, 1811. (Victoria & Albert Museum)

The same shape was used for a remarkable jug in Bristol City Art Gallery (Plate 79). It depicts Bristol, seen from Clifton Wood on one side, with the arms of Bristol City and County on the reverse. Below the lip is an unidentified crest, initials S H and the motto *Amicitia*. The armorial devices and the landscape view are unsophisticated but the gilding, like that on so much early Grainger, is outstanding. The mark Grainger & Co. Worcester is in black script.

Bristol was a major trading centre in the early nineteenth century and the Worcester factories seem to have had an important market there. Another important outlet was Cheltenham and from the number of pieces surviving,

79. The views of a magnificent early Grainger presentation jug, one side painted with the arms of the City & County of Bristol, the reverse with a view from Clifton Wood; 8 inches, marked Grainger & Co Worcester, in black, c.1810. (Bristol City Art Gallery).

Grainger clearly regarded the town very highly as a retail outlet. The earliest known view of Cheltenham on a Grainger mug is shown in Plate 80, on an example in Cheltenham Art Gallery and Museum. It is painted with a view of Royal Crescent, Cheltenham and is marked Grainger and Co. Worcester Warranted.

Early Grainger views of Worcester are surprisingly uncommon. One splendid example is the presentation jug (Plate 81) now in a collection near Rugby. It has an orange border with gilding, the gilding perhaps less intricate than on other examples, while the painting in black monochrome is a remarkably detailed view of the city from the north-west. The jug is marked Grainger & Co. Worcester and would have been accompanied by a pair of beakers, which were usually unmarked. The example illustrated in Plate 82 was sold as Chamberlain in a recent major auction, but an identical example has been seen with a Grainger mark.

80. An early mug with characteristic Grainger gilt sprigs flanking a view of Royal Crescent, Cheltenham; marked Grainger & Co Worcester Warranted, c.1810. (Cheltenham Art Gallery & Museum)

81. Two views of a presentation jug with a distinctive handle and orange border, painted in black with a view of Worcester from the northwest, 5⅞ inches, marked Grainger & Co Worcester in gold, c.1810. (Private Collection)

82. *A beaker which would have accompanied a jug similar to Plate 81. Unmarked but identical examples are marked Grainger & Co Worcester, 3¾ inches, c.1810. (Phillips)*

83. *A fine large porter mug similar to the pair show in Colour Plate II, but with a salmon-orange coloured ground, also richly gilt. Marked Grainger & Co. (Christie's)*

84. *A miniature jug only 1⅘ inches high inscribed 'North view of Worcester, Grainger Lee & Co. Worcester'. The image is remarkably fine. (Private Collection, Canada).*

85. *A lidded jug for toast and water, Old India pattern 391, 6¾ inches, marked Grainger Lee & Co; the handle has been riveted together at a later date. (Private Collection)*

86. A presentation piece inscribed 'View of Worcester Regatta 1846', the gilt inscription 'E.R. Rowlands No. 2' added after the race; 4 inches, marked George Grainger Royal China Works Worcester. (Victoria & Albert Museum)

87. Three marked Grainger mugs, 1840s and 1850s, the central loving cup with badge of the Worcester Rowing Club. (Central mug, Worcester City Museum; others, Private Collection)

88. Three English porcelain mugs (not Grainger) decorated by Conningsby Norris and presented to the Dyson Perrins Museum by a descendant.

Oddly, while the teawares in this period are normally marked Grainger Wood & Co., the presentation pieces never include Wood's name and are always styled Grainger & Co. We can offer no explanation for this anomaly, although it is discussed further in Appendix 7. The Grainger mark is usually more crudely written than Chamberlain's or Flight's name marks and indeed can be almost illegible at times. Such a mark occurs on three of the finest Grainger pieces from this early period, hunting mugs of large size, the square panels completely filling the front of the mugs.

Chamberlain made some fine examples of this sort of subject, while Grainger only occasionally attempted anything so elaborate. Colour Plate II shows a pair of mugs sold at Phillips in 1987 for £7,150. Of the large size known as 'Porter' mugs, they were 4½" high and while the painting is dramatic, the gilding on the reverse of the mugs is even more exceptional. One mug is entitled 'Drawing Cover', the other shows 'The Death'. The same hand is seen on a mug sold at Christie's in 1981. On this occasion, a salmon-orange ground was used and again the gilding is of the highest merit (Plate 83).

Grainger Lee & Co. period mugs are surprisingly uncommon. Virtually all of the examples known are of a single shape, cylindrical with a turned circular foot and gnarled *tau* or T-shaped handle. Colour Plate III shows a pair with different views of Worcester, painted with painstaking detail and bright gold around the panel. Most examples of this shape are painted with Worcester from the north-west, the bridge in the foreground, and some even used a printed outline as a guide to the painter. A range of miniature jugs and some tiny toy washbowls are known, usually painted with views of Worcester and Malvern, the nearby spa town. The example in Plate 84 is only 1¾" high and is painted with a 'North View of Worcester', copied from a well-known print of the city from the gardens of Henwick House. The base just has room for the name of the view and Grainger Lee & Co. Worcester.

89. A marked Grainger mug with exceptional flower painting and characteristic handle shape, c.1840. (Dyson Perrins Museum)

One other jug shape from around 1815–20 is worth a mention, shown in Plate 85. It is a toast and water jug designed with a pierced strainer and rather loose fitting cover. Burnt toast, crushed and mixed with water, was popular as a medicinal drink around 1820 and many factories made jugs, sometimes titled 'toast' or 'toast and water' on the front. The Grainger Lee & Co. example is in the popular 'Old India' pattern, 391.

90. Two views of a mug inscribed and dated 1862. The original copper plates for the outline prints survive in the Grainger archives but this mug, and many like it, is unmarked. It is possible the porcelain was not made at Grainger. (Dyson Perrins Museum)

91. Two cups and saucers with inscriptions relating to the Bradford china dealer Charles Rhodes, one presented by the Chamberlain factory, the other by George Grainger & Co, c.1850. (Private Collection)

The gnarled *tau* or 'T' handle was, it seems, replaced by a simple scroll handle with a leaf finial and single inward-pointing spur. Single and double-handled examples were made and the decoration ranges from very plain to rich presentation pieces. The factory had a close connection with the Worcester Rowing Club and made presentation pieces for the Worcester Regatta over a period of some seventy years. The piece in Plate 86 was awarded to E. R. Rowlands as the prize in Competition No. 2 in 1846. On the front is a view of the Regatta taking place on the River Severn and the mug is marked George Grainger, Royal China Works, Worcester. A later example is the loving cup made in about 1870, again showing the Regatta in progress but bearing on the reverse just the crest of the Worcester Rowing Club, with no winner's name or date. The scene appears painted, but Fig. 10 is a pull from the original copper plate which printed the outline. The artists have added the Regatta boats to an existing view of the river.

Only one other shape is occasionally seen on mugs and this has a double scroll handle with a single spur at the top. Plate 90 shows an example with a turquoise ground and view of Worcester and Malvern, inscribed 'Frank Waldron, Born July 6th 1862'. These two views are, in fact, coloured-over transfer prints and the engraved copper plate for these scenes still survives at the Worcester factory. We must admit to serious doubts about the origins of mugs of this type. Although the views match Grainger copper plates, we have never seen marked examples of either shape or decoration. They could be the work of outside decorators on Staffordshire blanks.

92. A poor photograph of a standard Grainger presentation shape of the 1850s, in this case given to Charles Rhodes of Bradford in June 1852. 7¾ inches, marked G Grainger Worcester, 28 Princess Street, Manchester.

93. A presentation punchbowl, probably a leaving gift, given by the potters at the Grainger factory to Joseph Scragg in 1860. 14 inches diameter. (Private Collection, Australia)

About twenty years ago a small number of mugs were given to the Dyson Perrins Museum by a descendant of Joseph Grainger and all came through the Grainger family. One is inscribed 'Mary Ann Grainger 1841' and two others are signed by Conningsby Norris who had married Mary Ann Grainger. The danger of accepting family history at face value is evident here as it is likely that none of these mugs was made at Grainger. Conningsby Norris worked as a free-lance decorator in Worcester and seems mostly to have painted on Coalport or Staffordshire blanks. The three mugs in Plate 88 are not Grainger shapes and must be treated with great caution. Another presentation mug in the Worcester Museum which is more likely to be Grainger is inscribed 'Harriet Ann Gosling. A birth day gift from her Affectionate Uncle Wm. Daniel'. A William Daniel was a gilder at Grainger and it is likely he made this piece for his niece.

A number of other presentation pieces and services are referred to in other parts of this book. A few others are worth mentioning here, particularly a number of items given by the factory to Charles Rhodes, a china dealer in Darlay Street, Bradford. For some reason, Rhodes was presented with special pieces by a number of English factories in about 1850. Plate 91 shows two cups and saucers inscribed to Mr Charles Rhodes by 'the Proprietors of Chamberlains Works' and 'by George Grainger & Co. Worcester'. A large goblet with turquoise ground is also known, inscribed 'Presented to Mr. Chas. Rhodes, Bradford, By George Grainger of

Worcester as a token of respect June 1852' (Plate 92). The same shape of goblet was given by the factory to the Worcester Glee Club and a pair of these are in the Dyson Perrins Museum.

Finally, a large punch bowl painted with flowers and a view of Worcester is inscribed 'Presented to Joseph Scragg as a Mark of Respect by the Potters Employed at Messrs. Grainger & Co's., Jan'y 1860'. The decoration includes gilded hops and barley. This example is 14″ in diameter, marked Grainger & Co. and is now in Australia (Plate 93).

Figure 6. *The underglaze portion of a rare printed pattern, c.1825, illustrated by a modern pull from a Grainger copper plate.*

CHAPTER SIX

VASES
AND ORNAMENTAL JUGS

When we began our research into the Grainger shapes we thought that recording the vase shapes would be the easiest part, as a great many pieces are fully marked, and the factory shape books illustrate a large range of vases beautifully drawn out. It soon became apparent, however, that there were going to be many problems. The shape books do not record any shapes made before about 1825, and Grainger tended to copy other makers so closely that finding a matching shape in the books is not conclusive proof in itself. Our biggest problem has been to explode the myth that any unmarked vase with a Worcester feel but not attributable to either Flight or Chamberlain, must therefore be Grainger. This notion goes back a very long way and numerous vases which we now know to be Staffordshire are illustrated in old books and catalogues as Grainger. Our worldwide appeal for information resulted in us receiving photographs of a great many vases believed by their owners to be Grainger. Many were inspired by Flight's rich styles of the Regency period but Staffordshire factories were just as keen to copy a popular range as Grainger would have been. Even a view of Worcester painted on an unmarked vase does not mean much, as we know of many independent china painters in Worcester who used Staffordshire or Coalport blanks.

We have been careful, therefore, to eliminate any shape which is not absolutely certain to be Grainger. All of the shapes illustrated in this book are either fully marked or tie up conclusively with the shape books. Unmarked vases have been seen which are exactly the same as marked examples and a few of these have been included where we have no doubt that the piece in question is Grainger. Significantly, there are very few unmarked vases. Grainger were in fierce competition in Worcester with the other factories and decorators and consequently proudly marked most of their richest productions. We do no believe that many vases were sold without marks, except possibly before 1825 when Grainger examples are particularly hard to find.

The earliest vase which can be attributed to Grainger, and indeed the only one known in the hybrid porcelain body, is shown in Colour Plate XIV. It belonged in the nineteenth century to R. W. Binns, who believed it to have been painted by John Wood. The shape is similar to early Coalport from the first decade of the nineteenth century, and the mark 'Grainger & Co. Worcester' does not exclude the possibility that this is John Wood's painting on a Coalport blank, before Grainger Wood & Co. were producing their own porcelain. The subject of hare coursing was later to become important to George Grainger, who bred his own greyhounds.

Except for the magnificent vase on the front cover of this book, the only other vase marked Grainger & Co. is in the bone china body and must date from 1812–14. It is copied from a Derby pastille burner: the shape was particularly used at Derby in the centre of an inkstand. Grainger also made an inkstand with this central design (Plate 140) but smaller than the vases in Plate 94. These examples are both missing their covers and are the only ones known to us.

The popular pattern Old India, with a coloured-in underglaze print, was used on a pair of massive vases which can be seen at Sudeley Castle in Warwickshire. A third example was sold in Leeds ten years ago and is illustrated here (Plate 95). It is marked 'Grainger Lee & Co. Worcester' and stands approximately three feet tall with its gilt eagle and globe finial. The vases were hand thrown on a wheel and must have been immensely difficult to fire in Grainger's bone china, and so the fact that three have survived nearly intact is remarkably fortunate. They must date from around 1820.

94. The central section of a Derby inkstand seems to have served as the model for these curious Grainger pastille burners made in bone china, c.1812–14. The example on the right is marked Grainger & Co. in red, and both would originally have had covers. (Authors' collections)

95. *A massive vase, the largest shape made at the factory, using the Old India pattern which had been designed for large meat dishes or tureens. Approximately three feet tall to the eagle and globe finial and marked Grainger Lee & Co Worcester; c.1820. (Phillips, Leeds)*

96. *A simple cylindrical spill vase with a view of Tremadoc, 3¾ inches, marked Grainger Lee & Co Worcester, c.1825. This shape was made by many factories and without a mark would be impossible to attribute. (Private Collection)*

A notebook preserved at the factory records the production costs of some of the ornamental shapes, with occasional dates between April 1826 and November 1831. The following references are to forms of spill vases:

Spill cans 3″
Spill cans or paper cases flanged 3½″, 4½″, 5″
Iacynth paper cases scalloped tops & square plinths 5½″ high, 6½″, 8½″
Spill can or paper cases, upright 4″, 4½″, 5″
ditto flang'd & with square feet and beaded by hand 3¾″, 4½″, 5⅛″
Flang'd spills double beaded 4¾″, 5¾″
Spills flang'd double bead and pierced at top 4½″, 5½″, 6″
8-sided paper cases 6″ grounds, gt [gilt] & flowers 7/6d [see Plate 98]
Square spill with gothic work bold gilt landscape & grounds 12/- [see Plate 100]

97. *Titled views of country houses were a popular form of decoration on English porcelain, c.1830. This spill vase and a cabinet cup (lacking its stand) are both marked Grainger Lee & Co. Worcester and elaborately titled underneath, the base depicting 'Lathum House, Lancashire, the Seat of E. B. Wildbraham Esq. MD.' The quality of painting is disappointing and the simple borders suggest that these were intended as inexpensive souvenirs. Simple spill vases were made in large numbers according to factory records, although few survive. (Authors' collections)*

98. A spill vase corresponding with the '8-sided paper cases' referred to in the Grainger archives. This example has a panel entitled 'Schoolboy', which is in fact painted over a lightly printed outline. 6 inches, marked Grainger Lee & Co Worcester, c.1830. (Private Collection)

99. An elaborate spill vase with a titled view of 'Trevan House – St. Columb – Cornwall', marked Grainger Lee & Co W'r, c.1830. (Private Collection)

100. A spill vase corresponding with the 'square spill with gothic work' mentioned in the factory records. The interior is marbled and the painting is characteristic of the factory; 5½ inches, marked Grainger Lee & Co Worcester. (Authors' Collections)

101. A view of Malvern painted on a plain vase shape of the 1820s, marked *Grainger Lee & Co. Worcester* in red; the gilt border occurs on many Grainger vases. *(Private Collection)*

102. A vase with swan handles in the French Empire style popular around 1820, 7½ inches, marked *Grainger Lee & Co Worcester*, striped gilding on the reverse. *(Private Collection)*

103. A naturalistic bird painting, unusual on Grainger vases, marked *Grainger Lee & Co Worcester*, 7⅞ inches, c.1820–5. *(Private Collection)*

104. A simple shape with a scalloped rim, painted with a view of Gloucester House, Malvern, 8 inches, marked *Grainger Lee & Co Worcester*, c.1825. *(Thornton Taylor Antiques)*

105. A fine pair of vases with views titled 'Old Bridge Bath' and 'Pulteney Bridge Bath'; 8¼ inches, marked Grainger Lee & Co Worcester, c.1825. (Andrew Dando Antiques, Bath)

Several very small flared (flang'd) trumpet spill vases have been seen marked Grainger Lee & Co. and we know of at least one with a rim of modelled beads or pearls. The Iacynth paper cases were probably similar to the drawing in the ornamental shape books (Colour Plate XVII) of which a single marked Grainger Lee & Co. example has been seen. In the same notebook, we are informed that Iacynths cost 4/7d to make, including 1/6d for modelling in clay, 6d for burning (firing), 2/- for painting and 3d for colour burning. Dahlias cost the same amount, while common flowers cost from 6d to 12d each to model and from 6d to 12d each for painting. In this way the factory could estimate the cost of making an elaborate flowered vase according to the number of flowers used to decorate it.

A very few wasters from plain spill vases were found on the factory site. These included a cylindrical shape such as that in Plate 96 and one flared or flanged rim. Some paw feet were also found and these would have been from examples such as those in Plates 97 and 99, or the gothic square spill in Plate 100. We have seen only one eight-sided spill, the decoration of a schoolboy and a dog being painted over a printed outline. This is 6″ high like the example mentioned in the notebook.

Simple shapes of spill vases were made by many small Staffordshire factories. Most were unmarked, and it is likely that some will be from Grainger. We would stress once again, however, that we believe Grainger marked most of their vases, and no unmarked example can be attributed without very good reason.

We believe that the ornamental shape books start in about 1832. Any elaborate vase shape not listed can reasonably be assumed to date from the 1820s and there are, in fact, relatively few basic forms. We have illustrated as many as we have been able to because we feel it is vitally important to publish marked Grainger shapes. In twenty years of searching these are all that we have come up with, and while undoubtedly some others will come to light, any unmarked vase which does not match our illustrations is unlikely to be Grainger.

106. An example of Grainger Lee & Co's most popular vase shape, painted with an extensive view of Bath, the handles similar to the plain vases shown in Plate 105; marked Grainger Lee & Co. Worcester, c.1825. (Bath Museum)

There are some interchangeable features and variations worth noting. The plain vase with scalloped rim (Plates 104 and Colour Plate XV) has been recorded with the same handles as the vases in Plate 105 showing views of Bath. Very similar handles were used on the most popular large vase shape which came with a pierced domed lid. We illustrate several examples and know of many others, all superbly decorated. The example with flowers believed to be by Evans has lost its handles altogether, showing how clever restoration nowadays can create a new shape out of a badly damaged vase.

It is surprising how frequently Grainger vases depict Bath. The factory clearly had a major outlet in the spa town and some of their finest products were aimed at the wealthy customers who settled in Bath to take advantage of the beneficial effects of the water. The magnificent set in Plate 109 depicts Bath and Bristol and here again the same handle shapes occur on a campana-shaped vase drawn in one of the factory shape books. The page is illustrated here in Plate 110 along with a corresponding pot-pourri basket and cover.

107. *A finely painted view of Worcester is here matched with Warwick Castle on a superb pair of large vases with matt blue grounds. These examples retain their original flat inner covers; 13½ inches, marked Grainger Lee & Co Worcester, c.1825. (Sotheby's)*

108. *A vase of the same shape as Plate 106, but sadly lacking its handles. The painting, by David Evans, is very fine, and the gilded border is typical; unmarked. (Dyson Perrins Museum)*

113

The pair of vases in Plate 112 are unmarked and this is uncharacteristic. The views are fully described but not as well painted as on other vases and this may account for the absence of the factory's name. The shape is more usually found on a tall plinth (Plate 111), and apart from these identical handles, the gilding on the stems should be compared with the fine pair of tall vases in Plate 113. This motif has been seen on other vases of this period.

The most flamboyant vase shape from the 1825–30 period is represented here by a pair with views of Bath (Plate 114). The handles are formed as swans and rococo scrollwork smothers the borders and bases. Like most Grainger vase shapes they came in two sizes so that a garniture could be made up with a larger single vase.

109. Bath and Bristol are again the subjects of three fine vases, the handles corresponding with the factory shape books (Plate 110). The central vase is 10 inches and marked Grainger Lee & Co Worcester in red, c.1825. (Phillips, Bath)

The set in Plate 115 is painted with all three of Grainger's most popular views, Cheltenham, Worcester, and Bath. The town of Rochester is known of on three Grainger vases, two of which are of a distinctive shape (Plate 116).

A complete contrast to any of these shapes was a pair of vases sold at Sotheby's in London in 1986 (Plate 118). Painted with views of New London Bridge and the Pavilion, Brighton, the border has modelled strawberries and the ground is of tiny mayflowers. The rims are beaded and the bases marbled in more typical Grainger

110. A page from a Grainger shape book of about 1825. The slightly later pot-pourri vase is painted with a view of Spetchley House, near Worcester and is marked G. Grainger Worcester in orange. 4¼ inches wide including handles, c.1840. (Private Collection)

111. A tall vase with matt pale blue ground, painted with a very rare figure subject, titled underneath 'Cupid & Psyche', 12 inches, marked Grainger Lee & Co Worcester: the shape was also made without the tall plinth, c.1825–30. (Private Collection)

style. These are marked 'Grainger Lee & Co. Worcester' and so there can be no doubt. Another pair of vases are known where the mayflower ground reserves a panel of Worcester from the north-west. The handles are modelled figures of putti and the finial is a rose. These vases are unmarked, and so we cannot make a definite attribution, but because of the similarity to the marked Brighton Pavilion vase, we have decided to illustrate the shape here as probably Grainger (Plate 119).

112. A pair of unmarked vases of shapes well known to be definitely Grainger products, with distinctive handles and gilding, painted with views of Sheffield and Shaugh Bridge, Devon, c.1825–30. (Phillips)

During the 1830s the neo-rococo style of Grainger vases became more and more flamboyant, verging on the eccentric. Scrollwork became more foliate and plant forms began to take over. The goblet-shaped vase (Colour Plate XV) points the way with its shell modelling and a bright pink ground to further illuminate the shape. This vase does not appear in the ornamental shape books, although it must date from the 1830s. Generally from about this time all of the ornamental shapes are drawn in a series of books which survive at the factory.

113. One of a pair of large vases painted with views of Worcester and Malvern. The gilding and painted borders are exceptionally fine on these examples which have unusual leaf-moulded rims, 23¾ inches, marked Grainger Lee & Co Worcester, c.1825. (Sotheby's)

When the books commenced, the shapes were consecutively numbered beginning at 1, and it is probable that some shapes had already been in production. The first two books are both watermarked 1825 but they begin with a series of biscuit vases and ewers which do not appear quite this early. In a separate notebook an entry seemingly for 1833 mentions a 'Biscuit Ewer Vine Border & C.' costing 4/6d to model, and the date October 1832 is in the front of the second shape book beginning with shape 41. A separate price book was kept which is watermarked 1841. It lists all the shapes in ornamental shape books 1 and 2, although no costings are recorded for any shape before 55. We therefore assume that the shape series began in 1832 with 1 and had reached 55 by 1841. The date 1860 appears against shape 200. Figures and animals had their own number sequence beginning also in 1832, although a note dated November 1831 lists many of the animal models. Candlesticks, baskets, inkwells, and sundries were given separate numbers.

Some of the drawings from the shape books are reproduced in Appendix 2. You will note that some of these are very meticulous and perfectly to scale, while others are more freely sketched and probably not very accurate. We list in Appendix 2 all of the ornamental shape numbers, although it should be noted that none of these numbers will appear on any of the finished pieces.

114. A pair of vases with elaborate leaf moulding and swan handles, the ground in pale turquoise blue. Once again the panels depict views of Bath, titled 'Crescent and Lansdown, Bath' and 'North View of Bath'; 13 inches, marked Grainger Lee & Co Worcester on the bases which are marbled underneath, c.1826–30. (Phillips)

The books commence with a range of vases and ornamental ewers which were applied with finely-modelled flowers. This was Grainger's speciality and it must be said that the quality of flower modelling at this period is exceptional, equal if not finer than any other English factory. Plate 120 shows shapes 1 and 2 and it can be seen that these were made in up to four different sizes and in three finishes: 'Bisque', totally unglazed and uncoloured; 'finished', which means that the flowers are glazed and then coloured; and 'Cold', which we take to mean cold-painted, straight onto the biscuit without any firing. Some of the shapes are further specified, such as 'white and gold' which we have seen on a vine-bordered ewer, the scrollwork glazed to take the gold while the vines are in biscuit. Others were done with 'cold small flowers intermixed with bisque grapes'.

The biscuit work at its finest is seen in Colour Plate XIII. This pair of vases are shape 24 and were sold at Phillips in 1987 for a very modest £480. When they were brought in for sale the vendor mentioned that they had a few links of extra bisque flowers which did not seem to belong, and these had not been kept. The drawing of this shape in the ornamental price book shows a garland of flowers hanging down from each handle. Several shapes seemed to have had these available as optional extras but we doubt that any will now have survived.

A remarkable shape in every sense is the Arabian Vase, shape 3, which was also made in two sizes. A single example was brought into the museum in Worcester twenty years ago and we were able to photograph it (Plate 122), while at the same time marvelling at how it could possibly have survived without any damage. The horses are not wonderfully modelled, but there has been some attempt to depict an Arabian stallion. The same shape was made without the horse handles.

A few other elaborate vases are drawn at the beginning of the shape books but are not numbered, presumably because they had been discontinued by 1832. One is a variant of shape 2, with a pointed pagoda top and pierced crescents and rays on the neck instead of modelled flowers. Another has a similar pagoda top and heavy foliate scrollwork, the handles shaped as leaping stags complete with antlers. A shell-shaped inkstand on a base of weed and coral is also lightly sketched, while a

115. A full garniture of the same shape as Plate 114, here painted with the three most popular Grainger views, Cheltenham, Worcester, and Bath. The ground is rich claret, the centre vase 12¾ inches, marked Grainger Lee & Co Worcester, c.1826–30. (Phillips)

116. An elegant vase with a red ground and named view of Rochester, 9 inches, marked Grainger Lee & Co Worcester. (Private Collection)

monumental vase heavily bedecked with vines has a cover surmounted by an eagle. A final shape is a basket-moulded jar, rather like a fishing basket, which has a figure of a naked boy beside the base. The drawing is very faint, but it looks as if a lizard or sea monster is climbing up the side. None of these drawings are finished off and do not have costs written alongside.

Shape 30 is fully drawn in the shape books with specific instructions for the decoration. Once again an example was bought into the museum at Worcester more than twenty years ago and a photograph was taken (Plate 123), showing just how accurate some of these drawings are. Another cornucopia shape is illustrated in Plate 124, this example marked Thomas Grainger & Co. Worcester. This shape does not appear drawn in the books, but is possibly 28, 'Cornucopia flowered full both sides'.

Many of these vase shapes appear to be unique to Grainger, but this is probably not the case. A note against shape 23 (re-entered as shape 53) reads 'Copied from Staffordshire', and there are examples known of a number of the vase shapes which are certainly not Grainger. We thought we had discovered a version of shape 1, a fine vase in parian with superb modelled flowers, but when a second coloured example was seen with an underglaze pattern number we knew we were looking at pieces from Samuel Alcock's factory. Alcock made ewers with modelled vines in parian during the 1840s and their vases also seem later in date than Grainger's. Some have printed marks and so the Alcock attribution is not in doubt. The

117. A garniture of three vases of the same shape as Plate 116, but here with an underglaze blue ground and fine gilding, reserving unusual shaped panels, the large vase 11 inches, marked Grainger Lee & Co Worcester. (Private Collection)

118. A remarkable vase, one of a pair painted with views of the Pavilion, Brighton and New London Bridge, the ground modelled with tiny mayflower blossoms in the Dresden style, 8¼ inches, marked Grainger Lee & Co. Worcester, c.1825–30. (Sotheby's)

119. A typical view of Worcester and a similar ground to the vase in Plate 118 point towards Grainger, but the lack of a mark prevents definite attribution. The putti forming the handles do not match any known Grainger figure models, 9¾ inches. (Private Collection)

question remains, did Grainger copy earlier Alcock biscuit vases in the 1830s, or are the Alcock vases copying Grainger? Shape 22 in the Grainger list is a vase, 'New as Allsup'. Could this be a bad attempt by the shop hand to record Alcock? A number of Grainger vase shapes were also made at Coalport in the flower-encrusted 'Coalbrookdale' porcelain, and Minton examples are identical to at least one Grainger shape, the square spill vase shown in Colour Plate XVII. Finally the perfume bottle, shape 54, is copied from Rockingham. The glaze and the decoration on most Grainger is so distinctive, however, that with experience it is reasonably simple to recognize an unmarked vase. Shape 93 is a 'Brameld Leaf Jar & Cover', also presumably copying Rockingham.

The large vase shown in Plate 125 could not really have been made by anyone else but Grainger. It stands 16½″ high and is marked G. Grainger, Worcester. It matches exactly with shape 51 in the books and exhibits the thick white glaze and bright gilding seen on so much Grainger. Beneath the handles is gold twigging, another Grainger feature (see Chapter Nine).

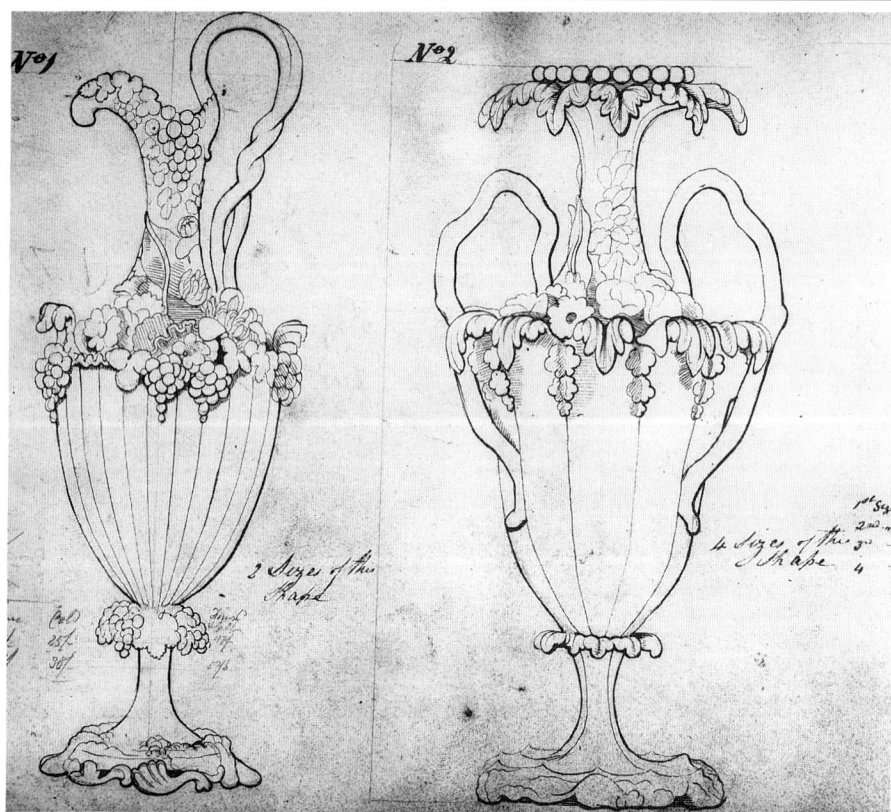

120. A page from the Ornamental Shape Books showing the first two vase shapes together with details of costings. (Worcester Royal Porcelain Co.)

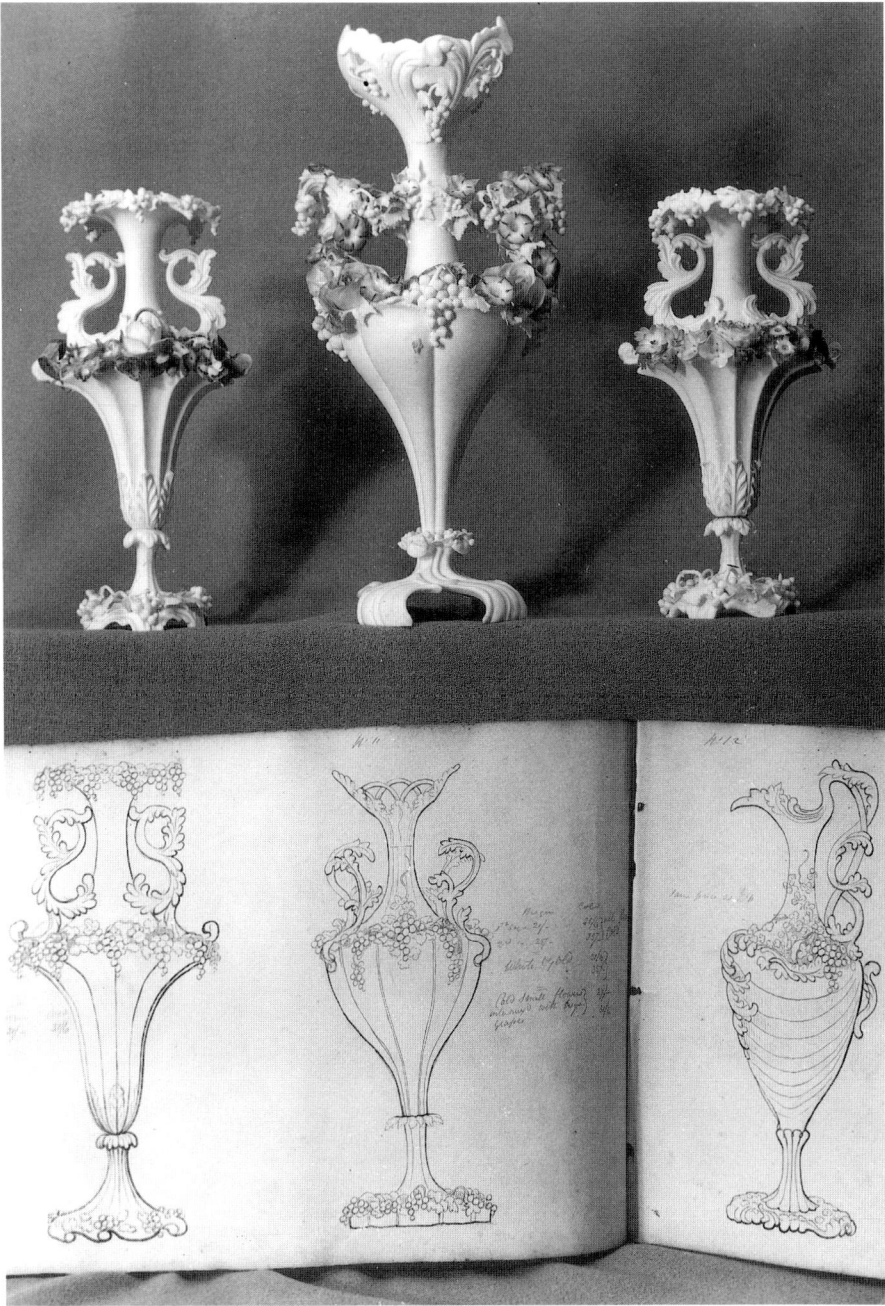

121. A pair of vases corresponding with vase shape 10 but with the flowers instead of vines, 9 inches, flanking a vase of shape 20, 12¼ inches, the flowers are glazed to allow delicate colouring, c.1832–5. (Private Collection). Shown below is the factory Ornamental Shape Book showing shapes 10, 11 and 12. (WRPC)

123

122. The Arabian Vase which is vase shape 3 in the Ornamental Shape Book. This example in biscuit has survived without any damage, something of a miracle, c.1832–5. (Private Collection)

By the 1840s the Grainger shapes had, in keeping with the taste of the time, become more and more florid and in a way eccentric. Plant modelling seems to have taken over, either combined with a vase shape, as in Plate 125, or else the whole piece became a fantastic plant. Pieces such as shapes 55 and 56 were inspired by contemporary Bohemian and French porcelain, and indeed the Grainger glaze can closely resemble Continental 'hard paste' if it has not crazed. We are sure that many of these flower vases are currently masquerading as French, for we know of only a single example from this period, the thistle vase illustrated in Colour Plate XII. A rough sketch appears as shape 69, and the glaze and gilding on this example are so distinctive that there can be no doubt whatsoever that this vase is Grainger.

123. A flowered cornucopia on a characteristic Grainger rocky base heightened in gold, the flowers coloured, shown alongside vase shape 30, unmarked, c.1832–5. (Private Collection)

125

124. An elaborate cornucopia, one of a pair applied with fruit and flowers in typical delicate colouring, 6⅛ inches, marked Thomas Grainger & Co Worcester in script, c.1835–40. (Private Collection)

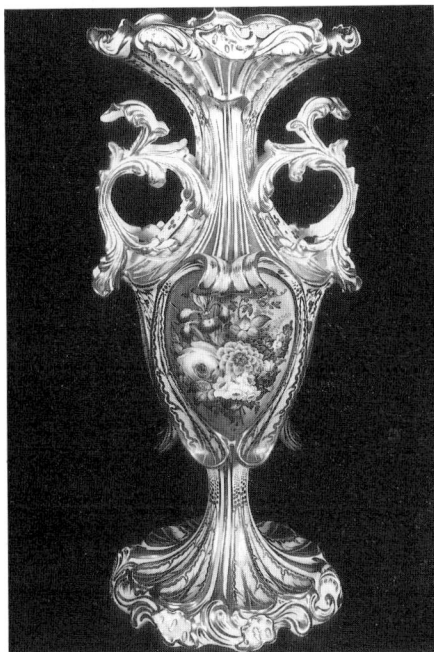

125. A large vase corresponding with vase shape 51, pale green ground with characteristic gilding, 16½ inches, marked G Grainger, Worcester in red script, c.1840. (Phillips)

126. A simple vase compared to others, but still heavily decorated including a view of Windermere Lake. Vase shape 70, 8½ inches, marked G Grainger Worcester. (Private Collection)

Similar vases were made in the shape of convolvulus flowers and tulips, and while tulip vases are commonly seen in Staffordshire, no Grainger example has yet been recognized. Some of the flowers, particularly a convolvulus vase, were also made in parian from the 1840s and revived much later in the nineteenth century. Examples with printed or impressed shield marks are not uncommon, with deep green stained leaves and white flowers, either glazed, semiglazed or completely matt.

Covered vases, bowls, and jugs in porcelain or parian where often ingeniously conceived and were a considerable success at the time of the Great Exhibition. A very great variety of jugs and vases was made in imaginative forms. The *Art-Journal Illustrated Catalogue* of the 1851 Exhibition generously devoted a whole page to these Grainger wares. They were described as

a peculiar fancy in design, combined with much simplicity of decoration . . . The difficulty of adapting this mode of decoration to the forms and uses of the articles is considerable: it has been contrasted with judgement but not always with success. We consider some of the objects we engrave as among the curiosities of earthen-ware manufacture, but are not prepared to enforce their claim to unqualified approval . . .

The star exhibit was a coffee set embossed with wheat ears and stalks on a ground pierced with honeycomb. The interior was solid and the double-walled effect, shaded inside in rich blue, was well received with the comment that, like most products of Grainger's factory, it was manufactured at comparatively small cost. Where are all of these leaf jugs and vases today? Probably in parian, maybe combined with coloured parian for the backgrounds, all of the examples must have been unmarked and have proved impossible to find. Every shape seems to have been made as a jug or without a handle as a vase, with only slight modification to the neck. Some of the most outrageous shapes are 139, the swan jug, and 142, a tall ewer with a swan on top fighting with a snake amongst the bulrushes, their heads locked in combat to form the handle.

Not all of the shapes produced in the 1850s were 'over the top'. Some very elegant classical shapes and very plain forms were also made, decorated with scattered painted flowers or festoons from narrow banded borders popular at the time. Plate 134 shows a page of shapes dated 1 May 1860. These are shapes 200–8 and represent the detailed modelling popular at the time on plain shapes. These would have been made in parian, probably glazed. The extinguisher photographed alongside is in a matt ivory finish called by the factory 'muffin'. The parian body was used almost exclusively for ornamental wares for the duration of the factory, as will be seen in Chapter Ten.

I An important large mug in rich 'Japan' style, marked in red 'Grainger & Co Worcester, Sepr 26 1807', 5 inches. (Authors' Collections)

II A pair of early Grainger porter mugs painted with hunting scenes, 4½ inches, both marked Grainger & Co Worcester, c.1808–10. (Phillips)

III A pair of mugs with finely painted views of Worcester and Cheltenham, the gnarled *tau* or T handle popular in the 1820s, 4¼ inches. (Private Collection)

IV A cabinet plate of Full Gadroon shape with typical high-quality gilding, 8 inches, marked Grainger Lee & Co Worcester, *c.*1820. (Private Collection)

V A dinner plate from the same service as the tureen shown in Plate 46, 9½ inches, marked
Grainger & Co Worcester, *c.*1812–14. (Private Collection)

VI A very rich tea service, unmarked except for pattern 575, the shapes corresponding with
drawings which appear in the factory pattern books *c.*1818–20. (Phillips)

VII A tea service of so-called London shape decorated with Grainger's most popular pattern known as Old India, mostly marked Grainger Lee & Co Worcester, *c.*1829 (Private Coll.)

VIII A truly magnificent dinner service of pattern 1358, *c.*1825, with typical Grainger style of flower painting, from a service of 117 pieces sold in 1986. (Phillips)

IX A tea service *c*.1835–40 painted with characteristic birds and insects amongst gold 'Twigging'. (Private Collection)

X Part of an important service presented by the citizens of Worcester to the mayor, William Lewis, for his work in getting the Oxford to Wolverhampton railway to come through Worcester in the early 1840s. Shown here are scenes of the Guildhall and Cathedral. (Private Collection)

XI Worcester Cathedral seen in the distance in this view of the city from the north-west painted with great care on a large plaque, the border richly gilded, marked Grainger Lee & Co Worcester, *c*.1835. (Phillips)

XII The 'Thistle Vase', an eccentric creation corresponding with shape 69 in the Ornamental Shape Books, unmarked, *c*.1840. (Authors' Collections)

XIII A pair of biscuit vases with delicately-modelled vines, the flowers glazed and then
coloured, 12¼ inches, unmarked, c.1832–5. (Phillips)

XIV An early vase said to have been painted by John Wood, similar to a Coalport shape,
marked Grainger and Co Worcester, c.1806–10. (Dyson Perrins Museum)

XV David Evans's delightful wild flowers used most successfully on a plain vase shape,
marked Grainger Lee & Co Worcester, *c*.1825 (Private Collection)

XVI The rococo revival seen at its best on a vase of *c.*1835, 13 inches, marked Grainger Lee and Co Worcester. (Dyson Perrins Museum)

XVII Two square spill vases drawn in the Ornamental Shape Books. (WRPC)

XVIII Cupids Building a Gothic Arch, one of the most delicate and exceptional Grainger products, 9½ inches, *c.*1835. (Dyson Perrins Museum)

XIX A fine reticulated vase, the panel signed by James Stinton, 11 inches, shape G693; such pierced work was a speciality of the factory in the 1890s. (Dyson Perrins Museum)

CHAPTER SEVEN

OTHER ORNAMENTAL SHAPES

During nearly a century of ceramic production the range of shapes and objects made by the Grainger factory was astronomic. Comprehensive records give us the names and occasional descriptions of a great many of Grainger's products, but tracing actual examples is more often than not an impossible task. In this chapter we list the more important shapes which the factory made, as well as some of the most absurd.

Artichoke Cups
A small jar and cover in the shape of an artichoke was made around 1850. Similar examples were made by several factories including Flight, Barr & Barr at an earlier date. As yet, no Grainger examples are known.

Baskets
From the 1820s numerous ornamental baskets were produced. The smallest were just cabinet pieces, not intended for use. Deeper baskets held flowers or pot-pourri, while larger examples were trays for visiting cards. Some baskets were decorated with modelled flowers, possibly to be sprinkled with scent (see Flower Baskets). Early Grainger Lee & Co. examples are rare. One remarkable example from about 1825 is square with overhead rustic handle and has groups of large modelled rose leaves around the rim. The illustration is of very poor quality (Plate 127) but we feel worth including to show David Evans's flower painting in the middle.

When the first ornamental shape book was started, basket shapes 1–7 were carefully drawn out and are shown here in Plate 129. Shapes 8–10 were on the following page. Some of these shapes were copied from other factories' popular shapes of the 1820s and 1830s. No. 1, the Gadroon basket, was based on Flight, Barr & Barr, and Plate 128 shows an example with a view of Worcester marked Grainger Lee & Co. No. 2, the Vine Corner basket, is the most frequently seen, and was also used as flower basket No. 2 with modelled flowers or, in the case of Plate 139, mushrooms. Basket shape 4 is called 'Albert' and this was introduced in 1840, the year of Queen Victoria's marriage to Prince Albert. An example with bisque vine border edged in blue and gold is recorded as having a 'group of painted flowers in bottom, as dessert ware plants Mr. Daniel, November 27 1840'.

127. A poor photograph of a large basket with modelled leaves around the border, the centre painted by David Evans, marked Grainger Lee & Co, c.1825. (Private Collection)

128. A miniature basket known as a 'Gadroon Basket', painted with one of the popular views of Worcester within a matt blue enamel border, marked Grainger Lee & Co. Worcester, 3¾ ins, c.1830. (Private Collection)

No. 6, the shell, was copied from Coalport, which in itself was copying Meissen. No. 8 is a circular lobed basket (as No. 6 and No. 7 in the flower baskets drawings, Plate 138) while No. 9 is the same as a ringstand. No. 10, the Princess basket, was very thinly cast with fine moulded basketweave, probably introduced in 1841. The border was left in bisque to show the modelling.

Another shape from the 1840s, not listed in the books, is shown in Plate 133, again with a view of Worcester and marked G. Grainger Worcester. Another larger version for cards is in Cheltenham Art Gallery and Museum (see Plate 130). Baskets were not generally made much after 1840.

Bread Plates

Called 'Loaf Plates' by the factory, the same design was made in two sizes in the early 1850s. They had raised Gothic lettering around the border with a motto including the word Joy, but the rest of the inscription is not recorded. Gothic bread plates were made by many factories, including Minton, to designs by Pugin.

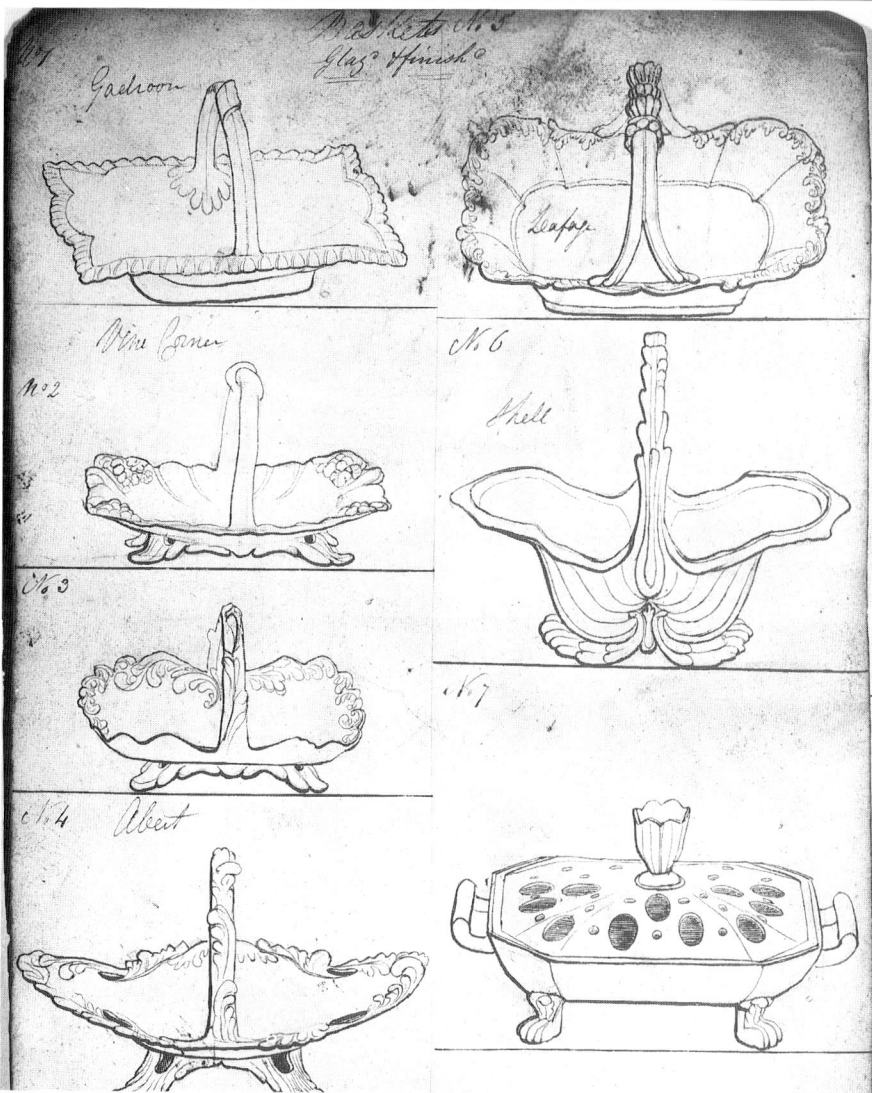

129. *A page from the Ornamental Shape Book showing basket shapes available from the 1830s and 1840s. (WRPC)*

130. *A large basket probably intended as a visiting card tray, in the revived rococo style, marked Thomas Grainger & Co Worcester, c.1835–9. (Cheltenham Art Gallery & Museum)*

Brooches

A variety of brooches were supplied with gold or pinchbeck mounts. They were made during the 1840s and were mainly oval. Recorded decorations are:

Nos. 1–2 Oval, view of Worcester or flowers & ground.
No. 3   Oval, Worcester or Malvern.
No. 4   Circular, birds.
No. 5   Oval, birds or flowers.
No. 6   Oval, single plant only.
No. 7   Oval, doves with love letter.
No. 8   Oval, single flower.
No. 9   Oval, a little larger than 5, bird & . . .

The views of Worcester and Malvern were printed in outline and coloured (see Plate 131) and the original copper plate survives at the factory. Usually unmarked, they sometimes have the printed title 'Worcester' on the back. An example painted with Leda and the Swan is shown in Plate 132. This is larger and marked Grainger & Co. Worcester.

During the late 1840s a wide range of modelled flower brooches was made in a form of glassy glazed parian called 'cryolite'. Some were single flowers such as roses or a convolvulus, others a spray of small flowers on a heart-shaped leaf. The most elaborate were a wreath of roses, a garland of fruit and flowers, and a 'Union Brooch' made up of a rose, thistle, and shamrock. They sold for between 4/- and 15/6 mounted.

131. A small brooch in a pinchbeck frame, the view of Worcester following a faint outline print, 2¼ inches without frame, marked 'Worcester'. (Private Collection)

132. Leda and the Swan on a gold-mounted brooch, 3 inches high, marked Grainger & Co Worcester, c.1840. (Phillips)

Butter tubs

Circular drum-shaped containers with matching stands were made in the 1830s and 1840s and many wasters were found on the site. The tubs have moulded hoops and staves like a barrel and raised square handles. The decoration included several underglaze prints. More elaborate moulded butter tubs were made in the 1840s, and a design with moulded primrose flowers and leaves was made in parian and china.

Buttons

The first ornamental shape book includes drawings of plain circular buttons decorated in eight different patterns. Chamberlain made a very large range of porcelain buttons, but they do not appear to have been a major part of Grainger's production.

Candlesticks

Upright or pillar candlesticks are rare in English porcelain and we know of only one pair by Grainger. These accompany the inkstand in plate 140, made c.1820. By the 1830s a shape on an octagonal base was drawn as candlestick No. 5 in the Ornamental shape book, although we have not seen a finished example. A number of chamber candlestick shapes were produced ranging from plain circular saucer shapes to elaborate examples with modelled mayflowers or scroll borders. In a separate notebook is recorded:

June 1826:

Flat gaddaroons candlestick with extinguishers 5½" across 5/- each

ditto   4½" across   4/- each

ditto   3½" across   3/- each

Candlesticks gilt with claret, green or any other grounds. . .

		beaded	no beads
ditto	9" across	31/6 pair	29/6
ditto	8" across	28/- pair	26/4
ditto	7" across	22/- pair	20/8
ditto	6" across	16/- pair	15/-

Mention is also made of 'Dresden Candlesticks in three pieces, flowered, Sept. 1835'.

Plate 133 shows an early miniature taperstick of 1820–5 painted with a minute view of Worcester. A larger example from the 1840s is shown alongside.

Two versions are recorded in the shape books with matching conical extinguishers, and one has a slot in the nozzle for metal fittings. Shape 98 is a hawthorn taperstick with delicately-modelled blossom. Others appear as shapes 84 and 85 decorated with 'vermicelli'. From the 1860s onwards candlesticks frequently accompanied dressing table sets which were usually simply decorated.

Candle Extinguishers

Chamber candlestick No. 2, in about 1830, was made with a matching conical extinguisher finished off with a studlike finial. No finished example has been recognized. In Grainger shape book 20, begun c.1860, shape 203 is a conical leaf-moulded extinguisher. A finished example is shown alongside in Plate 134. The same page shows shape 204, a lady's-head extinguisher closely copying examples from Minton or France. We know of examples in white-glazed parian and it is likely some were fully coloured. Various extinguishers were made during the 1870s and 1880s, the most usual being a Tyrolean hat, a shape continued well into this century by Royal Worcester. The monkey-head extinguisher (Plate 135) is very much rarer.

133. *Three pieces painted with views of Worcester. Centre: a miniature taperstick with pierced rim, 2¹⁄₁₀ inches, rare mark Grainger Lee & Co. Royal China Works, Worcester, c.1825. Left: a basket marked G Grainger Worcester, 5¹⁄₁₀ inches, c.1840. Right: an unmarked chamber candlestick, probably Grainger, c.1845–50. (Private Collection)*

134. *An extinguisher and stand in 'muffin' colour and gold, with a page from the Ornamental Shape Book dated 1860. The design was made by several factories. (Private Collection)*

135. *Two later Grainger extinguishers in white glazed parian. The Tyrolean hat was extremely popular, while the monkey head is very rare indeed, the hat with printed shield mark, c.1880–1900. (Dyson Perrins Museum)*

Chandeliers

Shape 57 of *c.*1840–3 is described as a 'chandelier for drops, glass'. It has a candle nozzle at the top above a leaf-moulded flange from which would have hung glass lustres or drops. These were very fashionable in glass during the 1840s and 1850s, although porcelain examples are rarely seen. Shapes 174 and 175 are called vases for chandeliers and were probably mounted as the stem of a hanging metal chandelier. They have embossed leaves and flower moulding.

Chemical Porcelain

A new 'chemical porcelain' body was introduced in 1848 and brought the factory an immediate claim to fame. Very highly regarded in its day, Grainger chemical apparatus was used in almost every laboratory. We reproduce here a fascinating page showing an extensive range of vessels sold under the title 'George Grainger & Co.'s Worcester Chemical Porcelain, Capsules, &c.' The sheet is undated although some additional notes have been added, including the dates Sep 30/54 and Oct 10/54. Sadly no descriptions survive, but many of the shapes are used almost unchanged in laboratories today. The only example we have located is FF, a medicine spoon which must have had a wide sale through chemists' shops. Plate 136 shows an example with the name of a homoeopathic chemist corresponding with factory records. The price list shows that these spoons sold for 8/- per dozen. Pestles and mortars, shape V, are listed as being glazed outside. They were made in ten sizes, the smallest 2½″ in diameter, selling for 1/- each, the largest 10½″, selling for 10/- each. A great many of these Grainger chemical wares must survive, but all will be unmarked and impossible to recognize.

On the reverse of this sheet is a drawing of a 'Photographic dish', a flat rectangular tray with lips at the corners, made in five sizes ranging from 7″×8″ at 6/6d to 14″×11½″ at 12/-. On p. 23 we reproduce two interesting testimonies published by Grainger to publicize the quality of their Chemical Porcelain. During the 1850s the factory appears to have put much effort into chemical apparatus.

136. *Three examples of Grainger's Chemical porcelain. Left: a sauce bottle made for Edward Moore of Cheltenham. Right: a medicine spoon inscribed 'From Healand's Homeopathic Pharmacy, 15 Princes Street, Hanover Sq. London'; and a pot lid. All unmarked, c.1850–60.*

Chess Table
A circular flat tray with a raised scroll rim. One side is painted with the black and white squares of a chess board, the reverse with flowers so that it could be inverted as a decorative tray when not in use. One example has been seen, unmarked but corresponding with a drawing of about 1845. It is recorded as selling for 4½ guineas.

Commemorative Wares
Only one reference is made to a relief-moulded jug, although an example has not been traced. Shape 233 of the early 1860s is described as 'Jug, illuminated in parian, Garibald' (*sic*). Garibaldi, the Italian patriot, visited England during the 1840s and remained a popular figure. Several Staffordshire jugs with his likeness are known. Copper plates survive at the factory for printing the following inscriptions, probably used on mugs, although no finished examples have been seen: 'In Commemoration of the Majority of George William 9th Earl of Coventry, May 9 1859' and 'Presented to James Levich, Esq. by a few of his Worcester Friends and Admirers in Remembrance of his Gallant Contest for the Representation of the City in the Conservative Interest at the General Election, July 12 1865'.

Cup Plates
A service of Gloster shape dating from the late 1830s included small circular almost miniature plates, about 3½ inches. These were used to place the cup on while tea was drunk from the saucer, a pastime popular in America from the 1830s. Several factories made cup plates, including Rockingham, although they are rarely identified as such.

Dog Troughs
A footed dish of commode shape used to feed dogs. The shape was popular in Staffordshire pottery but no Grainger example has been seen. It was made in opaque 'semi china' in the 1850s.

Door Furniture
A major production of the Grainger factory, an entire pattern book is devoted to the hundreds of different designs. The doorknobs were mostly plain circular, although some were fluted. They had matching 'roses' or 'flats', which fitted against the door. Finger plates came in many sizes and 'Escutcheons' were made to cover the keyholes. Some of the decoration used on door furniture was particularly elaborate but it is a pity that marked examples are so rare. Grainger probably produced more even than Copeland & Garrett, the best-known British maker.

Dressing Table Sets
Usually composed of a tray, candlesticks, ringstand, and various covered pots. Rare before the 1850s and most popular in the 1860s. The circular flat powder pots were sold on their own fully decorated at 3/- each in the 1850s. Most sets of this period were in the 'semi china' body.

137. A dressing table set with very simple decoration, marked Grainger & Co Manufacturers Worcester, c.1860, the tray 10⁷⁄₁₀ inches wide. (H & B Wolf Antiques)

Epergnes
An elaborate four-tiered centrepiece is described in the ornamental price book as an 'Epurgham'. Each section is scroll-moulded with rustic sections between. It dates probably from the 1850s.

Ewers and Ornamental Jugs
See under Vases, Chapter Six.

Feeding Bottles
The following three-line inscription appears in the Grainger print book and would have been used on a baby's bottle or invalid feeding cup. No finished example has been noted. 'Lang's Universal / London & Paris / Shilling Feeding Bottle'.

Flower Baskets
A range of porcelain ornaments was made to contain finely-modelled flowers. When produced in bisque the quality of the modelling is almost unbelievable. Sadly, these ornaments were so fragile that we know of only one surviving example, badly damaged now. Part of the range is shown in Plate 138 from the first ornamental shape book. Shapes 6 and 7 have the date Nov. 27 1840 against them. Shape 2 with a plain handle and modelled mushrooms is shown in Plate 139, but this is glazed and coloured. Shape 14 is a remarkably elaborate large circular basket with the most intricate woven sides. Flower baskets were probably issued with glass domes, to protect the delicately-modelled blossoms.

A small number of pot-pourri baskets are known with modelled flowers in much lower relief, dating from about 1825. Others had no modelled flowers except for a central bud finial.

A notebook from 1826 to 1831 gives some prices the workers were paid for modelling the flowers for these baskets, per gross. April 1826 (round baskets with handle and cover, cover and rim covered with flowers): 4″ size, white 6/-, coloured 9/-; 4½″ size, white 8/-, coloured 12/-; 5″ size, white 10/6, coloured 16/-; 6″ size, white 12/6, coloured 1/1/-. Date unspecified (biscuit baskets filled with flowers and handle across): 2″ size, white 1/6; 3″ size, white 2/-: round basket with twig work, 2¾″ size, 4/6.

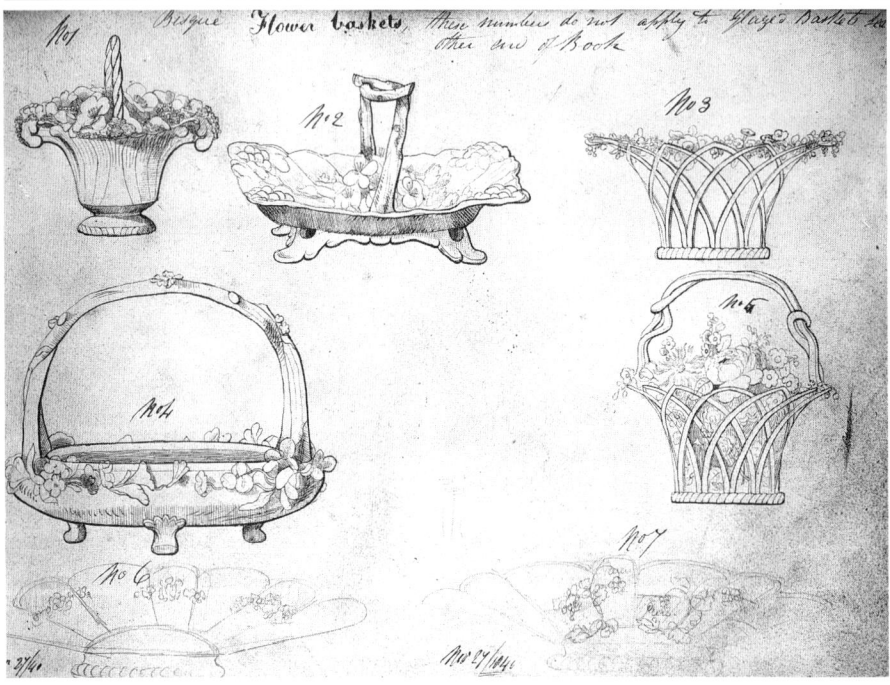

138. A page from the Ornamental Shape Books showing baskets containing finely-modelled biscuit or coloured flowers. These were issued with protective glass domes, but few seem to have survived, c.1832–40. (WRPC)

139. A 'Vine Cornered' basket containing realistic modelled mushrooms and cob nuts, unmarked but the basket shape exactly matching a Grainger Lee & Co example, c.1830. (Phillips)

Flower Pots

Jardinières or small pots for plants were popular at Chamberlain but Grainger seem to have made very few. One shape is recorded around 1830–5 as 'Opaque flower pot with porous linings, 3 sizes'. This was bucket-shaped with a flanged rim. The factory advertised this for sale as the 'Patent Drawing Room Flower Pot'. The outer case could be decorated to match a table service, while plants would be grown in a greenhouse in the porous containers, which were placed in the flower pot when in bloom.

Gas Meter Dials

Oval shapes with two printed dials on one side. Made in the 1850s. No examples are known to have survived.

Honey Pots

A service of Gloster shape of about 1840 included a honey pot of domed shape on a fixed circular stand. A pot in the form of a beehive has in the past been attributed to Grainger but we can find no evidence to support this.

Inkwells, Inkstands, and Desk Sets

Only one early example is known, illustrated here in Plate 140. It probably dates from about 1820 and bears a crude printed pattern copied from Spode. The border

140. *An early Grainger desk set with a popular printed pattern lightly coloured. The inkstand is copied from a version manufactured at Derby of an approximately similar date. 10 inches high, c.1815. (Phillips)*

141. Grainger's inkstand shape number 1, with chrome green stripes and characteristic flower painting, marked Thomas Grainger & Co Royal China Works Worcester, c.1837–9. (Phillips)

142. An unusual scroll-moulded inkstand corresponding with inkstand shape number 3 in the Ornamental Shape Books, painted with a view of Worcester, marked Grainger Lee & Co Worcester, c.1835. (Private Collection)

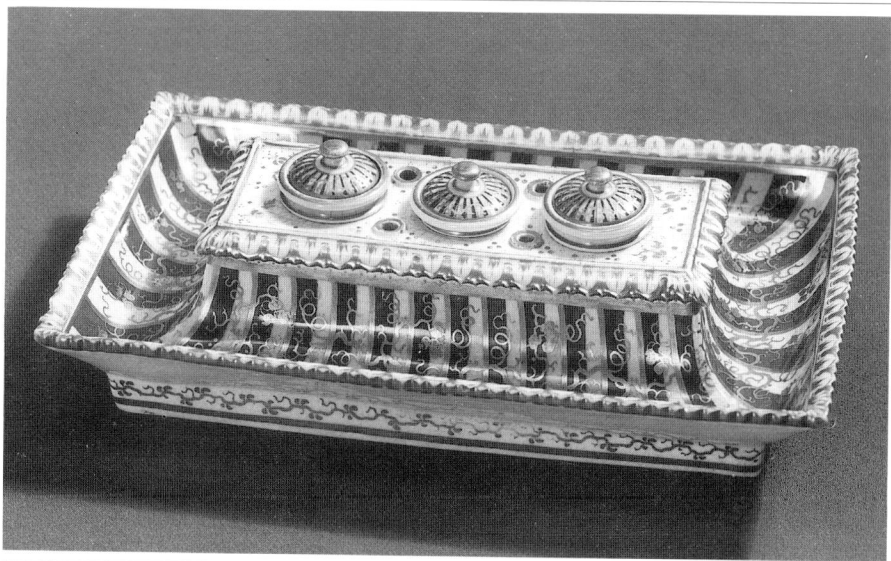

143. A rectangular inkstand with gadroon edge, introduced around 1840 to replace inkstand shape number 5, decorated with deep ultramarine and gold stripes, 11¼ inches, marked G Grainger Royal Porcelain Works Worcester. (Private Collection)

144. A 'Schlesinger's Patent Hydraulic Ink' with original metal fittings to pump the ink, 6¼ inches, unmarked but corresponding with factory records, c.1850. (Private Collection)

is Full Gadroon and the piece is set with a central well similar in shape to a larger Grainger vase (see Plate 94). The basic form is copied from Derby of roughly similar date. Ornamental shape book 1 includes the same shape as Inkstand No. 5, but with added handles and paw feet. The inkstands in this 1830s and 1840s book are as follows:

1. As Plate 141, with curious step-shaped lids.
2. As 1, but with plain gadroon edge, pointed knops to lid.
3. As Plate 142, scroll shape with high scroll handle at back. Should have covers with pointed finials.
4. Gadroon-edged small rectangular basket with a central vase-shaped well, pointed finial.
5. As Plate 140 but with added handles and paw feet. (Withdrawn by 1841, replaced by the shape shown in Plate 143, rectangular with gadroon rim.)
6. Rectangular tray, 'holding sand box & stick rings'.
7. Tray only without fittings.

Drawings of two other inkstands are included in Plate 110, one of which is based on a popular Coalport shell basket.

Later inkwells included 'Ratcliffe's Ink with Plunger', a plain cylindrical shape with very complicated metal fittings which pumped the ink during use (Plate 144). These were sold under the name 'Schlesinger's Patent Hydraulic Ink'. A wonderful novelty from the 1870s and 1880s is an inkwell in the form of a packing crate, the lid inscribed 'China from Worcester'. We have only ever seen one example, which is a pity because the idea is great fun (Plate 146).

145. An inkwell fixed to an oval pen tray, the blue-green ground reserving a view of Worcester, 10 inches wide, marked George Grainger 19 Foregate Worcester, c.1850–60. (Sotheby's)

146. *An amusing model of a crate of Worcester china, the box lifting off to reveal an inkwell inside, realistically coloured, printed shield mark, c.1880. (Dyson Perrins Museum)*

Incense Burners

A curious reference in an untitled notebook datable to between 1826 and 1831 refers to 'Tash's ornamental incense burner token from Yorkshire gold lids, tips chas'd well painted flowers & little gold mixed.' Prices were: 5″ high, 16/-; 6″ high, 22/-; 7″ high, 30/-.

Jug Stands

Usually thought to be teapot stands today, a range of simple flat circular stands was made by the factory in the 1850s. Shape 184 is a 'jug stand on balls', painted either with plants or wreaths, and came in either 6″ or 7″ sizes. They were painted with plants, wreaths, or heather wreaths, and also came in cheaper printed versions. Shape 161 had a modelled hawthorn border and similar ball feet.

Lemonade Sets

Popular in the mid Victorian era, possibly as a reaction against strong drink, sets for drinking lemonade were produced at many factories. Several Grainger examples have been seen, usually comprising a jug and a pair of tumblers or beakers on a tray. It is unusual to find such a set in the shape of a barrel (Plate 147), because they would not normally have been used to serve alcohol, but this set, made in about 1870 for the Corporation of the City of Worcester, may have been used for beer.

Lithophanes or Berlin Transparencies

Grainger has long been thought to have made these objects and, indeed, had a British patent for them in about 1828. However, the Public Record Office were not able to trace a reference to Grainger. On 13 March 1828, however, Robert Griffith Jones of Middlesex patented a method of ornamenting china and other compositions which he denominated as 'Lithophanic Translucid on opaque china'

147. *A lemonade set decorated with the arms of the city and county of Worcester, printed marks, c.1880. The Grainger factory produced many wares decorated in this way. (Private Collection)*

(ref. c54/10535/m.15). Whether Grainger actually produced lithophanes in translucent porcelain or not, there are two moulds at the Worcester Royal Porcelain Co. which were always said to have come from the Grainger factory. They are rectangular and one depicts a young lady dressing, or undressing, by her bed and struggling with her stays; the other is a portrait of a gentleman, looking not unlike William IV, wearing dress clothes and holding a top hat. There is a scene of soldiers in the courtyard of a castle that might be Grainger, but the greatest collection of lithophanes in the world, the Blair Museum of Lithophanes in Toledo, Ohio, USA, does not possess a single Grainger marked example out of some 2300 items.

Nightlights

A single example has been recorded, illustrated in a photograph provided by

Geoffrey Godden (Plate 148). It corresponds with shape 103 in the second ornamental book, produced in about 1845. The top lifts off and the light glowed softly through the angels. This example is in glazed porcelain, although a note in the price book indicates that they were also made in parian.

Grainger also made some sort of container or base for commercial nightlights. A printing plate survives for 'The Family Night Light', manufactured by Simpsons Payne & Co., London.

Oil Lamp Bases

No. 176 in the ornamental shape books, dating from c.1855, is a plain globe raised on a spreading, scroll-edged foot. They were made in white or gilt, in two sizes, 7½″ and 8½″ high.

Pen Trays

Several versions are mentioned in the shape books, including one with scroll borders and painted flower centres. Another is a very plain rectangular shape.

148. A rare nightlight in two sections, corresponding with shape 103 in the Ornamental Shape Books, 5 inches high, marked G Grainger Royal Porcelain Works Worcester, Sole Manufacturers of the Semi Porcelain Prize Ware, c.1845. (Geoffrey Godden, Chinaman)

Perfume Bottles

Several early nineteenth-century small scent bottles have been attributed to Grainger but we can find no evidence, although a flat pointed shape was popular at Chamberlain. A pair of perfume bottles and stoppers are shown in Plate 149. They correspond with shape 54 in ornamental book 2 and were made *c*.1835–40. The shape closely copies a Rockingham model although the flower modelling and gilt weed confirm a Grainger attribution. Later in the century a number of reticulated scent bottles were made in the parian body, either glazed white or shaded in ivory. Examples are frequently unmarked.

149. A pair of perfume bottles like a Rockingham model but with typical Grainger decoration, 6½ inches, unmarked but as shape 54 in the Ornamental Shape Books, c.1835. (Phillips)

Plaques

China painters always regarded it as an honour to be able to paint plaques, as they felt this placed them in the realm of the artist rather than the craftsman. Firing a good-sized flat plaque was extremely difficult, especially in bone china, and any Worcester plaque is a great rarity. Plaques tended to be painted by independent decorators and marked examples are always rare. We know of only one marked Grainger flat plaque. This is a rectangular, with a view of the Royal Crescent, Bath (Plate 150). While not the best painting by a long way, the composition is attractive and links up with many examples of Grainger vase painting.

We know of three plaques signed by David Evans, who had joined Grainger from Swansea in 1819. They are not marked or dated, but it seems reasonable to assume that they were painted while he was at Worcester. It is possible though, that they were bought-in blank plaques painted by Evans in his own time and for this reason he was able to sign his work. It is tempting to call them Grainger plaques, but we have no evidence to support this; indeed one of the plaques is inscribed in pencil on the frame 'painted by David Evans, Worcester', suggesting that he was working as a free lance in some way. Similar still lifes, unsigned, were painted by Evans on marked Grainger vases and a basket (Plates 4, 108, 127).

Several pairs of plaques are known with elaborate moulded gadroon rims and scrollwork corners. All clearly marked Grainger Lee & Co. Worcester, they date

150. A porcelain plaque painted with a view of Royal Crescent, Bath, marked Grainger Lee & Co Worcester, c.1825. (Bath Museum)

from c.1825. Most depict Worcester, although we have seen some with views of Cheltenham and Lincoln. The painting is always of the highest quality, as can be seen in Colour Plate XI showing Worcester from the north-west. The painter seems to have enjoyed concentrating on the river boats and coach in the foreground and Worcester Cathedral is almost unimportant in the distance.

While we have tried to illustrate only items which are undoubtedly Grainger, we must confess to have nagging doubts about the plaques shown in Plate 151. They are of a type which includes a very elaborate moulded border cast in one with the plaques, the moulding in gold against a coloured ground, usually pink. The popular subjects of Worcester and Malvern have been noted on these plaques, but we have never come across a marked example. The style of modelling and the look of the glaze shouts Grainger to us, but we do need to see a marked example before we are totally convinced.

Finally, Grainger made a series of advertising plaques with copies of letters proclaiming the qualities of their 'semi-porcelain' body and Laboratory porcelain.

151. While very much in the Grainger style, these plaques, and many like them, are totally unmarked and therefore there is some doubt as to their origin. The pink ground and painting style occur on many marked Grainger Lee & Co. vases, however. 9¾ inches, c.1825–30. (Phillips)

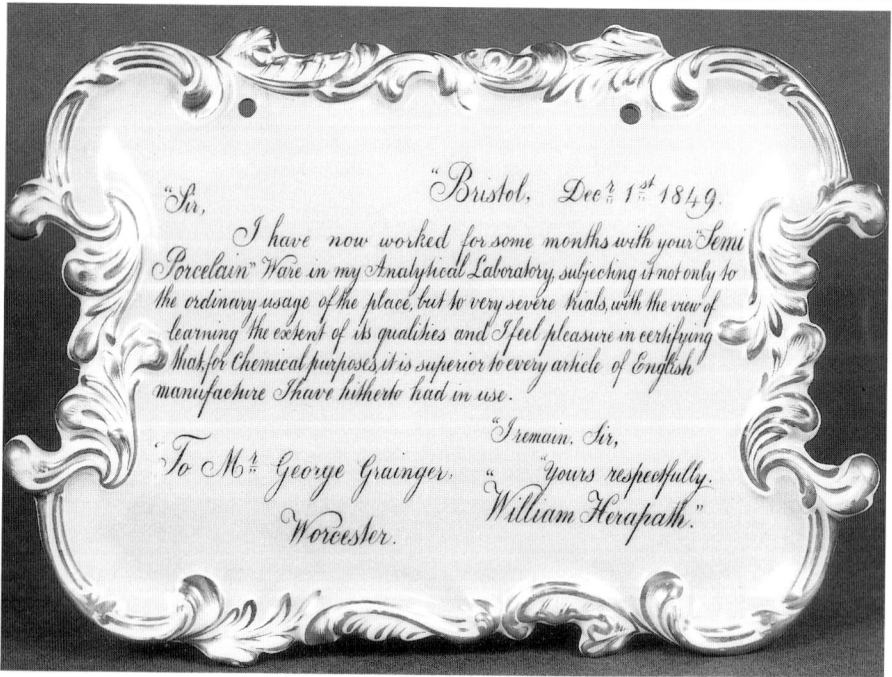

152. An advertising plaque for display in shops selling Grainger's 'Semi Porcelain' ware, the testimonial finely painted in black, c.1850. (Dyson Perrins Museum)

Although the design may seem too elaborate to have been made purely as an advertisement, we have not yet found others of this shape painted with subjects suited for general sale.

Pot Lids

During rebuilding work in Worcester in 1973 a group of workmen found a dump of Victorian glass bottles. Alongside were a number of white porcelain pots and lids which we now know to have been made by Grainger. The same dump yielded a single printed pot lid, illustrated here in Plate 136. In the archives at Worcester is the copper plate used to print this lid, together with designs for a variety of other lids and jars. All were sold by the Malvern chemists, Lea, Perrins & Burrows, and promoted a hair restorer called 'Muroma'. The lid illustrated was made in three sizes of which this is the smallest. The small size came in a different design inscribed:

MUROMA

A FRAGRANT POMADE

FOR

Promoting the growth of the hair

PREPARED

FROM THE RECIPE OF DR. GULLY

BY

Lea Perrins & Burrows

CHEMISTS

GREAT MALVERN

Labels for the side of deeper jars or the bases for Muroma pots were inscribed:

LEA PERRINS & BURROWS

Chemists

Sole Proprietors of the

MUROMA

and

Mertons Cooling Hair Wash

GREAT MALVERN

The single Muroma lid from Worcester is still the only recorded example, and we can assume from this that Dr Gully's recipe was not as successful as he probably claimed. Dr Gully himself achieved notoriety in Victorian society for his involvement in the celebrated Charles Bravo murder trial.

One other Grainger pot lid survives, 3″ in diameter, bearing the name of 'Rendall, Ho'c Chemist, Exeter, Torquay & Taunton. Member of the Royal Pharmaceutical Society of Great Britain'. The underside is marked 'Homeopathic Graduated Medicine Vessels, Chemical Porcelain, Grainger & Co. Worcester Sole

Manufacturers'. J. M. Rendall commissioned several designs from Grainger and this lid is datable to c.1850–7. Appendix 6 lists many other names which could occur on Grainger pot lids, made for specific china retailers or chemists.

Rose Labels

Introduced. in about 1850, plain sticks with rounded ends were made in large numbers. They were priced per gross with 'not less than 3 Doz. of each name'. A small hole was pierced at one end. Presumably these were tied to rose bushes, the names fired on so that they would not fade.

Sauce Bottles

A copper plate survives at the factory for printing the design on a bottle of 'Cheltenham College Sauce' and ever since discovering this we have searched for an example. We eventually tracked one down in the reserve collection of Cheltenham Art Gallery and were recently able to buy another in a small auction in Cheltenham. Neither is marked but there is no doubt about their origin. They are made in semi-porcelain body and must have been made very cheaply. Edward Moore was a chemist, rather like Lea & Perrins, and sauce-making would have begun as a sideline. Lea & Perrins's 'Worcestershire Sauce' became a worldwide success, but Cheltenham College Sauce was a short-lived concoction. However, considering how badly whatever was in the sauce had stained the bottle illustrated (Plate 136), it is probably just as well.

Spittoons

A spittoon was a circular flat vessel with central opening, within radiating flutes. A rough sketch is titled 'Spitoon Star Hotel' in the ornamental price book, 1850–60. The Star Hotel is in Foregate Street, Worcester and is still in business, although no Grainger spittoons seem to be!

Stoneware Jugs

A most remarkable example is illustrated in Plate 153. Moulded in a thick marbled agate-type stoneware in shades of brown, the surface is finely stamped with dots to resemble saltglaze. The front is embossed with the crest of a greyhound. The base is incised with the name 'George Grainger Worcester'. Probably made in about 1845. No other wares in brown stoneware have survived and George Grainger may have had this specially made, since he kept greyhounds himself.

Sugar Sifters

A page of shapes dated May 1860 (Plate 134) includes a sugar sifter with leaf moulding. A note mentions that it would have been decorated in 'Muffin', a matt ivory colouring not generally popular until the 1880s. No complete example has yet been seen.

Teeth

In the Dyson Perrins Museum is a fascinating metal tin containing false teeth! Incredibly realistic, they were made in very hard porcelain tinted to match the patient's own teeth, and attached to simulated gums. Apparently made by Grainger during the 1850s, a note book, also in the Museum, details their manufacture.

Telegraph Insulators

Ceramic insulators mounted on telegraph poles used to be a common sight before modern technology. Grainger were sufficiently proud of their insulators that they were part of the factory's stand at the 1862 International Exhibition. *Berrow's Worcester Journal* of December 29, 1866 also describes their manufacture. No examples have survived.

153. A remarkable jug in marbled brown stoneware, moulded with the crest of a greyhound, the incised mark of George Grainger confirming the unlikely origin, 8¾ inches, c.1845. (Private Collection on loan to the Dyson Perrins Museum)

Tie (or Cravat) Pin

A copper plate at the factory includes the outline of a fox's head to be printed on a tiny medallion. Fully coloured, this would have been mounted on a tie-pin or similar item of gentlemen's jewellery. We have seen an example attributed to Royal Worcester, but it was not marked and could well have been Grainger.

Toast Rack

Shape 227 from the early 1860s is the only reference to a Grainger porcelain toast rack. Its form is not known.

Toilets

Included in the review of Grainger's stand at the International Exhibition of 1862 is the note that the factory also manufactured toilets. It is possible that this refers to toilet sets (washbowl, jug, chamberpot, etc.) but it is not inconceivable that the chemical porcelain body was used to make toilet pans and other sanitary fittings. We know of no other references to such items.

Toys

Most factories made miniature ornaments, known at the time as toys. Plate 84 shows a miniature jug with a view of Worcester, and most of the miniatures made by Grainger were jugs, some with matching basins. Marked examples are mostly from the Grainger Lee & Co. period. Shape 132 of *c.*1850 is a 'Toy Jug, Parian', 2¼″ high with moulded flowerheads and scroll panels.

Whist Counter

A single example in the Dyson Perrins Museum (Plate 154) is marked G. Grainger, Royal Porcelain Works, Worcester. It corresponds with shape 78 and is fitted with a bronze bolt which allows the top to revolve. The price recorded in the shape book is white and gold, 1/8 each, grounds and gold, 2/- each.

Work Boxes

Shape No. 44 in the second ornamental shape book is a 'ladies work box & Ink'. It is shaped as a casket with elaborate scroll moulding and a loop handle at each side. The cover would lift off. Introduced in around 1832, the shape was withdrawn by 1841. Shape 45 is a 'basket box & cover' probably serving the same purpose, and shape 217 from the 1860s is an 'Embossed Box'.

154. A very rare surviving example of shape 78 in the Ornamental Shape Books, a 'Wist counter' painted in red and gold. Records show that such items sold for 2/- each in about 1840, marked G Grainger Royal Porcelain Works Worcester. (Dyson Perrins Museum)

CHAPTER EIGHT

ANIMALS AND FIGURINES

Up until the middle of the nineteenth century the Worcester factories were not figure makers. John Toulouse modelled a few in the 1760s for Dr Wall's factory and again around 1790 for Chamberlain, and Chamberlain issued a range of figures during the 1820s, but they lacked the qualities of those produced elsewhere, Derby in particular. As there had never been a tradition for figure making in Worcester, it is satisfying to be able to record the success of Grainger's excursion into the field, which certainly surpassed the efforts of their rivals in Worcester.

The factory records list in detail all of the models which were made, with some of them drawn out, and so we know almost the entire range. The ornamental shape books commenced in 1832 and it is possible that some of the animals not included pre-date them by a year or so. Models of animals were made extensively at Derby and in Staffordshire, the most prolific maker apparently being Samuel Alcock. Rockingham made some models, as did Minton and many smaller makers such as John and Rebecca Lloyd at Shelton. Grainger followed Chamberlain in joining in the act, producing a small range of rather amusing studies.

In a way, the drawings which survive in the shape books are almost better than the actual pieces. The models were cheap novelties and lacked the detail seen in other models of the period, but they do have a certain charm. Most seem to have been made as matching pairs, the models either reversed, or used with another companion model. The three studies in Plate 155 are all from matching pairs and show three different finishes. The giraffe is in glazed white porcelain while the doe is edged simply in gold. The companion has gold antlers. The dog is fully coloured and on a base which is a characteristic of many Grainger animals. In addition most models were issued in unglazed biscuit, such as the poodle in Plate 157. All of the animals illustrated here are marked Grainger Lee & Co. Worcester, impressed neatly into the base, with the exception of the mouse in Plate 158. This has a very Grainger look to the glaze and we feel confident enough to include it with a slight note of caution.

The giraffe is an amusing subject introduced slightly later, probably in 1836, when the first live giraffes ever seen in England arrived at Regent's Park Zoo. The animals were captured in the Sudan by M. Thibout, a French trader who brought them through London and caused quite a sensation. George Scharf produced a lithograph showing three of the giraffes and it is most likely that Grainger copied this rather than sending a modeller to the Zoo. The colouring is rather imaginative (Plate 159) suggesting that no one at Grainger had actually seen a real giraffe.

In addition to the animals illustrated, the following are recorded in the ornamental shape books:

A pair of greyhounds, one seated upright with forepaws crossed, the other lying with its nose resting on outstretched paws, the rounded bases edged with ferns and leaves; also issued together on a single base.

A King Charles spaniel standing with left forepaw raised, the base edged around with a rope.

A pair of a stag and a doe, both standing, the stag with gilded antlers and chain collar, a single gold line around the rocky bases.

155. *Three of the small animal subjects photographed alongside pages from the Ornamental Shape Books. All are marked Grainger Lee & Co Worcester, impressed, and illustrate the different finishes available, c.1830–5. (Private Collection)*

A dog looking at a mouse in a cage. A finished example shows the cage made of wire fitted over the fixed porcelain mouse, the base moulded with floorboards.

A pair of a pointer and a setter (shown in Plate 155).

A pair of groups of 'two deer compleat', the same as the lying stag and standing doe placed on a single base with tree behind. The companion group has a lying doe and standing stag.

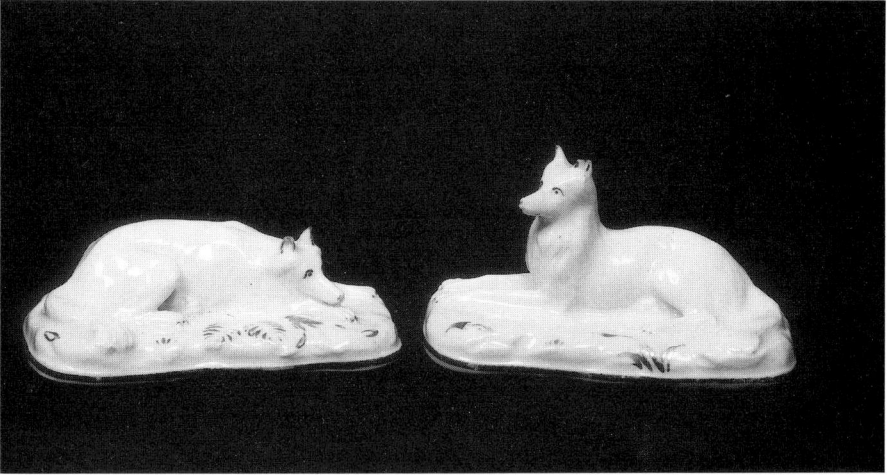

156. *A pair of dog models, possibly to be identified with the model named 'Tirrier lying' referred to in an early Grainger notebook on a list of animal prices, undated but around 1830. The models have a simple gold decoration, 4⁴/₁₀ inches long, with the impressed mark Grainger Lee & Co Worcester in the base. (Christie's)*

157. *A model of a French Poodle in biscuit porcelain with a 'Ruff'd' coat, 3⅛ inches high; and a model of a squirrel, fully coloured, 2½ inches high, both marked Grainger Lee & Co Worcester impressed, c.1830–5. (Private Collection)*

A model of a Russian setter, standing, with a chain hanging from its collar (model No. 50).

An earlier notebook includes an entry for April 1826 listing the cost of making a pug dog. The model 'Ruff'd all over' was costed at 8d while the same, 'half Ruff'd' cost 6d. On another page, not dated, is a list as follows:

Price of Animals nett	gilt	coloured proper	plain
Deer standing	3/6	4/-	3/-
Deer lying	3/-	3/6	2/6
Giraff or Camel L'pard	3/6	4/-	3/-
Greyhound lying down	3/-	3/6	2/6
Indian hare dog	3/-	3/6	2/6
Spaniel standing	1/10	2/2	1/6
Tirrier lying (sic)	1/8	2/-	1/4
French Poodle	—	—	1/4

158. A page from the Ornamental Shape Books showing a range of small animals. The poodle is shown in Plate 157. The finished mouse is unmarked but corresponds so closely with the drawing, and has a glaze of typical Grainger appearance, that there can be little doubt as to its origin. (Private Collection)

159. A giraffe or 'camel leopard' as it was known, introduced c.1836 and probably taken from George Scharf's lithograph of the first live giraffes delivered to London Zoo. The colouring is most extraordinary; impressed Grainger & Co Worcester. (Christie's)

160. Three Cupids building a Gothic Arch, also called 'Gothic Flowerists', finely modelled in biscuit with glazed and coloured flowers, 9½ inches, impressed Grainger Lee & Co Worcester, c.1835. See Colour Plate XVIII. (Dyson Perrins Museum)

159

161. *A magnificent 'Bower Group' with two Cupids below finely-detailed flowers, 6½ inches, impressed Grainger & Lee & Co Worcester. (Private Collection)*

The first human figures are drawn in the ornamental shape books with their own numbering from the early 1830s, beginning with a series of Cupids. It appears that certain models could be made up from individual figures and sections. Shapes 1 and 2 are single kneeling Cupids, holding wreaths. These two were combined with a third to make a group entitled 'Gothic Flowerists' (Plate 160 or Colour Plate XVIII). The Cupid held aloft was used on his own standing below the same gothic arch (shape 4) and shape 5 was the same with a wall at the back. Shape 12 is a Bower

Group or Cupid and Bower and has the same standing Cupid in the front as used on the gothic arch. In the background is a sleeping Cupid, which was also placed alone on a couch, as Plate 162. This is shape 14 entitled 'Cupid & Sofer' (sic) and was also issued on an extra base covered with lace. This base also supported two standing Cupids holding a basket of flowers (shape 16) and other versions had two Cupids with a shell or a single Cupid with a shell. The most elaborate of all is shape 18, 'Double Bower & Flowerists', with three Cupids within a very ornate flower arbour. The cost of this piece is given as 52/6 bisque and 73/6 coloured.

The Cupids are chubby and weakly modelled, possibly copied from Derby, but the quality of the Grainger flower modelling puts these pieces into a class of their own. Some are impressed Grainger Lee & Co. Worcester, while another has had the same mark altered at the factory to remove the word Lee, probably after the dissolution of the partnership in 1837. Others are unmarked and very often attributed to Derby or Minton, both of whom specialized in biscuit figures. These two rivals both made versions of the figures variously titled 'Infant Samuel' or 'Goodnight and Good Morning'. The similarity of the modelling and body lead us to believe that the example in Plate 162 is Grainger, but several much inferior versions were made in Staffordshire over a considerable period.

The full list of shapes is given in Appendix 2. We would like to point out a few other special models, as they are particularly fine and charming studies of the Royal Family. The group of Queen and Prince, shape 20, was published 14 January 1845 to protect Grainger's copyright. Queen Victoria is seated beside a box on which the

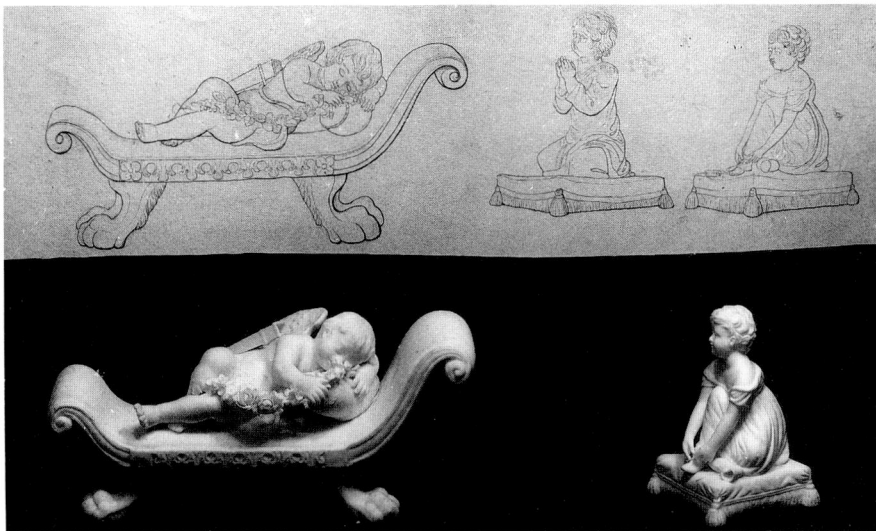

162. Two biscuit figure subjects which, although unmarked, correspond in every detail with the factory shape books. Left: 'Cupid on Sofer', 5½ inches long. Right: The companion to 'Girl at Prayers', 2⁹⁄10 inches high; several factories made versions, c.1835–40. (H & B Wolf Antiques)

young Prince of Wales stands, reaching up to kiss his mother's cheek, a dog stands to one side on the wide circular base heavily edged with scrollwork. We have not yet heard of a surviving example of this most delightful study. An unnumbered sketch entitled 'Royal Couch' shows an infant sleeping in a shell-shaped crib below an elaborate heavy velvet awning surmounted by a Royal crown. It probably depicts the Princess Royal, born in 1841, and a single example is known to us. Without the canopy, which presumably was an extra, it is in the Dyson Perrins Museum.

Most of the Grainger figures are only known from the books, no finished examples having survived. The exception is a group of large female figures which was published by George Grainger in 1845. They depict characters from literature and were made in bisque porcelain. Originally adorned with the most delicate lacework imaginable, it is hardly surprising that little of this still survives. Very fine lace netting was dipped in wet clay and placed on the figures. In the kiln the real lace burnt away leaving just the porcelain lightly attached to the figure. The slightest touch made the lace crumble to dust, meaning that the figures were doomed right from the start. Minton and Copeland parian was available from about this time and their figures were far superior. Grainger could make parian but does not seem to have attempted any figures. Therefore the biscuit ladies illustrated here (Plates 163–4) are rare survivors from the most ambitious Worcester figure venture

163. Two large biscuit figures. Left: Hermione, retaining some of the original lace, 13¾ inches, incised on the reverse 'Published Sepr. 22nd 1845 Geo Grainger, Worcester'. (British Museum) Right: Haide, a character from Byron made as a companion and with impressed factory mark. (Dyson Perrins Museum)

164. Left: a biscuit figure of Medora, 12¼ inches, impressed 'Published Nov 1st 1845 by George Grainger Worcester'. (Private Collection) Right: a biscuit figure of Parisina, originally hung with fine lace, 11⅓ inches, incised 'Published Sept 22 1845 by George Grainger Worcester'. (Phillips)

of its time, but the scruffy appearance explains why they failed. Their original cost was two guineas each.

A few figures were made in parian during the 1840s, namely shapes 46 and 47, 'Italian Boy and Girl', and 64, 'Cupid and Pedastle' (*sic*), but we cannot know how successful they were. The only other surviving figure we have traced is shape 60, 'Wellington Bust', a miniature portrait only 3¾" high. At the other extreme, a group was made of four children gathered around a base 'feeding rabbits'. A note says that this cost four guineas. The only clue is a copy of an invoice found in a Grainger notebook from the 1830s, which reads:

Edward Warner
No. 59 Brearly St. Birmingham
Modeller, Chaser & Repairer &c.

	£	s
General Washington	2	15
Pickwick		10
Wesley		12
	£3	17

None of these subjects are known in Grainger or listed in any other records, and so the significance of the invoice remains a mystery.

Figure 7. The popular pattern called Bamboo in the factory records, and used by Grainger for more than sixty years: a modern pull from an original copper plate.

CHAPTER NINE

THE DECORATION OF GRAINGER PORCELAIN

PAINTING AND GILDING

There really is no need to go into great detail about the enormous variety of painting seen on Grainger's porcelain as the illustrations in this book try to cover the whole field as thoroughly as possible. We feel, however, that it is worth explaining a few distinctive factory characteristics which help in identifying Grainger porcelain.

Every factory employed a team of painters who would all have their own mannerisms and peculiarities. When they worked together they would learn from each other and gradually follow a 'house style' which can be as vital a clue to identification as a mark or a key handle form. Grainger copied many of their designs from Chamberlain and a number of features suggest a 'Worcester' origin, even if they are not unique to Grainger. Other styles are much more individual and can only point to the Grainger factory.

It is nearly impossible to ascribe any piece of Grainger to a particular artist. Some pattern numbers give a painter's name but this alone is no guarantee that that painter would be responsible for that pattern every time an order was placed for it. Two important painters whose work should be distinctive are John Wood and David Evans, but even here the task is far from easy. The hare-coursing vase (Colour Plate XIV) was said by R. W. Binns in the nineteenth century to be the work of John Wood, but Binns was writing some time after the vase was made. Wood had learnt his trade at Chamberlain and it is tempting to see in the fox-hunting mugs (Plates 83 and Colour Plate II) the hand of a former Chamberlain employee. Positive identification is impossible in the absence of any signed pieces.

David Evans, 'the finest wild-flower painter in the trade', came from Swansea and his work can be traced back to examples on Welsh porcelain. There is little doubt that the vase in Colour Plate XV is by him, and on the strength of the signed plaque (Plate 4), other pieces can be attributed to Evans. The difficulty is that Evans would have influenced those around him, and the others clearly painted in a lighter, freer style as a result. A certain style of flower painting is seen on a great many Grainger wares from the 1820s. On the dinner service (Colour Plate VIII) this style is impressively shown, with soft pink roses shading into white grounds and other semi-formal flowers grouped round. Evans must have painted some of these, but there is no way of telling. Plate 165 shows a page from the pattern books with a similar spray in the centre of a table plate (pattern 1325). This is not ascribed, but

165

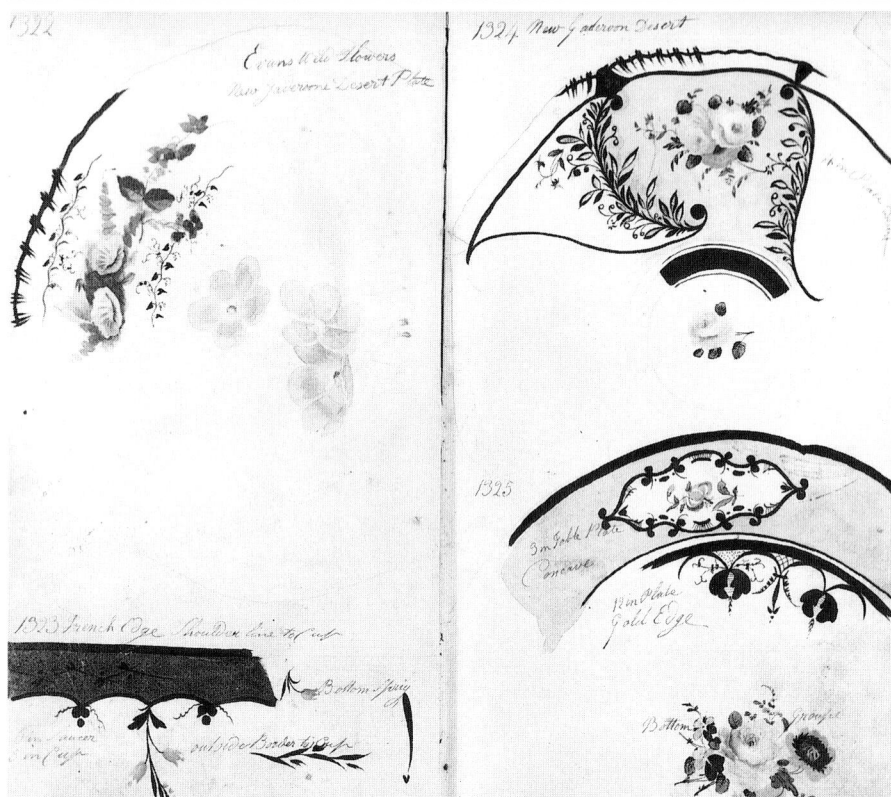

165. *A page from the factory pattern books including patterns 1322–5, c.1825. (WRPC)*

pattern 1322 has 'Evans wild flowers' written against it. His Swansea style of painting is seen clearly here.

Another distinctive painting style is the use of a type of exotic bird usually placed among gold branches and foliage, but also with bird's nests and, occasionally, landscapes behind. Very popular from about 1830, these can be seen at their best in the pattern book pages reproduced here (Plate 166).

Landscape painting on Grainger belongs to a 'Worcester' school which is remarkably similar on Flight, Chamberlain, and Grainger wares. Outside decorators such as Doe and Rogers and Sparks in Worcester painted in a similar way. It is therefore impossible to pick out any characteristics which are certainly Grainger. Generally, the standard of painting was not as fine at Grainger, but at its best it could be outstanding. The quality does vary greatly, however. The views were always copied from published engravings, many of which have been traced, such as Middleman's *Select Views in Great Britain*, and Jones's *Great Britain Illustrated* published in 1829, and it is sad to have to relate that even the popular views of Worcester were copied from prints. It is tempting to think of the Grainger

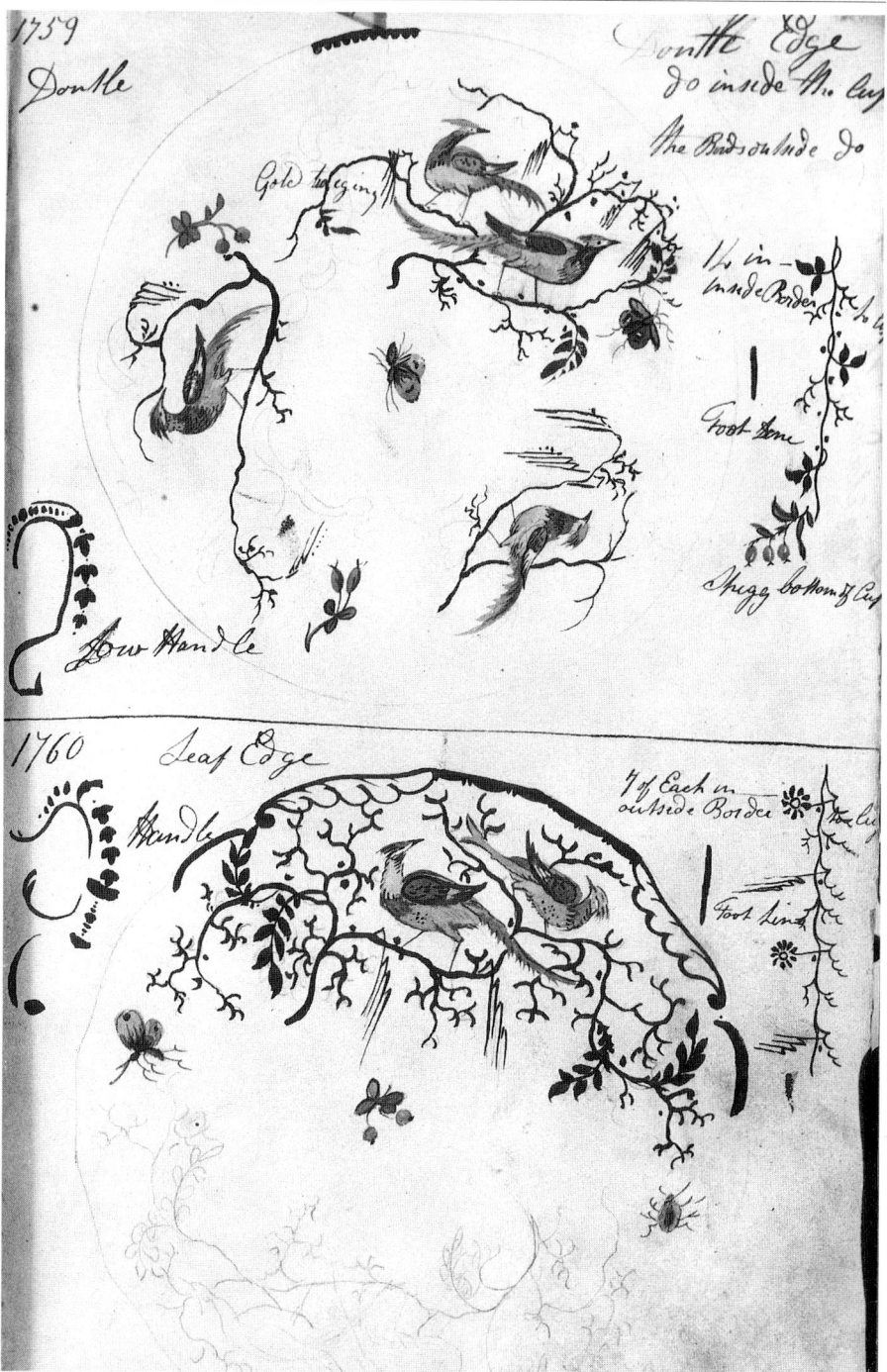

166. *A page from the factory pattern books showing characteristic bird painting and gold 'Twigging', patterns 1759 and 1760, c.1825–30. (WRPC)*

painters sitting on the banks of the River Severn sketching the Cathedral beyond, but this just did not happen in china factories.

Figure subjects were almost always avoided by Grainger, it seems, as we know of very few. They did paint a few figured vases but these are not of high quality.

Gilders have their own characteristic styles, just as painters, although they are much harder to pinpoint. Each factory seems to have stuck rigidly to certain styles of gilding and it is possible to recognize patterns which almost always point to a particular factory. Worcester gilders as a rule loved to put dots along the handles of tea and coffee cups, almost to the point of absurdity. Why this should be we cannot imagine, but there are certain pieces of Flight and Chamberlain as well as Grainger which have dots all over the handles, a feature used only occasionally elsewhere. This is a very dangerous area in which to be dogmatic, but the presence of dots on the handle does suggest Worcester to begin with.

The gilding on early Grainger is remarkably rich and very high quality. The gold tends to exhibit a slightly red tint and is often streaked, almost as if every brush stroke has remained visible. There are certain motifs which recur frequently in the early patterns, in particular a bell-like flower which is cross-hatched on one side only (see Plates 102 and 108), but it is in the late 1820s and throughout the next twenty years that the most distinctive feature was used time and again.

167. An unusual circular tureen printed in grey with the 'Challie' pattern, in this case partly filled in colours and hung with gold 'Twigging', the stand 7 inches, marked G W and pattern name, c.1840. (Private Collection)

168. A gadroon-edged dinner plate decorated with 'Blue Ball Japan' pattern 1472, together with a number of wasters of this and other 'Japan' patterns, the plate 10¼ inches, c.1825. (Authors' Collections)

It appears that the factory name for the style of gilding was 'twigging' and this is how we have elected to refer to it. A thin pattern of hanging gold foliage, like short wispy creepers, was used again and again and must have been very popular in Grainger's retail outlets. True, it is fairly unexciting and inexpensive, but it can be very effective.

The gilt twigging is seen at its best on the circular tureen of Challie pattern (Plate 167). The design of delicate flowers is printed in underglaze grey and then lightly coloured. Gilt twigging has been hung all over the pattern and produces a spikey, rustic charm. The pair of perfume bottles (Plate 149) link up with the shape books, but it is the gilding which points immediately to a Grainger origin, as distinctive as the thick crazed glaze and fine flower modelling. Samuel Alcock occasionally used gilt twigging, but never to the same extent as Grainger.

One other decorating style worthy of special mention is the so-called Japan patterns, perhaps better known today as 'Imari'. These use the primary colours of underglaze blue, red, and orange enamel, and gold, with the occasional green and purple. The style is best known on Derby, although it was popular throughout England and every factory seems to have produced some Japan patterns in the first quarter of the nineteenth century. The earliest Grainger piece known, the mug dated 1807 shown in Colour Plate I, is in a very popular Japan pattern used at many factories, especially Chamberlain and Coalport. Even Geoffrey Godden, who has written the standard works on both these rival factories, has admitted to us that this early Grainger mug is the finest example of its class known to him, and it is certainly much more finely produced than Coalport. Grainger's early hybrid porcelain body was well suited to Imari designs, and in addition to the pattern used on the mug and tea service in Plate 6, we show in Plate 168 a waster of an early saucer in 'finger and thumb' pattern, a rich Japan design also much used at Coalport and Chamberlain. As yet we have never seen a finished Grainger example, which should be on the New Oval shape with Bute-shape cups.

Pattern 1472 is referred to in the pattern books as Blue Ball Japan, an appropriate name considering the underglaze blue portion includes three round blobs in the border. The blue is used in two shades, and we have found several unfinished fragments of the pattern on the factory site. Some of these are shown in Plate 168 alongside a complete dinner plate dating from about 1820. Such designs at this period are much more usual on Staffordshire ironstone pottery, and Grainger is rarely thought of, although they made great quantities of this pattern.

TRANSFER PRINTED DECORATION

Almost from the outset Grainger made use of transfer printing, but in a very different way to other manufacturers. Overglaze 'bat' prints, finely-stippled engravings usually in black or grey, were widely used in England in the early nineteenth century, but only one pair of such prints is recorded on Grainger (Plates 9 and 10). A teapot in the Dyson Perrins Museum of standard Grainger New Oval shape from about 1810 is printed with travellers and their donkeys in a rural scene, a signpost to one side inscribed 'To Worcester'. The reverse has a print of a figure on a horse outside of an inn and again the name 'Worcester' appears, this time on a milestone. It is tempting to believe that these were printed at Grainger but the evidence is conflicting. The same prints occur on both sides of an oblong teapot datable to about 1812, in a bone china body. The shape is close to a Coalport form but with a different handle. The prints appear identical, except for the signpost and milestone, which have been blacked out. Are we looking here at an unrecorded Grainger teapot shape? Or did Grainger sell their copper plates to another manufacturer or decorator? The quality of the illustration of the oblong teapot is poor, but we reproduce it here in the hope that other examples might be identified to help solve this puzzle.

Printing played an important part in the decoration of Grainger, but not in the field of high quality overglaze decoration. Instead it was used as the underglaze outline on a number of coloured-in patterns, and other teaware and tableware designs were printed in underglaze colours. Blue was the most used, but examples are known in grey, brown, and green. Some overglaze printing in red or black was

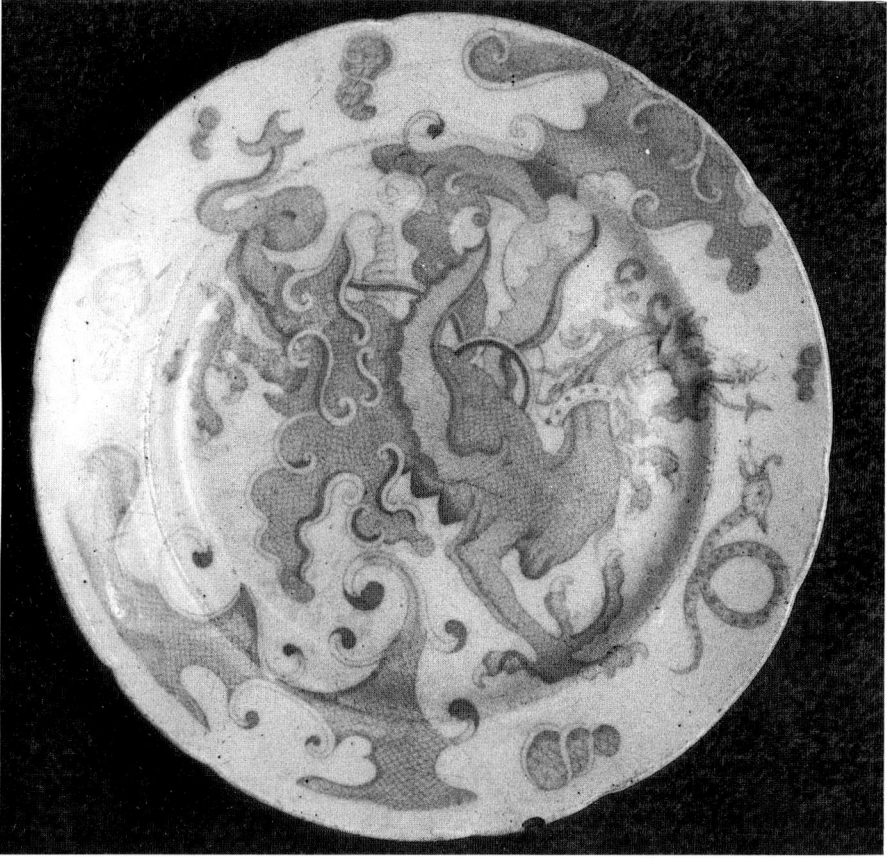

169. *A lobed dinner plate of Broseley shape printed with the Dragon pattern in underglaze blue. Many factories made this shape. 10¼ inches, marked Grainger Lee & Co Worcester, c.1815–20.*

attempted, again mostly just for outlines which would be painted-in with enamel colours.

A great many Grainger copper plates survive at Worcester and from these we have taken 'pulls', just as they would have been used in the Grainger Lee & Co. period. We have chosen to illustrate just a small selection here, but give the names of all the Grainger printed patterns in Appendix 3. These are mostly taken from a list prepared in 1844 recording the number of plates of each pattern and the weight of copper for insurance purposes. The number of plates of each which were in use gives an approximate idea of which patterns were the most popular. Some are well known to us while others have yet to be identified.

The best-known patterns are Broseley (Plate 14), Dragon (Plate 169) and Old India (Colour Plate VII). These designs were in no way unique to Grainger and their attribution needs to be confirmed by shape, pattern number, or marks. Some

171

others, such as Red India, were copied from Chamberlain or Spode prints, but most of the other designs are only found on Grainger porcelain. Many of the designs were 'sheet' patterns which could be used to cover almost any shape. This kept costs down and accounts for the popularity of Moss Fibre, Weed, Challie, and Leaf Ground. In about 1850 a particularly harsh bright blue was used for underglaze printing on the chemical porcelain body and this is almost instantly recognizable as Grainger Worcester.

As mentioned elsewhere in this book, some of the prints were of light outlines intended to be fully coloured-in. Views of Malvern and Worcester were available in

170. Transfer printing was rarely used on Gloster shape but this cake plate is decorated with a printed pattern called 'Vase', in this case in a very bright underglaze blue. The Grainger factory used this distinctive colour a great deal and it can easily be recognized. Marked with the pattern name and G W, c.1840. (Private collection)

several sizes to suit any panel and any piece of Grainger with a popular view needs to be examined closely to tell if there might be an outline print. Usually the title of the view will be printed underneath the base from the same copper plate, a useful clue to look out for. The vase shown in Plate 98 with a schoolboy is another outline print, carefully coloured in.

During the 1880s and 1890s a very extensive range of souvenir pieces was made, mostly taking the form of small posy vases. They frequently bear an ivory or 'blush ivory' ground and the print is lightly coloured. From surviving prints and records we have listed most of the views which were used (see Appendix 4) but there will undoubtedly have been a few others.

OUTSIDE DECORATION

Just as Thomas Grainger and John Wood probably began their partnership decorating white Coalport porcelain, Worcester attracted a large number of china painters to work at the factories and many settled in the city as independent artists. Training and inspiration came from the close proximity of Flight and Chamberlain but there was little chance of acquiring undecorated white porcelain on which to paint from these sources.

With such intense competition in Worcester, it would have been suicidal for the principal factories to provide rival decorators with modern shapes and the pastes and glazes which had taken years to perfect. Factories in Staffordshire, and particularly Coalport, were more than happy to supply free-lance Worcester decorators with any white porcelain wares they needed. Some Chamberlain and Grainger, however, was painted by independent decorators.

Several decorators apparently had connections with the Grainger factory, although there is little concrete evidence to work with and few marked pieces.

George Rogers and Enoch Doe

worked together at the Chamberlain factory. By the 1820s they had established a decorating kiln in Worcester specializing in well-painted landscape views, raised gilding and coloured grounds. The partnership survived until Rogers's death in 1835, although Enoch Doe continued as a free-lance artist until the 1850s. Geoffrey Godden suggests, in his *Encyclopaedia of British Porcelain Manufacturers*, that vases and teawares marked 'New China Works, Worcester' could be the work of Doe & Rogers, but we remain unconvinced.

A number of Grainger dessert wares of the 1820s have been attributed to the Doe and Rogers partnership. In particular an extensive service of undoubted Grainger shapes was split up and dispersed by several dealers in 1985–6, apparently unmarked, but we have been told that a few pieces were in fact marked 'Doe & Rogers Worcester'. We have not ourselves seen a marked example on Grainger porcelain and would appreciate further information. The similarity of this service to the work of J. Hadley accentuates our doubts.

Figure 8. Grainger's version of the popular pattern known as Broseley, a modern pull from a copper plate including the printed mark Grainger Lee & Co. Worcester.

Figure 9. A modern pull from the original copper plate of a saucer of 'Fountain' pattern, c.1840.

George Sparks

bought Coalport blanks and was proud of the fact, marking his wares as 'Coalport Porcelain' together with his name, address in Broad Street, Worcester, and, usually, 'By Appointment to Her Majesty Queen Adelaide' or 'to the Late Queen Adelaide'. The Queen had died in 1849 and this gives us the latest possible date for the establishment of Sparks's decorating workshop. Marked examples are known on Minton porcelain, but no Grainger or Chamberlain wares seem to have been used.

Sparks's connection with Grainger is confirmed by the pattern books. Patterns 1993–9 include the curious note 'with Sparkes' (sic) against each pattern, including patterns featuring underglaze blue or else gilt twigging, firm indications that these were decorated at Grainger. These patterns would date from approximately 1820 and we therefore suggest that George Sparks was a senior decorator or supervisor at Grainger before setting up on his own. He later used the mark 'Sparks, Royal Porcelain House, Worcester', to distinguish his wares.

Conningsby Norris

began his career at the Grainger factory where he is recorded as a decorator in the pattern books. Pattern 1356 is ascribed to Norris and James Meigh. Godden records that by 1835 Norris had set himself up as an independent decorator. Bentley's Local Guide of 1840–1 lists him as a china gilder and enameller. By 1851 he claimed to be a 'manufacturer of . . . tea and breakfast sets, desserts, ornaments &c.', although he clearly did not make any porcelain at Worcester.

Conningsby Norris married Mary Anne Grainger, daughter of Joseph Grainger, and a descendant gave to the Dyson Perrins Museum twenty years ago a series of mugs painted by Norris, including one bearing his wife's name. In spite of the Grainger name, we are certain that none of these are Worcester mugs. Godden suggests that a class of wares just marked 'Worcester' and a low pattern number could be Norris's work. The idea is attractive but we can find no evidence to support it, except to mention that very few pieces have Conningsby Norris's name on them so they must either have been unmarked or marked in some other way.

J. Hadley

is recorded on the bottom of a coffee cup shown by Michael Berthoud, item 490, and on a full dessert service with named landscape views. Many of the views are local to Worcestershire, but exhaustive searches in the Worcester public record office have failed to establish his identity. The decoration is high quality and with good gilding, and the landscape painting suggests that J. Hadley was trained in one of the main Worcester factories. Another unmarked dessert service attributed to Doe and Rogers looks very similar to signed Hadley pieces. There is no connection with the later Worcester modeller and manufacturer, James Hadley.

J. Derbyshire

is the final name regularly occurring on Grainger pieces. He is known to have bought Worcester vases and services for decorating, usually signed, and occasionally giving his address at Fort Royal Hill, Worcester. Pieces with the impressed shield mark of the 1870s have been seen with deep blue borders edged in gold, suggesting that Derbyshire bought finished wares with plain centres and simply added the centre painting. Usually flowers, occasionally somewhat crude landscapes have been noted. Most signed Derbyshire pieces are on Grainger porcelain, and some bear the name of another partnership, Padmore-Derbyshire.

While it is very difficult to say whether the decoration on unmarked early wares was added at the factory or not, most later Grainger pieces are marked and it is therefore likely that many more pieces of unmarked Grainger were painted outside the factory. This is clearly an area which would benefit from further research.

Figure 10. A modern pull from an original copper plate showing the view of the River Severn that occurs on the loving cup shown in Plate 87, where the artist added two rowing boats.

CHAPTER TEN

LATER ORNAMENTAL WARES
1870 1902

In the two decades spent working on this book, we have seen a noticeable change in collecting habits. Twenty years ago Worcester collectors were very interested in the early Grainger porcelains while the later wares, with few exceptions, were considered decorative novelties of little academic interest. This attitude has now changed totally, with an increasing number of collectors seeking the later reticulated wares and ivory grounds.

With the heavy competition in Worcester it is surprising just how many pieces from the 1870–90 period are unmarked. The printed or impressed shield marks occur on little more than half of the rich ornamental wares made at Grainger during this period, the remainder having the sole distinction of a pattern number. The numbers relate to the decoration as well as the shape, and each shape was given a different number, depending on the particular pattern used. Usually painted neatly in red, these numbers are fractional, running from the earlier shape number sequence which had reached 1/250 by about 1865. By 1890 the numbers were well over 1/3000, the 1 fraction representing ornamental wares. After the factory was sold to Royal Worcester the shapes were all given a new number with a G prefix, to distinguish them from Royal Worcester's own lists. The G shape numbers occur on some later Grainger vases, although this sequence was mostly used after the final closure of the Grainger works.

Classical shapes seem to have influenced Grainger production from 1870. Whereas the Worcester Royal Porcelain Company were completely dominated by Japanese designs in the 1870s and 1880s, Grainger looked toward Greek and Roman forms and the ornament of the Renaissance. The magnificent swan and bulrush vase (Plate 171) is more traditional Grainger and could well have been modelled in the 1850s. The only example known to us is this one in the Dyson Perrins Museum, done in parian with a green stained ground, popular around 1870. As mentioned previously, some of the Grainger flower shapes of the 1840s were reissued at this time, with other new shapes of posy vases and wall pockets made in the same green and white parian, sometimes glazed just on the inside or occasionally all over with added gilding.

The same combination of stained and white parian, in this case glazed, is seen on the eagle vase in Plate 172. The shape proved very popular from its introduction in the early 1870s, continuing at Royal Worcester well into this century. Most

171. An exciting vase in parian, the swans and bulrushes in white, the ground stained deep green. Grainger used plant forms to great effect and this is one of their most successful, 11 inches, c.1870. (Dyson Perrins Museum)

172. An eagle and amphora vase in glazed white parian, the vase in salmon pink with pâte-sur-pâte decoration probably by Kate Locke, impressed shield mark, c.1880. (Private Collection)

examples are in the matt ivory of the 1890s, but this earlier piece was left plain, except for *pâte-sur-pâte* on the pot-pourri vase between the bird's wings. *Pâte-sur-pâte* had been revived in England at Minton by the great French artist Marc Louis Solon and a team of fine craftsmen. Few factories attempted this difficult technique but a certain amount was made at Royal Worcester. Grainger *pâte-sur-pâte* is very delicate, mostly used for finely-detailed flowers in white against a plain-coloured ground, rarely with any border or even a gold rim. The flowers were built up in white clay mixed with water to form a paste called 'slip'. We know of three pieces of Grainger *pâte-sur-pâte* signed by Kate Locke, and we believe she was responsible for most of the Grainger wares, although it is possible her father, Edward Locke, did some *pâte-sur-pâte* work. The vase in Plate 173 is unusual in that the leaves are unglazed and have been gilded to contrast with the celadon ground. This vase is signed with Kate Locke's monogram, K , scratched into the base.

Grainger were great experimenters and tried out numerous decorating techniques. Curiously beautiful, although short-lived, was a method of simulating variegated stones and marble. Two very clever examples are in the Dyson Perrins Museum (Plate 174) but this technique is rarely seen outside the factory's own collection. The same is true of Grainger's architectural porcelain. During the 1870s, and early 1880s, the factory made a large number of tiles moulded in relief with formal motifs, flowers or leaves. Some were stained in different colours and others

173. A rare signed example of the work of Kate Locke, the pâte-sur-pâte decoration unusually gilded, printed shield mark and incised K+L monogram, c.1875–80. (Phillips)

174. Grainger's experimental marbled grounds used to good effect on tripod vases, about 6 inches, unmarked except for pattern numbers in red, c.1870. (Dyson Perrins Museum)

175. A pair of vases reproducing early Worcester blue scale ground, in this case with painted scales although later printed scales were used, 11 inches, marked Grainger & Co in red script, c.1870. (Private Collection)

176. A pilgrim or moon vase in the popular classical style with simulated pearl border, the rustic landscape by John Stinton Senior, 8½ inches, unmarked, c.1870. (Dyson Perrins Museum)

177. A vase with 'old ivory' and 'blush ivory' grounds, decorated with a coloured-in print of Stratford-upon-Avon Grammar School, 4 inches, printed mark with date letter for 1897. (Private Collection)

were left in unglazed parian. Mouldings for borders and cornices were produced to accompany the tiles and a large number survive at the Worcester museum. Being in parian, they were probably not as hard wearing as pottery tiles and very few seem to have survived any period of use.

The factory apparently had a certain success with reproductions of early Worcester porcelain decorated with a deep 'blue scale' ground. The vases illustrated (Plate 175) are marked Grainger & Co. in red script and date from about 1870. In this case the scale ground is painted, although later a printed scale pattern was used, the surviving copper plate bearing a copy of Worcester's square mark and dated 1886. We have seen several examples where Grainger's name has been removed by grinding in the hope of passing the pieces off as early Worcester but, as the shapes are purely Victorian, we cannot see how anyone could really have been taken in.

The use of a deep blue ground was a Grainger speciality. A range of pieces were decorated on top of the ground with classical figures printed in outline and coloured and gilt, in the styles popular during the 1850s, but the Grainger examples appear to be from the late 1860s or 1870s and for this reason are not seen frequently. The blue ground was much more successful as a frame for painted panels, usually embellished by brilliant enamel jewels simulating pearls. We illustrate two examples of this type, one a plate from a full dessert service, the other a moon vase or pilgrim's flask, with gorgon's head handles. Both were painted by John Stinton sen. with delightful landscapes inspired by the water-colours of Miles Birkett Foster and others. Not all of the landscapes painted in the centres of dessert services were by John Stinton sen., as some are clearly inferior and care must be taken in attributing these pieces. Stinton's work has tremendous detail and particularly atmospheric backgrounds.

John Stinton's two sons, John jun. and James, both painted at the Grainger factory. They probably started out as apprentices, painting birds on ivory ground vases such as the pair in Plate 179, or else colouring-in printed souvenir wares such as the Stratford-on-Avon vase in Plate 177. A very large number of these views were produced on small vases and trinkets, and a long list of subjects is given in Appendix 4. All of these appear to have been coloured-in prints.

John and James Stinton soon developed their own individual painting styles and

178. A range of later Grainger pieces by the three principal members of the Stinton family. The plate by John Stinton Senior, c.1870, the vases with pheasants by James Stinton and cattle by John Stinton Junior, the latter with typical ivory grounds, date codes for 1897 to 1902. (Dyson Perrins Museum)

became Grainger's foremost artists. They were the only painters ever permitted to sign their work on Grainger porcelain and typical examples from the 1890s are shown in Plate 178. James specialized in game birds, particularly pheasants emerging from woodland, and he seems to have painted little else in his later years at Grainger. John Stinton jun. could paint fine English landscapes, although in a different style to his father. His speciality was cattle, and while at Grainger, only English cattle. Later, after the transfer to Royal Worcester, he took up painting the Highland cattle for which he was to become famous. Two other Stintons, Walter and Arthur, began at Grainger, but left with Edward Locke in 1895.

Other painters began their careers at Grainger before moving to Royal Worcester but do not appear to have signed any pieces until after the closure of the Grainger factory. One artist, George Cole, was a fine flower painter, specializing in roses. The rose on the neck of the perfume bottle in Plate 180 is probably his work.

At the Great Exhibition in 1851 Grainger had displayed pierced porcelain, and this was a field they were to make their own during the last quarter of the nineteenth century. True, they did not have a George Owen, whose freehand

179. Later Grainger reticulated porcelain, printed marks, c.1890. (Dyson Perrins Museum)

180. Reticulated porcelain including jewelled decoration in raised enamels, the perfume bottle painted probably by George Cole, printed marks, c.1885–90. (Dyson Perrins Museum)

piercing for Royal Worcester was in another dimension entirely but, by carefully following a moulded outline, Grainger craftsmen were able to produce intricate reticulated porcelain which could be made commercially. No other factory consistently produced such fine pierced wares, which at their best were breathtaking. The tea service in Plate 181 was done with the double-walled technique developed forty years earlier. The matt ivory-glazed parian is set off by jewelled borders which are beautiful in themselves. At their most impressive, as on the large vase in Plate 182, these creations were most fitting memorials to the skill of the Grainger factory. The vase stands 19″ inches high yet is as light as a feather,

181. A reticulated tea set of exceptional quality produced c.1885–90 under the direction of Alfred Barry. All are double-walled so that in spite of their fineness the pieces are perfectly functional, shield marks. (Dyson Perrins Museum)

182. An unusually large example of Grainger's reticulated porcelain bearing the date code for 1894, 19 inches overall, shield mark. (Sotheby's)

185

wonderfully controlled and faultless. At the other extreme, a pierced scent bottle no more than two inches across exhibits the same meticulous attention to detail.

The pierced work was under the control of Alfred Barry, who supervised the many craftsmen employed to cut out the delicate tracery. The moulds, some created by Barry himself, produced thin, evenly cast blanks and this was very important to prevent the pieces warping and splitting in the intense heat of the kiln. After eighty years, here at last was an art form at which Grainger could excel.

183. A typical page from the Pattern Books showing x-series numbers from about 1840. Some are fully drawn and described, while others just have a single line entry. Note the gold 'Twigging' represented by black enamel in the pattern books.

184. A cup and saucer of Malvern shape photographed alongside the corresponding entry in the Pattern Book, where the gilding is attributed to Parry, pattern 1866x, c.1840.

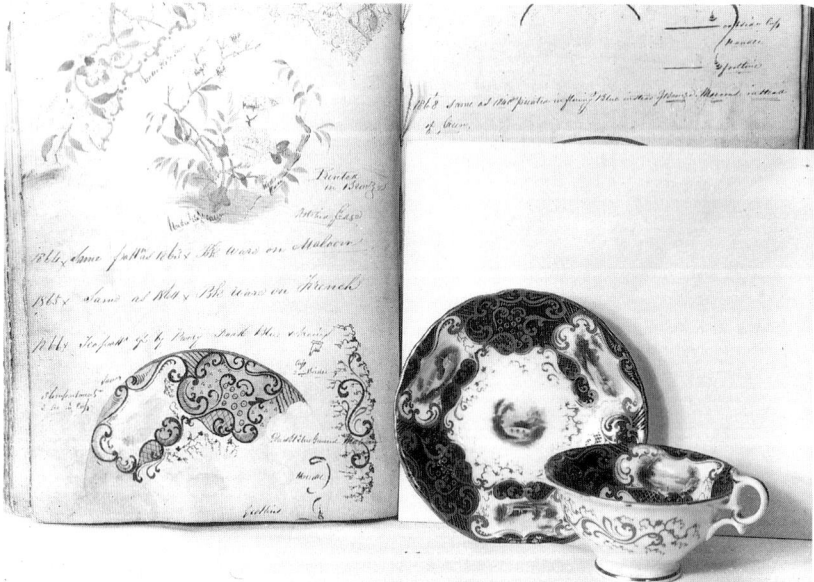

GRAINGER PORCELAIN MARKS

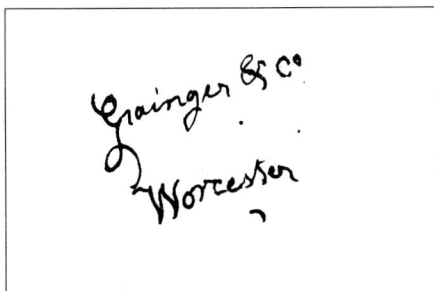

In script under covers or bases *c.1806–11*

Printed in underglaze blue *1814–37*

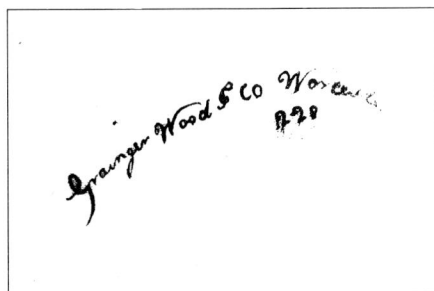

In script under covers *c.1806–11*

Painted in red script *1814–37*

Painted or printed *c.1811–14*

Rare printed mark *1814–37*

GRAINGER LEE & CO
WORCESTER

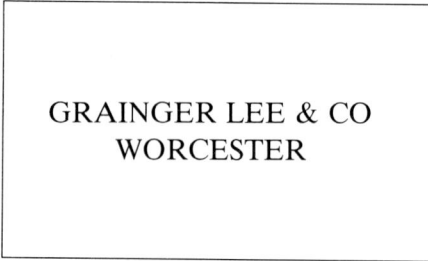

Impressed under figures or animal models
c.1825–37

Rare printed mark *c.1820–30*

Script mark, usually red *1837–9*
 (possibly from c.1830)

Printed marks including pattern name
c.1830–50

Rare printed mark *c.1820–30*

Many marks include the initials G W, G G, or
G & Co. W with the pattern name *c.1825–30*

Rare printed mark *c.1820–30*

Printed mark *c.1840–60*

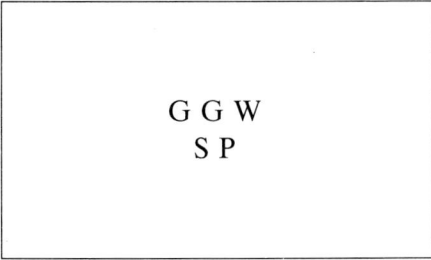

G G W
S P

Impressed mark on semi-porcelain
c.1848–60

Printed mark   c.1850–70

Printed mark   c.1850–60

Printed or impressed mark   c.1870–89

Printed mark   c.1848–60

Printed mark on blue scale reproductions
c.1870–1902

Printed mark   c.1860–70

Printed mark   1889–1902

189

From 1891 a letter date code was used under the printed mark:

A	1891	J	1900	H	1898
E	1895	C	1893	L	1902
I	1899	G	1897		
B	1892	K	1901		
F	1896	D	1894		

After 1891, 'England' is usually added.

ORNAMENTAL SHAPE LIST

The shapes below are recorded in the ornamental shape books which commenced in about 1832. These descriptions have been extracted from several volumes and in some cases are our own where a shape is merely drawn with no title. We have made no attempt to standardize original spellings.

Figures and Bowers

1	Single Cupid and wreath	24	Girl and butterfly, 'Butterfly Catcher'
2	Companion to ditto	25	Girl and rock
3	Single Cupid and shell	26	Hermione
4	Cupid and Gothic arch	27	Parisina (various spellings)
5	Cupid and Gothic arch with wall at back instead of vine tree	28	Heidi (various spellings)
		29	Medora or Madora
6	Cupid and shell with further cupid and flowers below	30	Contemplation small
		31	Girl and basket
7	Country girl with lace	32	Flower girl
8	Companion to No. 7	33	Fellow to 31 and 32
9	Girl at prayers	34	Fellow to 31 and 32
10	Sappho and lace, holding flowers	35	Bat filled with flowers
11		36	Cupid and tree
12	Cupids and bower	37	Large Cupid and open bower (sleeping)
13	Venus and lace, large figure		
14	Cupid and Sofer on extra large stand and lace (no number without stand and lace)	38	Group 'Feeding Rabbits', 4 figures of boys
		39	Basket of flowers
15	Male figure hawking	40	Two boys and rabbit
16	Two Cupids and basket	41	
17	Small Eve	42	
18	Double bower and flowerests (3 Cupids)	43	
		44	
19	Lady hawking and lace	45	
20	Queen and Prince (pub. 14 January 1845)	46	Italian girl, Parian
		47	Italian boy, Parian
21	Large Eve and lace	48	Greyhounds
22	Fellow to large Eve, Contemplation	49	2 greyhounds with chain
23	Boy and bird with chain and dog	50	Russian setter (with chain)

51	2 deer complete	59	
52	2 deer	60	Wellington bust
53	Giraffe	61	Jenny Lind
54	Pointer	62	Taglioni & fellow (ballet dancer)
55	Setter	63	Taglioni with or without lace
56	Candour	64	Cupid and pedestle Parian
57	Innocence	65	Girl with flowers
58	Melancholy and Water Nymph	66	Flower girl with basket, flowers

Vases and Other Ornaments

1 Ewer with twisted handle, applied vines, fluted body, 2 sizes
2 Vase fluted, two handles, applied flowers, 4 sizes
3 Arabian Vase in 2 sizes, horses' handles, applied vines
4 Arabian Vase, without horses
5 Clarence Vases with embossed leaves, 2 sizes
6 ditto without leaves, 2 sizes
7 Clarence Ewer with leaves, 2 sizes
8 ditto without leaves, 2 sizes
9 ditto with scrolls on the shoulder, 2 sizes
10 Vase, scroll handles, vines
11 ditto
12 Ewer, shell-like with scroll handles and flowers
13 As No. 10, no handles
14 Vase, fluted, foliate handles and neck, pierced sides, filled with modelled vines, 2 sizes
15 ditto, plain body, solid and not pierced
16 Same as No. 15, no handles
17 Fish tail bottles flowered, scroll handles
18 Ovoid vase twig handles, flowered
19 Rickuss's China, vase wide lip, flowered, 2 sizes
20 As 19, altered top, foliate
21 ditto, ribbon top
22 New as Allsup, trumpet, hanging flowers, 2 sizes
23 Copied from Staffordshire, see No. 53
24 Vase, fluted, scrolls, flowered, 2 sizes

25 Trumpet Vase, one flower on each side, small sprigs crossing
26 As 25, without handles
27 As 25, without flowers
28 Cornucopia Vase, flowered full both sides, foot as Allsup, 3 sizes
29 Cornucopia, 1 slight rose raised at foot
30 Cornucopia Vase, bluebells on foot, 3 sizes
31 Flower holder, leaf base, cane coloured top (also made in parian)
32 ditto blue top
33 ditto green top
34 Oval flower holder, cane ground and green leaf
35 ditto blue leaf
36 ditto, biscuit blue ground, cane leaf
37 Flower vase, overlapping leaves green and gold
38 ditto, pink and green top
39 ditto, green and blue
40 ditto, green and blue
41 Vase, pear shape, trellis neck, flowers, scrolls
42 Flower vase, scroll, blue and green
43 Indian Jars, also made as coffee pots, 3 sizes
44 Large Ladies Work box & ink
45 Basket-box and cover
46 Convolvulus flower Vase, Tazza shape with cover
47 ditto, deeper
48 Water leaf flower vase and cover
49 Pear shaped Vase, scroll handles
50 As 10, chrome green, matt blue, v. flowery

51	Large Vase, scroll shape	87	Pot-pourri & cover, octagonal, vermacilly and view
52	ditto, bird handles, scroll shape	88	Oak leaf jug, green and gold
53	Leaf handled Vase	89	ditto, white and gold
54	Scent bottle, flattened pear shape, flowered	90	Cornucopia Vase
55	Flower shaped Vase, tall trumpet flower	91	Etruscan Ewer, figures, 1 handle
56	ditto, Cornucopia flower, flowered base	92	Pear shaped Ewer, plain
57	Chandelier for drops, glass (lustre type)	93	Brameld leaf jar and cover (primrose leaves)
58	Flowered ovoid Vase, pierced flowered neck	94	Leaf moulded tazza and cover
59	ditto, no flowers, quite plain	95	
60	Flower-like Vase, pointed leaf design, flowered	96	Ovoid Vase pink stripes, views Malvern or Worcester
61	ditto, plain, no flowers	97	As 96 pink bands and gilding
62	Tulip shaped Vase	98	Hawthorn Taper
63	Convolvulus shaped vase	99	Large York Vase, scroll handles flowered. ditto, small
64	Elaborate scroll centrepiece	100	As 99 glazed all over and gilt
65	Scroll-cornucopia Vase, flowered	101	Figure boy by tree and vines
66	Two handled Vase	102	ditto, no flowers and vines
67	Rickuss's Violet basket, tazza-like with lid	103	Angel nightlight
68	Pen tray, scroll shape	104	Bird on a tree, shaded in green, leaf base
69	Thistle Vase	No Number	Chess Table, scroll rim
70	Vase, leaf modelling, 2 sizes, China or parian	105	Poppy Vase, parian or china, 8¾"
71	Fellow to 72, China or parian	106	Lily Vase, parian or china, lily of valley flowers, 8¾"
72	Vase with convolvulus (priced in Parian)	107	Fushia Vase, parian or china, 7¼" and 8½"
73	Scroll handled Vase, leaf modelling, 2 sizes	108	Violet Vase, parian or china, 7¼" and 8½"
74	Convolvulus Vase	109	Trellis Vase, 7¼" and 8½"
75	Fellow to 74	110	Cylindrical Vase, spiral flowers
76	Ovoid Vase, floral modelling, castleated top	111	As 109, grounded and gilt
77	Convolvulus violet stand, circular	112	As 108, ditto ditto
78	Wist Counter [sic]	113	Lilly Jug parian
79	Two handled jar and cover	114	Ovoid Vase petal rim, views or flowers, 2 sizes
80	As 79, no handles	115	As 114 with handles
81	Amphora Vase, marbled or Egyptian figures, 2 handles	116	Slender vase, high handles
82	ditto, 1 handle	117	Flower moulded Jug, parian or china, 6"
83	Flower Vase, scale moulded neck	118	Water Lily Jug, parian 5½" and larger
84	Leaf Taper Vermicilly, printed in Antwerp blue, stiff leaf rim	119	ditto, no handle, as a vase 5½" and larger
85	Vermicilly Taper, flat leaf rim	120	Grape jug, twig handle 7½"
86	Vine basket, vermicilly & view or flowers	121	Flower Vase, modelled 9½"
		122	Vine bottle as 120, no handle
		123	Flower jug as 121, handle

124	Lily jug 5¾″
125	Bull Rush Vase 9⅜″
126	Ewer, trailing leaves, pear shape 7⅞″
127	Lily Vase, as 124, no handle 6″
128	Bull rush jug 6″
129	Bull rush bottle 5⅞″
130	Vine jug 5¾″
131	Vine Bottle 5⅞″
132	Tulip Vase 8″
133	Toy Jug parian, mayflower ground 2¼″
No Number	Tea Plant Dejeune
134	Pear shaped Vase, ribbed, flower band 6½″
135	as 134, no flower band, just ribbed, 6½″
136	Double fluted cup 2¾″
137	Cabinet Cup, stand, and cover as 152 3″
138	Jug, Eastern design, straight neck 5⅞″
139	Swan Jug, 4⅜″
140	Same as 77 but Parian
141	Primrose Jug 3¾″
142	Jug, bird, snake & bullrushes 9⅛″
143	Oak leaf Jug, 2¾″
144	Cornucopia Vase 4⅛″
145	Temple shape, 3⅞″
146	Rose labels per doz, or per gross
147	Fluted jug, floral band and handle
148	Fluted pear shaped Jug
149	Artichoke Cup and Cover
150	Fluted Jug, wavy handle
151	as 134 but coloured berried leaves
152	as 137 coloured berried leaves
153	as 126 but coloured leaf spirals
154	Loaf plate 'Joy', large and small plain
155	ditto coloured
156	ditto emerald green ground
157	ditto Hard kiln pink
158	ditto letters in Celeste
159	ditto white gold
160	ditto blue rim
161	Jug stand, hawthorne border
162	ditto red ground
163	Loaf plate, blue and gold
164	ditto, green and gold
165	Leaf moulded jug
166	Jug, 4 festoons of flowers
167	Jug, decorated Hearts ease & rose & forget-me-nots
168	Jug, 4 festoons
169	Fluted Vase, convolvulus band, scroll handles
170	ditto, no handles
171	Vase leaf base, handles with modelled grapes
172	ditto, no handles
173	Ovoid Vase, vine handles
174	Ovoid Vase, leaf moulding, for chandeliers
175	Bottle Vase for chandeliers, floral
176	Oil Lamp base on spreading foot
177	As 174 with foot
178	Ovoid Vase with foot
179	Persian style Vase with pierced handles
180	Tall egg shaped vase
181	As 177 pierced
182	As 179, no handles
183	Squat Jug, flower wreath
184	Jug stand on balls, 6″ or 7″
185	Plain beaker Vase, sapphire ground, gold stars
186	ditto, floral band, blue rim
187–199	not listed
200	Cylindrical spill, fluted and leafage
201	ditto, fluted with flowerheads
202	ditto, fluted
203	Extinguisher and stand, conical, leafage
204	Extinguisher, lady's head
205	Pear shaped Vase
206	
207	Ewer, fluted
208	Ewer fluted, keyfret band
209	Shaped box & cover, scrollwork
210	ditto, panel on cover
211	
212	Candlestick
213	Cornucopia Vase
214	Pierced circular pot-pourri bowl
215	ditto on foot
216	3 amphora vases, joined
217	Embossed box
218	Dogs
219	Dogs
220	Butter Tub
221	Tazza

222	Figure supporting dish		236	ditto, ditto
223			237	ditto, ditto
224			238	ditto, ditto
225	Shell on mound, weed base		239	Tazza
226	Squat jar on 3 feet		240	Tazza Top
227	Toast rack		241	Tazza
228	Jug		242	Jug and stand
229	Vase, moulded cherub head and scrolls		243	China spill
			244	
230	Loaf plate		245	
231	Jug		246	
232	Jug, parian		247	As 229, ivory
233	ditto, illuminated in parian, 'Garibald'		248	As 229, traced
			249	Cupid and basket
234	Tripod, as 216 traced in red		250	Duck
235	ditto, colourings			

This sequence of ornamental shapes reaches up to about 1865 and so covers the major part of Grainger's history. The series later goes above 3000 by 1890 and we have not had the space to continue listing the shapes here. We do however illustrate on pp. 195–201 some of the early drawings, copied from the shape books 1 and 2 and reduced in size.

Figures and Bowers

6

8

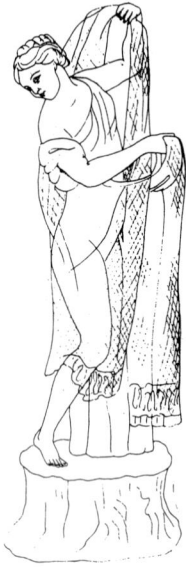

13

15

19

Vases

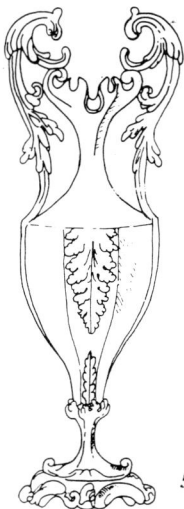

5

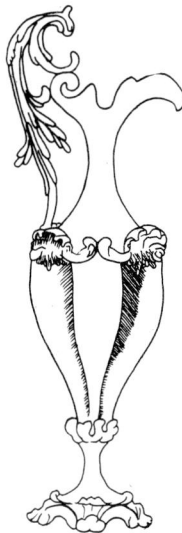

9

17

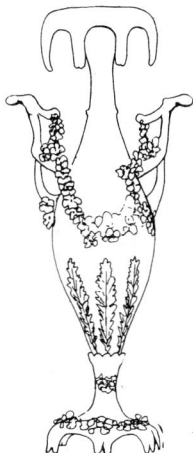

18

33

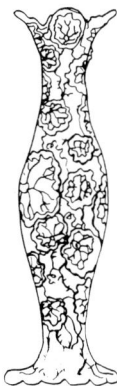

34

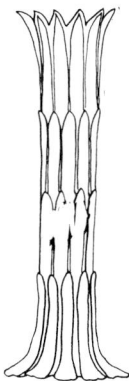

37

41

44

46

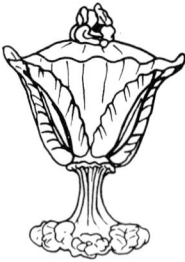

48

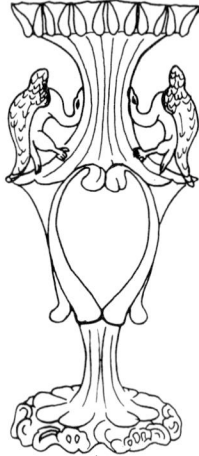

52

53

57

58

60

62

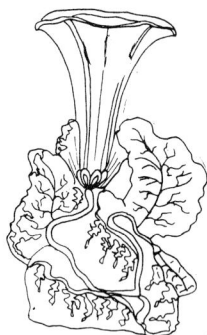

63

64

65

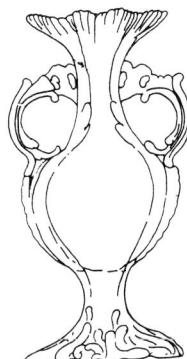

66

73

74

75

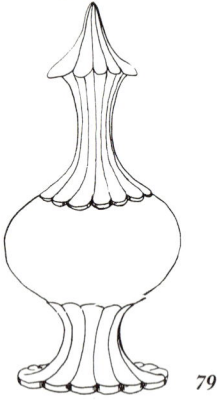

79

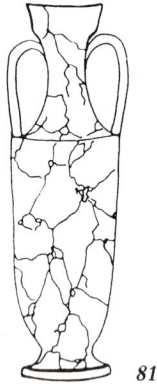

81

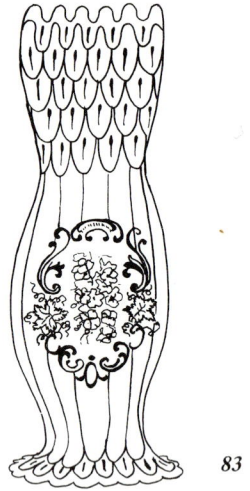

83

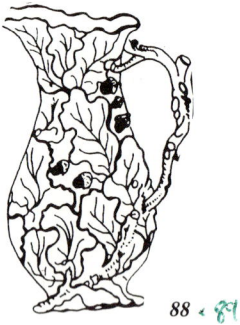

88 ‹ 88

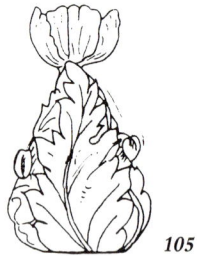

105

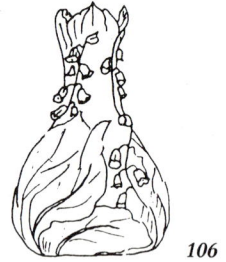

106

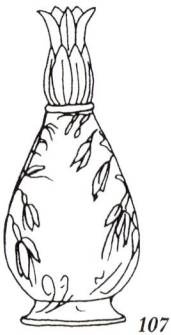

107

114

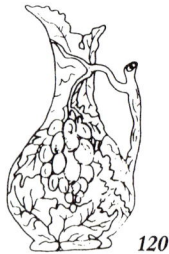

120

121

123

124

125

126

127

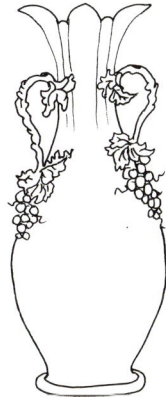

128

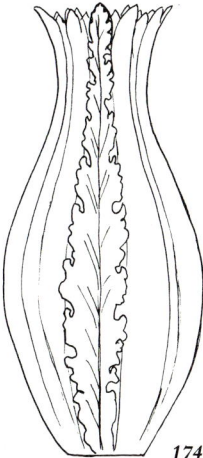

174

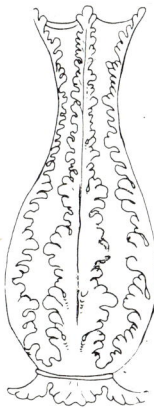

177

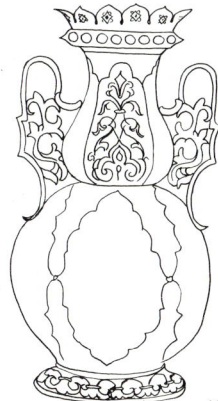

179

Appendix 3

NAMES OF PRINTED PATTERNS

The names of printed patterns as recorded in the pull book or from existing copper plates are listed below.

Blackberry or Blackberry Border
Blackthorn
Broseley
Bryony (trailing border of hanging berries and leaves)
Butterfly
Challie
Chestnut (beads)
Chinese (two men in boat, with bamboo border)
Convolvulus
Coral
Currant Border (continuous floral border)
Dahlia (large botanical spray)
Diamond Lace (all-over border of tiny circles)
Dragon (well-known blue printed pattern)
Dresden Trellis
Egyptian
Ferns (leaf sprigs)
Festoon (floral sprigs)
Fibre (same as Moss Fibre)
Figure Bead (keyboard border)
Floral Diaper
Ford's Wreath
Fountain
Geranium (large sweeping spray)
Gothic (triangle border)
Gown Border
Grass
Hawthorn Ground
Hawthorn Sprig
Honeycomb (all-over honeycomb diaper)
India Tree Outline (same as Old India)
Ivy
Japan
Kent Sprig (spray of flowers with central rose, within scalloped feather edge)
Key Border

Lace
Laviustinius or Larinistinus (ie. Laurustinus – a flowering shrub)
Leaf Ground
Leraxacum
Lily Sprays (rose group)
Little Print (dagger border)
Maidenhair
Maple
Minton Outline
Moss Fibre
New Wreath
Oak Leaf
Old Indian or Old India (also called Blue India)
Old Worcester (a Royal Lily-type formal pattern)
Palm Grass
Persian
Pearl Dots (border with black circles)
Phlox
Red India
Rock
Rose
Rose Borders
Scale
Scrawl
Scrowl
Sparke's Spriggs
Star Bar (starry border)
Star Bead (dagger border)
Taraxagum
Temple
Thistle (sprays of thistles and leaves)
Vase
Verandars
Vine
Weed
Wildflower

SMALL PRINTED SCENES

The following are small printed scenes which would have been hand coloured and used on inexpensive souvenir wares. The names appear under each scene or occasionally under the base of the vase or cup.

Abbey Church, Great Malvern
Abbey Gateway, Great Malvern
Alfreds Hall
Ann Hathaways Cottage
Birmingham Cathedral
Birthplace of Shakespeare
Bridge House, Ambleside
The British Camp
Calton Hill, Edinburgh
Castle Yard, Tynemouth
Chain Pier, Brighton, destroyed by storm
Chester Cathedral
Cirencester Church and Abbey
Clandeboye, seat of the Marquis of
  Dufferin & Ava
The Cliffs, Bournemouth
The Cliffs, Tynemouth
The Clock Tower, St. Albans
The College, Great Malvern
The Commandery, Worcester
Douglas Head Lighthouse
Dove Cottage, Grasmere
Dove Nest, Ambleside
Edinburgh Castle
Edgar Tower, Worcester
Friars Crag, Ullswater
The Gardens, Bournemouth
Great Malvern Happy Valley
Haddon Hall
Harlow Car Woods, Harrogate
Helen's Tower, Clandeboye
Hereford Cathedral and Wye Bridge
Highbury
High Street, Dundee

High Tor, Matlock
John Knox's House, Edinburgh
Lancaster Castle
Low Wood Hotel, Windermere
Malvern Abbey
Malvern Wych & Beacon Hill
Mumbles Pier
New Tay Viaduct
Newton Abbot
Old Castle & Black Gate, Newcastle on
  Tyne
The Old Gateway, St. Albans
Old Mill, Ambleside
Old Mill, Jesmond Dene, Newcastle on
  Tyne
Old Roman Wall, St. Albans
Royal Arch, Dundee
Royal Baths, Harrogate
Royal Pump Room, Harrogate
Ruskins House
St. Albans Abbey
St. Johns Ruins, Chester
St. Johns Priory, Chester
St. Nicholas Cathedral, Newcastle on
  Tyne
Slybarrow Crag, Ullswater
Stock-Ghyll, Ambleside
Torquay
Tower of Refuge, Douglas Bay
Wordsworths House
Worcester Cathedral
Ye Old Fighting Cocks Inn, St. Albans
York Minster, West Front
York, St. Mary's Abbey

Appendix 5

ESTABLISHMENTS SUPPLIED

The following clubs, hotels and restaurants, regiments, and other establishments used Grainger chemical or semi-porcelain decorated with their name or badge. A copy of each print was kept in a notebook, which survives in the present factory pattern room.

Clubs

Conservative Club
Caledonian United Services Club
Westminster Club
Stephen's Green Club
Junior United Services Club
East India United Services Club
The County Club
Army and Navy Club
Union Club
Worcestershire Club
New Club, Edinburgh
Club Valparaiso
Oxford and Cambridge University Club
City and County of Worcester
  Constitutional Club
Civil Service Club (BONITA)
Royal Thames Yacht Club
City Carlton Club
University Club
Carlton Club
Carabineers
Reform Club
Athenaeum MDCCCXXIV
The New Club, Cheltenham 1874
Liverpool Reform Club
Salisbury Club
Thatched House Club
The Birmingham Club Ltd.
Prince of Wales Club
St. George's Club

Hotels and Restaurants

The Russell, Ottawa (border design)
The Covent Garden Hotel
Tavern and Hotel, Rupert St., Haymarket
Dr. Johnson's Tavern
Reindeer Hotel
Saracen's Head

Beauchamp Hotel Company Ltd.
Claridge's
Tavistock Hotel
Molteno Hotel
Hop Market Hotel
Russack's Marine Hotel
Athole Arms Hotel, Blair Athole
The Craven Hotel
Alexandra Hotel
Royal Clarence Hotel
Golden Cross Hotel, London
The Douglas Hotel
The Grand Hotel, Manchester
Bold St. Cafe ⎤
Exchange Cafe ⎟ All in Liverpool
Westminster Cafe ⎬ with liver bird
Water St. Cafe ⎟ design
Merchants Cafe ⎦
Mountford's Restaurant
The Park Cafe
Wilberforce Cafe
Royal Marine Hotel, Hunters Quay, Bain

Regiments

Royal Sherwood Foresters
Royal Sussex Regiment
East Devonshire Regiment
G Battery, 9th Brigade
1st Royal Surrey Regiment
Royal Regiment of Ireland
Royal Scots Greys
Royal Horse Artillery
North Devon Regiment
2nd Staffordshire Regiment
Royal Welsh Fusiliers
Bermuda Mess

Many, many other regiments

Others

B.A.Y.R.
Worcester Station
Hull Peoples Public House Company Ltd.

Baptist Chapel, Cinderford, Dec. 4th 1876
College for Civil Engineers
London Road Chapel
Gateshead Station
St. John's School, Longsight

Appendix 6

SHOPS SUPPLIED

The factory produced porcelain for a great many china dealers and retailers, marked with the name of the shop rather than Grainger's name as manufacturer. They also supplied jars, pots, spoons, etc. for chemists. A record of the following survives at the present Worcester Royal Porcelain factory.

Retailers' and Chemists' Marks

Joseph Wood, York
H. Jackson, Liverpool
Lang & Co., London
Thos. Sharpus & Co., 43 Cockspur St.,
  London
Thornton & Co., Edinburgh
Eagland, Leeds
J. Hall, Bradford
Cullum & Sharpus, 43 Cockspur St., Pall
  Mall, London
J. T. Buckles, Dresden Rooms, Belfast
Gilbertson & Sons, Ludgate Hill, London
David Henry Jacobs, 64 Crown St.,
  Finsbury
Pearce & Co., London and Bristol
W. T. Copeland, New Bond St.
W. Thomas, Dublin
J. M. Rendall, 4 Cary Place, Torquay
H. J. Gardner, 63 & 453 Strand, London
T. Jarvis & Son, China Merchants, Church
  St., Plymouth
James Marshall, Buchanan St., Glasgow
Ritchie & Co., Royal China Rooms, Perth
J. H. Gray, Maker, Nottingham
J. Silcox & Co., Hull
G. Smith & Co., 57 Conduit St.
Morleys, Trafalgar Square
J. & A. Bradley, 47 Pall Mall, London
Lang Brothers, London

William Legge, 25 Thames Inn, London
Thomas R. Grimes, 83 New Bond St.,
  London
W. A. Norman, Promenade, Cheltenham
Latimer, Clark, Muirhead & Co. Ltd
Alfred Slatter & Co. Ltd
Reid Brothers
Tiffany & Co., New York
S. Woods, Malvern
Henry Green & Sons, 135 & 195 Cannon
  St., London Bridge
Manufactured for T. Goode & Co., South
  Audley St., London
Apsley Pellatt & Co., 21 Northumberland
  Ave., Charing Cross, London
Mander & Weaver, Wolverhampton
Thompson & Capper, 43 Bold St.,
  Liverpool
Madame Laffay, Geant des Battailles
James Green & Nephew, Queen Victoria
  St., St. Pauls
W. P. & G. Phillips, Late Chamberlain, 65
  New Bond St., London
J. Wippell & Co., Exeter
Sandbach & Co., Manchester
J. Denley & Co., Stamford Works,
  Cheltenham
John Mortlock, Oxford St. Pottery Galleries,
  Orchard St., London

John Miller, China Warehouse, South St.
Albans St., Edinburgh, Potter to Her
Majesty

Worcester China from James Notcutt, 24
Grand Parade, St. Leonard's-on-Sea

James M. Shaw & Co., New York

Specific Chemists

G. Anderson, Chemist, Worcester

W. Barrett, Trunk & Dressing Bag Maker,
372 Oxford St., London

W. H. Billin, Homeopathic Chemist,
Edinburgh

Bolton, Chemist, 146 Holborn Bar

J. Cochran, Homeopathic Chemist, Glasgow
& Leicester

James Craft, Homeopathic Chemist,
Reading

James Epps & Co., Homeopathic Chemists,
London

F. Foster, Homeopathic Chemist,
Scarborough

W. H. Gill, Homeopathic Chemist, 19
George St., Croydon

Grainger & Co, Makers, Clarks Patent,
Worcester

Edwin Hawker, Homeopathic Chemist, 52
High St., Above Bar, Southampton

Headland's Homeopathic Chemist, 15
Princes St., Hanover Sq., London

Lang & Co., Patentees, London

Lipscombe & Co., patent, Soda Water,
Temple Bar, London

N & Z Patent, Negretti & Zambra, London
(Patent) No.

J. C. Pottage, Homeopathic Chemist,
Princes St., Edinburgh

I. M. Rendall, Hom'c Chemist, London,
Exeter, Torquay & Plymouth, Member of
the Royal Pharmaceutical Society of Great
Britain

T. Shepperley, Druggist, Nottingham

Slade & Rapier, Homeopathic Chemist,
London St., Norwich

Thompson & Capper, Homeopathic
Chemist, Liverpool & Birkenhead

Twinberrow & Son, Chemists, 2 Edwards
St., Portman Square & 45 Westbourne
Grove, London

Twinberrow & Co., Worcester

H. Turner & Co., Homeopathic Chemist,
41 Piccadilly & 15 Market St., Manchester,
& 77 Fleet St., London

Appendix 7

GRAINGER PATTERN NUMBERS

Introduction

Our research into the wares of the Grainger factory would be incomplete if we had not had
the assistance of the pattern books which are preserved in the pattern room of the Worcester Royal Porcelain Company. The numerous volumes recorded each new pattern as it was
introduced, drawn out as a guide for the decorators. The books list the designs by number
and the pattern numbers usually appear on the bases of all Grainger tea and dessert wares.

Sadly the record is incomplete. The first books with the earliest patterns have not survived, and the other books have large gaps which either mean that the patterns were never
drawn out or that some blocks of numbers were not used. Some numbers are duplicated,
which further confuses the picture.

If any piece has a pattern number on the base, the pattern itself must correspond with the description given in the books for the piece to be attributed to Grainger. We have tried to provide as much information as we can, but it is often very difficult to give a brief description for a complicated decoration. Some patterns are not drawn and in these cases we record just the entry written in the books. These occasionally give a full description, but otherwise are just a cryptic name that provides little clue as to what the pattern actually looked like.

The entries frequently record what shape was to be used, whether the pattern was to be on gadrooned or plain shapes, or some of the complicated teaware shapes. Usually a pattern used on more than one shape will appear as a different number in each case, the books listing for example '1783 – The same as 1730 on Clarendon'. Pattern 1730 gives the shape as 'Dresden Embossed'.

Some entries start with a note of the border or rim design. The gold edge can be treated in different ways, the most standard being a plain narrow gold band which we believe was called 'French Edge'. Only rarely is any indication given about the artists who were to decorate the sets, but we list those which are mentioned. We should point out, however, that a pattern could be ordered some time after the named hand had left the factory, and a new painter would have been allocated the work. Also, to complete a large order on time it was sometimes necessary to use several painters and this is noticeable on some finished services. The decoration on the teapot in Plate 28 is given in the pattern book to William May, but we do not know for sure that May was the only painter who could have worked on that pot. The names in the book, therefore, can only be a general guide to the workmen whom we list in chapter 2.

The pattern books are mostly undated. Some have watermarks and from these we know that the first pattern in each book could not have been introduced earlier than the date of the watermark. The following watermarks are distinguishable:

Book	Date of Watermark	Patterns
2	1812	391–1642
3	1825	1595–464x
4	1831	396x–1229x
5	1840	1244x–2008x

also the complete 2/ series

The date 1845 occurs between patterns 2/680 and 2/682 and we know that a service of pattern 2/46 was given as a wedding present in 1846. After around this date most Grainger pieces were marked and we have not therefore reproduced the subsequent pattern books.

The first pattern book in this series is missing. We have various numbers occurring on actual marked services, and hope that in time we will be able to add to this early list. There are significant inconsistencies which lead us to the opinion that the factory had two different pattern number sequences. Miller and Berthoud, item 1510, show a marked Grainger Lee & Co. teapot of London shape with a coloured-in blue print. The cups in this service were marked 397, yet 397 is drawn in the pattern books as 'Bourbon Pattern' with scattered French sprigs. Another teapot in Miller and Berthoud, item 1179, is marked Grainger & Co. Worcester 816, yet the shape is 'New Oval' of c.1810 and the pattern number is much too high, the recorded numbers in the surviving pattern book being in the later bone china London shapes and beyond, after 1815.

Pattern 705 occurs on the blue-printed 'Broseley' pattern marked Grainger & Co. Worcester, putting it before 1814 when Grainger Lee & Co. commenced. This must be the first pattern series, but this is on bone china. 'Broseley' was probably used on the hybrid body previously.

The most likely explanation for these contradictions is that a new pattern number sequence began in about 1812–14, possibly for the new Grainger Lee & Co. partnership. Pattern book 2 which survives (watermark 1812), starts with pattern 391, on London shapes which were made in the thick bone china. A service of Old India print has been recorded with pattern 276, the earliest pattern noted on bone china. Other patterns in the 200s range seen on the hybrid hard porcelain body are much earlier, on New Oval shapes, and if the teapot of pattern 816 is to be believed, there must have been two series. This could account for the large gaps between patterns, especially between 900 and 1292. Was the factory confused by two sets of books and thus jumped these numbers to avoid further overlap? A teapot has been seen marked Grainger Wood & Co. 902 with blue floral motifs. This must have been made long before the pieces entered at the beginning of pattern book 2 in about 1814.

No one has ever suggested two sets of pattern books before and we still have difficulty in understanding just what was going on. There is no other explanation for the fact that one service marked Grainger & Co. Worcester No. 135 has a border of coloured and gold 'S' scrolls and gilt sprigs, while another service marked Grainger Wood & Co. Worcester Warranted No. 135 has a pattern of a waving stem of leaves and berries in puce and yellow. Were Grainger Wood & Co. and Grainger & Co. in some way different? Could this explain the two different versions of London shape, and such variety in the forms of the ring handles seen on early Grainger cups, as well as the absence of any marked Grainger Wood & Co. mugs or jugs? We realize that there is still a great deal to learn. The pattern numbers listed here between 391 and 900 will be in bone china. It is possible that other pieces of earlier Grainger will use these numbers on different patterns, probably in the hybrid hard porcelain. We look forward to hearing from any collectors about any Grainger pattern numbers not recorded here, to help sort out the problems.

First pattern number series

135   Border of S-shaped leaf motifs and gilt sprigs, seen on a service of apparently Coalport porcelain marked Grainger & Co. Worcester No. 135. Illustrated by Geoffrey Godden in his *Encyclopaedia of British Porcelain Manufacturers.* However, another 135 is recorded.

135   Waving stem bearing berries and leaves in puce and yellow, service sold at Sotheby's, 20/11/79, lot 192, marked Grainger Wood & Co. Worcester Warranted.

140   Japan pattern in iron red, underglaze blue, green, and gilding. Tea and dessert service sold at Sotheby's,

27/5/70, lot 361, script mark in iron red, Grainger & Co. Worcester Warranted.

204   Border of gold bell-shaped flowers and gold leafage between narrow bands. Sold at Phillips, 20/4/83, marked 'Grainger Wood'.

220   Blue border, gilded pattern of leaves on the blue and a hanging pattern in gold.

228   Shaded gold leaves on a gold ground divided by 2 crossed shaded red straps.

232   Straight fluted shape, red and gold weed pattern on opposite sides of a gold line. Marked Grainger Wood & Co. Worcester Warranted. See Plate 8.

302   The Chamberlain pattern books list for their pattern 636, 'Grainger's 302, enamelled gold edge and ring'.

397   Underglaze blue print with colouring-in, chinoiserie temple in a riverscape. Marked Grainger Lee & Co. teapot of London shape illustrated by Miller and Berthoud, item 1510. Possible later use of an earlier pattern.

705   Underglaze blue print, chinoiserie riverscape known as Broseley, on a scalloped cup marked Grainger & Co. Worcester.

816   Border of a white seven-petalled flower and gold scrollwork on a deep blue ground, teapot marked Grainger & Co. Worcester Warranted.

902   Flicks of blue to form floral motifs, seen marked Grainger Wood & Co.

930   Chamberlain's pattern 649 is 'Grainger's 930 enamelled & gold boss border of purple, red etc.'.

972   Chamberlain's pattern 638 is 'Grainger's 972, green leaf border etc., coloured edge'.

Second pattern number series. Noted on marked piece

276   Old India, printed in blue, coloured in red, green yellow and gold, marked Grainger Lee & Co. Worcester.

Pattern Books 2–5

The descriptions given for the several thousand patterns listed below were written over a period of at least twenty years' research and are for purposes of identification only. Many are direct transcriptions from the pattern books; some mix our own words with those of the original; and a number are entirely modern. In this present publication we have made no attempt to brush up what are essentially working notes made under varying conditions. For reasons of cost we end our list in the latter part of Pattern Book 5. As stated on p. 207, most Grainger pieces were marked after the 1840s, making further entries unnecessary here.

In the front of pattern book 2 a note in pencil reads: 'Any person found destroying this Book shall be prosecuted according to law'. In another hand is subscribed: 'Any person found looking in this Book will be transported'!

391 India flowers, popular printed pattern filled in. Also known as Old India.

394 French edge. Gold pattern of alternating spike and rays with stars above on a blue ground, gold line top and bottom.

395 Gadroon edge, orange ground, 3 reserved fan-shaped panels outlined in blue containing fabulous bird type paintings, gold pattern between the panels.

396 Scattered green and red sprigs below a red line.

397 Scattered French sprigs in blue, green, and red Bourbon Pattern.

398 Green border outlined in gold, reserved gold panel containing flowers and fruit, large group in the bottom, gold edge.

399 New (embossed). Solid handle and knobs. Moulded flowers pale blue with flowers.

402 Old embossed sprigs (modelled in relief) with common flower sprays in panels, gold edge.

411 Blue line and dot border, blue rim and dark pattern central large cluster of flowers.

412 French Edge purple leaf pattern.

413 French Edge, all-over Japan pattern in red, green, and blue, large blue rock and flowering tree at left hand side.

414 French Edge blue ground, octagonal oblong panels containing a Japan-style large red and green flowering tree left and a black, dead tree right, alternating leaf shape small reserve panels and gilding.

415 Blue border reserving long shaped panel containing a rose, with leaves and bud, border inside cup of a snake-like line and alternate dots.

416 Blue ground border, gilded flowing leaf pattern, holly berry pattern.

417 Broseley Edge. Wheel-like or snowflake-like pattern alternating with a leaf and flower spray.

418 French Edge. Blue border, two reserved panels central rose and flower clusters, joined by a shaded gold pattern.

419 Gilded panels of alternating simple and more complicated shapes, sprays of flowers in colours, gilding 1½d.

420 Green ground, 6 alternating flower groups around border, rose and small spray in centre.

421 5 panels of flower groups, alternating border panels of frogspawn, stippling, three dots, ermine and barbed wire. Note in pencil 'not priced, see 477'.

422 French Edge, pale blue border, diamond-shaped reserved panels

containing single roses, joined by a gilded Grecian pattern. (Drawing of London-shape cup.)

423 Alternating side and down-looking rose border, scattered roses.

424 Green border reserving small oval panels of roses, large flower centres. Note in pencil 'Not done'.

425 Japan pattern all over, blue, red, and green, large blue shape at bottom, palm tree-like shape at left and large central leaf and flower.

426 Common enamelled flowers on new embossed – same flowers as 402.

427 Shanked, rows of red and green stylized simple flowers.

428 Grecian shape, alternating rows of large roses.

429 Wellington Embossed shape, alternating rows of large roses and small rose buds.

430 Old Embossed shape, same pattern as 429.

431 Gold dentelle rim, scattered small roses and pansies.

432 Gold edge, large seven-petalled blue flowers divided by large and small feather-like leaves and brown leaves on a straw ground.

433 Full gadroon edge, large centre group of flowers, 6 small roses round border. Note in pencil: 'F 1/- Gadroon 2½', i.e. Flowers 1/-.

434 Embossed gold edge, small groups of stylized flowers.

435 Gold edge and line, 4 long sprays of moulded roses alternating with pointed sprigs around the border, in the centre one painted group and two small flowers.

447 Stylized sprigs in two tones of blue, with London-shape handle.

448 Wellington embossed shape, large groups of flowers alternating with small coloured sprigs.

449 Not a finished pattern. Panels of orange drum capitals.

450 Same embossed dessert as 435, border of 5 small double sprigs, centre of 4 large flower groups and 3 small sprigs.

451 French edge, blue border, reserved circles containing single roses, joined by gold stem and leaves, flower spray centre.

452 Gold edge and line, brown roses and leaves, 6 in saucer.

453 Brown leaf design and brown leaf sprigs.

454 Alternating rows of brown roses.

455 Tendrils of green leaves with red flowers and stamens.

456 Rows of brown roses.

457 Orangey red feathery flowering leaves, 12 in saucer.

458 Purply weed pattern.

459 Twining roses, alternating with purple and blue flowers, green leaves, and red buds.

460 French edge, yellow and blue leaves and flowers and small sprigs, 3 in saucer.

462 Not done, see 520.

463 French edge, large curled leaves alternating with weed, 9 in saucer.

464 French edge, small curled shapes alternating with weed, 12 in saucer.

465 French edge, flower sprigs, 3 in saucer.

466 Blue printed, leaves and rose buds, 12 in saucer.

467 Same as 452, white edge only.

468 French edge, rich gold target pattern, Nantgarrow, 3 double lines inside the cup, 5 outside, 6 lines in saucer.

469 Rich Nantgarrow Japan red and blue pattern, Japan diamond border inside, solid handle.

470 Nantgarrow Music in black. Gold musical instruments outside cup, gold star in bottom.

471 Taunton red printed filled in with gold and gold edge.

472 'India' green printed in red filled in with gold, gold edge, printed inside the cup, gold line outside.

473 Blue printed 'India' printed in red and coloured in rose colour and green and gold, gold edge.

474 569 Blue and gold musical

instruments etc. etc. gold edge.

475 Wellington shape, No. 1293 done in enamel blue instead of colours. 'B ½d G 3½d F 4½d'.

476 Blue border, alternating sprays of flowers and weed, roses. 'G 5d. Flowers 10d.'

477 Gold borders as 421, panels of flower groups, gold dentelle edge, 5 groups in the plate.

478 Blue group, pairs of large roses with leaves.

479 Fld Dragon – foot line 'G 1¼d'.

480 No. 3 shape, pairs of large roses, as 478, but divided by small pansies. 10 roses in cup, 10 in stand.

481 Large weed pattern round rim.

482 Blue border leaving waved reserves containing roses, rose centre, gilding on the blue.

483 Spear border inside a Grecian-style edge, square star-shaped centre. 'G 3½d'.

484 Diamond, leaf and dots shaped border.

485 Gadrooned edge, border with 5-leaved stylized flower centres and dotted V shapes.

486 Gilded blue border reserving 3 shaped panels containing bunches of roses, centre group of roses. 'B 1½d G 6d F 1/-'.

487 Same as 481, blue ground on No. 1 shape.

488 Elaborate border with onion dome shapes, centre an elaborate spray of exotic flowers.

489 New blue print filled in colour, see pattern (? like 490).

490 New red print, see pattern (1/4d per dozen) (Chinese print in red).

491 Sprigs of hanging bells below a line, 7 in saucer. '1½d'.

492 Trailing leaves and red flowers, 6 in saucer '1¼d'.

493 Trailing leaves with red lantern-like flowers, 6 in saucer.

494 Purple trailing leaves.

495 Gold dentelle border in and outside the cup, a line outside and footline, simple 4-dot flower

pattern.

500 Purple flowers, green leaves, and red berries.

501 Jigsaw-like pattern covered with red stippling, red line each side.

502 Green and blue bell-shaped flower sprigs, 5 in the saucer and a bottom sprig.

503 Red flower and green-leaved sprigs, 5 in the saucer and 1 in bottom.

504 Purple line, purple flowers, and ribbon-like leaves.

505 Waving leaf pattern surrounded with dots.

506 Printed in blue, lozenge border broken by flowers, similar central pattern, in between India flowers in red, yellow, pink, green, and blue.

507 Weed pattern in red with green tips.

508 2 toned blue spear-shaped flowers, green leaves and red berry-like shapes.

509 Large leaves, alternating with small leaves and bud.

511 Stylized 6-leaved flowers and leaves alternating above and below a line.

512 Large and thin line border from which depend green swags alternating with curled shapes.

513 Ermine shapes in a line, alternating red, ermine shapes below.

519 Double border of alternating vine leaves and bunches of grapes.

520 Large green and purple leaves alternating with 3 red hips, sprigs of 3 red hips.

521 Border of oval pearls.

522 Border of lines with 2 green dots at end of each space.

523 Border of diamonds joined by ovals, 4 dots outside and a green dot inside.

524 9-rayed and dotted border.

525 Elaborate border of 3 orange flowers, green leaves, and large flower on a pale blue ground above a dark blue border. '6½d'.

526 Pale ground border with large shaded leaf, yellow and red flower and pale 5-petalled flower and

leaves.

527   Border of alternating pink squares with roses.

528   Pink ground, shaded large leaf with green balloon-like shapes, alternating with 5 5-petalled flowers.

530   Nantgarrow B G Band and blue dots, gold scallops gold handle. (B G may mean B B for underglaze blue).

531   Blue ground border reserving 3 shaped long panels containing 2 roses and 2 other flowers, centre of large flower with sprays, gold, shaped edge.

532   Blue ground and gilded border reserving 3 shaped long panels containing flowers, gold edge. Wellington embossed shape.

533   Border of panels containing a flower and leaves, centre a flower surrounded by a gold leaf pattern, gold edge.

534   Large India pattern of a blue vase on a table, red and yellow flowers, blue and green leaves out of the vase, gold edge.

535   Wide blue border and gilding, large spray of flowers in the centre gold edge. 'B 8d per dozen, G 9d plate, F 1/-.'

536   French edge, wide blue border reserving small circles painted with single roses, large flower spray centre.

537   French edge, very wide blue and gilded border, reserving 3 crescent-shaped yellow borders containing rose groups, single rose centre.

538   French edge, very wide blue border, reserving 3 large shapes containing roses and 3 small shapes containing red and green spray, large single rose centre.

539   Table pattern, India green, gold edge.

540   Table pattern not Frapator (?). Table pattern Sèvres flower, gold line, green and blue flowers.

541   Wide blue and gilt border, reserving

3 octagonal shaped panels containing large flower sprays and 3 5-pointed panels containing small sprigs, centre panel of flower sprays.

542   'New printed India table sett not filled in with blue nor colour'.

543   Gadroon various and gilt exactly same as 533 in bottom and round border gold edge.

544   Blue printed India printed in red and filled in with rose colours and green and gold, gold edge.

545   Taunton printed in red and gold, gold edge.

546   Taunton in red and gold, no edge.

547   Green India printed and filled up with gold and gold edge.

548   Blue and gilded border reserving mosque-like shaped panels, centre with rose and flower spray.

549   Wellington embossed shape, blue ground and gilding, reserving 3 long shaped panels with roses and sprigs, tulip and roses centre, gold edge.

550   All-over India tree and leaf pattern in blue and green, gold edge.

551   As 550.

552   Wellington embossed, no centre line, blue border and gilding, reserving panels with butterflies, centre of fabulous birds. 'B 1d, G 9d, P 1/8d'.

553   As 552 but reserve panels of roses, rose centre.

554   Wellington embossed shape. Blue green ground, ground only on the border, reserving panels painted flowers, flower centre.

555   Dry blue and blue-green ground border, reserving panels of roses, rose centre.

556   Gadroon edge, green border reserving panels of roses, centre of roses surrounded by pointed triangle gilding. Note in pencil 'not done'.

557   Wellington embossed, flowers, same as 555, white edge.

558   New embossed, fancy green

stenselled flowers white, gold edge.

559 French edge, gold centre line, gold sprig.

566 1276 Table ware done in ornamental.

567 French edge, gold floral border, no foot line, sprig in bottom and centre line.

568 Derby Japan Table Plate (9d p plate, B 2½d).

569 Purple floral line, no foot line, French edge, sprig in bottom border inside the cup. Number crossed out and 619 added.

570 Blue sprig, 3 sprigs in the plate etc, 1 in the centre.

571 Bell-like flowers, 10 in saucer.

572 Gadrooned, blue border.

573 French edge, French sprig in red and blue.

574 Elaborate stippled border with scrolled circular shapes, 3 in saucer, two in cup, star in bottom.

575 Fence and floral pattern all over, 5 repeating sections around cup and 3 on saucer. 'Rich Japan, blue, red, and gold'.

576 Alternating rose and flower sprigs, gold edge, no foot line nor centre line, same as sent to Genl. Lashley.

577 Pale blue outlined border with roses, reserving long, scrolled edge panel, hanging border inside.

578 Alternate bow-tie scrolls and flower groups.

579 French edge, shoulder line to cup, alternating sprigs, bottom sprig to saucer and cup, 3 rose buds inside cup.

580 Scrolls and 5 flowing strokes, weed-like pattern in between, 5 in cup and 7 in saucer.

581 Old embossed shape, 2 small French sprig-like flowers in red and blue inside dotted semicircles, sprig in bottom, gold dentelle border.

582 'Chamberlain red table ware, only it is shaded in black'.

583 Large rose spray.

584 Trailing sprigs, thin border at top

(16 in border, 12 in cup), wider one with red at bottom, 8 in saucer and cup. 'H[andle] stripe slap down'.

585 French edge, sprays of grapes and trailing vines, 5 in saucer and cup, bottom sprig the same. Handle slap down with dots on side.

587 'Taunton India printed pattern filled in'.

597 Hanging sprig, feathered pattern, 3 in saucer and cup. Handle slap down, sides dotted, bottom sprig.

598 Hanging sprigs, 28 in saucer, 16 in cup, large hanging bells, 14 in saucer and cup, feathered middle, H Stripe.

619 See 569.

620 Shaded leaves alternate directions, 4 in cup and saucer, French edge.

621 Wide blue border, 3-shaded leaf pattern, 3 in saucer, no bottom sprig.

622 All over Japan pattern, red and blue, centre 3-leaved large flower, no edge.

623 French edge, spiky coloured flowers, blue, red, yellow, and green.

660 Japan flowers filled in. London-shaped handle.

683 French edge, all-over Japan, large tree with blue, pink, and yellow flowers at left, pagoda centre with Chinaman in boat, rocks at right.

684 French edge, hanging bells, alternating with red grapes, 6 in saucer, no bottom sprig.

685 Round edge. All-over Japan, tree with red leaves at left, flowers hanging top centre, two pagodas at right, Chinaman in boat.

686 French edge, dotted cross sword and scroll border, 12 in saucer, main border of shaded sideways bell, alternating with orange flower emerging from a cup, 3 in saucer.

687 Hanging leaf pattern, 6 in saucer and 5 in cup.

688 Common edge, 'OXO' border, large Japan centre, church-like building

at left, man in boat below a
2-arched bridge.

689 French edge, trailing sprigs with red
flowers, bottom sprig.

700 Small balls hanging from V shapes.

701 3-leaf motif under hatching at the
border above painted leaf pattern,
purple and gold.

702 Roses and other flowers and sprigs,
sprig in bottom.

704 Stylized leaf shape divided by
trailing sprigs, 12 in saucer, 8 in
cup.

706 Two pink bands enclosing 2 curled
scrolls divided by a sprig, gold
dentelle border.

707 Butterfly-like shape and small
3-leaved sprigs, above an
alternating loop and dot pattern,
gold dentelle border.

708 3 purple-leaved flowers with red
heart-shaped leaves, 8 in saucer
and cup.

709 Group of spiky hawthorn-like
flowers, red, blue, pink, and green
and a sprig. Spider.

710 Christmas tree-like shape above and
below a curl and dot pattern.

711 Similar to 710 but a more leafy tree.

712 Dry blue scaled border, flowers
hanging from scrolls, 4 in saucer,
3 in cup or can.

713 Flowers, 3 groups in dessert plate,
same as sent to Ashford by *G L*
on Gadroon, no edge.

714 Table ware Spider and same as Tea
pattern (709) Gold and French
line. (Spider is a spiky flower
sprig).

715 Table pattern Chamberlain blk
pattern in blue instead of blk. N.B.
printed in blk. not red.

716 Table pattern – blue sprigs blue lines
done for Mr. Bailey.

717 Dessert Spider (?) done by (?) Lloyd
for as before. (Mr. Bailey.)

719 Dessert gadroon blue sprig similar to
702 – gold lines same as sent to
Mr. Bailey.

720 French edge, 6 dots around a central
dot divided by a diamond and

scrolls, 6 in saucer, 4 in cup,
flowers and crosses across a line
outside border to cup, bottom
sprig.

721 Shaded 2-toned leaf pattern, trailing
vines and grapes, bottom sprig of
grapes and vine.

722 Ground reserving 3 octagonal panels
of flowers, divided by double
white lines with large dots and
leaves in between, sprig in centre.

723 French edge, hanging bells
alternating with leaves, 30 in
saucer, 24 in cup, 8 trailing leaf
and bow groups outside border to
cup, 16-pointed star centre.

724 Common edge, blue border inside
and outside cup, hanging commas
and leaves, bottom sprig, long
hanging dotted pattern in every
other flute.

725 French edge, double-dotted ended
scroll, 6 in cup and saucer, trailing
bell-like flowers outside border in
cup.

726 No. 1 shape, no edge, dotted border
outside a ground surrounding 3
half-diamond and 9 semicircles,
flowers in the diamonds, sprig
centre.

727 French edge, scrolled border, 12 in
dessert plate, 8-pointed star in
bottom.

728 Trailing leaves with 5-petalled pink
flower at each end, no edge,
bottom sprig.

735 Gadroon, gold border, strawberries,
roses etc.

737 French edge dentelled, line etc. all
gold.

741 No. 1 shape, French edge, blue
ground with alternating pattern of
barbed wire, dots and fish row
reserving continuous panel
containing roses at corners, joined
by sprigs, sprig centre, 15 horn
shaped patterns outside border to
cup, solid handle, shoulder line to
cup.

743 No. 1 shape, French edge, 2 blue
lines enclosing 5 blue diamond

shapes alternating with flowers in circle and dot pattern, sprig centre.

744 No. 1 shape, French edge, scrolled border with 3 octagonal shapes containing flowers surrounding fish row, sprig centre, 2 panels in cup, 3 in saucer.

745 Blue ground reserving 3 8-pointed irregular reserves containing flowers, sprig centre, 3 reserves in saucer.

746 Dentelle edge blue border, barbed wire pattern, above circles and red dots, bottom sprig.

747 New embossed, dentelle edge, dark blue, flowers, bottom sprig.

749 Gold edge, all over Japan flower pattern, large centre pink flowers and blue leaves.

750 Paris Flute shape, sprigs, dotted handle.

752 Gadrooned edge, gadroons left white, sprig in centre.

756 Gadrooned edge, blue border and bannisters reserving oblong panels of flowers, 3 in dessert plate, bottom sprig.

757 Gadrooned edge, 6 blue V-shaped panels in dessert plate, alternating with hatched panels and snail-like dots, blue arch pattern around centre.

758 Gadrooned edge, central flower spray surrounded by small sprigs.

759 As 758 but birds in bottom of plate.

760 French edge, 3 double octagonal panels containing flowers, joined by a blue ribbon, sprig in centre.

783 Paris Flute, bottom star-like sprig, solid handle.

784 French edge, snake-like scrolls with sprigs, 8 in saucer, 6 in cup, bottom sprig, shoulder line to handles and cup.

785 French edge, blue border reserving 6 Chinese lantern panels containing alternately flowers and onion domes, sprig centre.

786 Blue border reserving octagonal panels containing flowers, trailing leaf sprig outside border to cup,

shoulder line to cup, no foot line.

787 Paris flute, barbed and feathered shape in every other flute, ribbon and dot line inside, no foot line to cup, dotted handle.

788 Paris flute, double line surrounding trailing sprig, 3 pointed leaf pattern inside, border inside cup and line, no bottom sprig, no foot line to cup, same handle as 750.

789 Paris flute, curved line and dots from which hang vine leaves and grapes, 15 in saucer and 14 in cup, handle same as 788, French edge inside and out in cup.

790 Gadroon edge dessert, blue border reserving circles joined by ribbon containing small flowers, large flower spray centre.

791 Purple line French edge inside cup and shoulder, no foot line, 10 in ½-pint stand, 7 in ½-pint cup, bottom sprig.

792 The same as 791, common gold edge and line in place of the purple line.

794 Gadroon edge, blue border with stars inside and large flower spray centre.

795 Blue inside border with caillouté pattern, alternating shaped panels around border, with sprays alternating with octagonal panels with flowers, sprig centre.

796 Gadroon edge, large sprays of flowers inside border, centre sprig.

815 White border and gold line, 3 sprays of flowers and a central spray.

821 French edge, trailing French sprigs, alternating 2 growing up and 1 down, 20 upper ones and 10 lower ones in plate, bottom French sprig.

822 Gadroon edge, C-shaped scrolls, centre spray.

823 Chamberlain pattern in black, no edge.

825 French edge, small daisy-like sprigs, bottom sprig.

826 Dentelle edge, small daisy-like sprigs, bottom sprig.

827   Feathered leaf-like scrolls.

828   Sharp-edged leaves and small sprigs.

829   Blue sprigs.

830   Is 746 on Broseley which Border done on outside of cup, a line inside.

831   Is 195 on Broseley white. Loop and dot border.

834   Gold edge.

835   French edge, flower sprig with stamens, feather handle.

836   French edge, double shaded bell-like leaves, 6 in cup, 8 in saucer, shoulder line to cup.

837   Ground border, feathered curling leaf joined to a 14-petalled flower, 8 in cup 10 in saucer, Broseley shape, gold edge and foot line to cup and saucer, line inside cup, no bottom sprig, feather handle.

838   Gadroon white edge, gold line, ground border, 18 small dotted sprig outside in plate, hanging fleur-de-lys pattern and triangle of 3 dots inside, 12 in plate, no bottom sprig.

841   Gadroon, gold edge inside and out cup, scroll-shaped reserves containing 2 flowers and sprigs alternating with vase shapes with a sprig, bottom sprig, solid handle inside and out.

842   French edge, blue border with fleur-de-lys and triangle of dots (28 in table plate) fine line inside border from which hang small sprigs (26 in plate), large centre group of flowers.

843   New gadroon shape, large and small shaped reserve panels alternating with flowers and sprig, sprig centre.

844   New gadroon, ground reserving oblong panels with C scrolls containing flowers (4 in dessert plate), centre group of flowers surrounded by 14 patterns like Greek key motif.

845   French edge, blue border reserving large squarish panel containing gilding alternating with smaller squarish panel containing flowers, 3 in saucer, 2 in cup, solid handle number 1, shoulder line to cup.

846   Gadroon edge, no edge, 3-dot border, blue ground reserving 3 oval panels containing flowers, large flower spray centre.

853   Gadroon edge, interior sprig, blue border reserving 3 oval panels containing flowers, large central flower spray.

855   New gadroon edge, green and blue double stalk sprig alternating with red flowered thistle-like sprig, thistle-like sprig in bottom.

857   Broseley, 3 pink flowers sprig border, blue standing flower above a red circle pattern, 7 in cup, 10 in saucer, 12 on stand, 14 in table plate, blue sprig in bottom.

858   New gadroon, large and 3 small flower sprigs, sprig in centre, 3 small sprigs outside cup.

859   New gadroon, French edge inside cup, ground border, with small sprigs either side, 15 inside cup, small sprig centre.

862   New gadroon, pale ground, 2 large and 1 small spray of flowers, centre small rose.

864   New gadroon, pale ground, 3 large scroll-edged panels containing flowers, alternating with smaller mirror-shaped panels containing sprigs, pansy sprig centre, solid handle.

865   New gadroon, pale ground reserving alternating long scrolled panel containing roses and taller scrolled panel containing pansies, large flower centre.

866   New gadroon, maroon ground, small gilded sprigs, 16 in cup, 12 in saucer, flower centre, flowers inside cup, foot line to cup.

870   ? 3 Gold C scrolls containing rose and a flower, gold star-like centre.

876   All over Japan.

877   Pale ground border reserving circular panels with gilded commas containing single roses, 3 in

saucer, 2 in cup, bud sprig in bottom, shoulder line.

878 Gadroon, pale ground border, hanging leaf and hook gilding, 9 in dessert plate, large flower spray centre.

879 Gadroon, 3 oval outlined ground panels alternating with flower sprays, sprig centre.

887 New gadroon, double tulip shape, red top and purple bottom, French edge inside cup. 'Purple rose and gold pattern'.

888 Gadroon, ground border divided by line of reserved circles, large oval panel outlined with 3 dots containing sprig alternating with similar smaller panel containing flowers, sprig centre.

889 New gadroon, 3 painted leaf and 2 dotted sprig, 8 in saucer and cup, small sprig centre.

894 New gadroon, small trailing sprig pattern, 12 in cup, 18 in saucer, border outside cup and pattern inside.

898 New gadroon, bold blue and red-leaved Japan border, red Japan sprig centre.

899 New gadroon, no gold border inside cup, ground border hanging sprigs inside, flowers the same as 866.

Pattern numbers 900 to 1292 are not used in this pattern book.

1293 Embossed groups with groups of flowers.

1295 Gold French edge, nicked edge, border of trailing green leaves and red dotted flowers, purple flowers with green leaves scattered in centre.

1296 Gold edge, green border, inner comma pattern, 18 in table plate, concave centre, rose sprays.

1297 Nantgarrow shape, French edge, pink ground reserving oval panels containing rose sprays, 2 in cup and saucer, pansy centre.

1302 New gadroon, straight trailing

sprigs, French edge inside cup and a foot line to cup.

1303 Blue, red, and pink Japan flowers.

1304 Is the blue India table pattern as done for Abell similar to 714, Thunder pattern, orange line.

1305 New gadroon, double pale blue band divided by trailing leaf pattern, bottom sprig.

1306 The same as 1305, but rose colour band.

1307 Purple band, dentelle border inside, arrow and 3-dot pattern, centre sprig, no foot line to cup.

1308 Nearly the same as 1307, but green band and no 3-dots.

1309 New gadroon, ground reserving long octagonal panel containing flowers, alternating with smaller 6-sided panel containing small sprig, sprig centre, border inside cup and French edge, solid handle, foot line to cup.

1310 French edge, dentelle borders, large bunch and 2 small groups of flowers alternating with little sprigs, sprig centre, Nantgarrow shape.

1311 New gadroon, Imari-style border, red, blue, and green, small panel of red hatching with green spots, red and blue leaf spray centre.

1312 Cane ground, new embossed gold edge, rose groups, foot line to cup, loop border inside cups and bottom of saucer.

1313 Cane ground, flowers the same as 852, foot line to cup and no fine line to cup, French edge to cup.

1314 Gold edge, Grecian shoulder to cup, red, green and blue Imari-like flowers, bottom red and purple sprig.

1315 Gold edge, Grecian, blue, orange, and pink Imari-style pattern in centre surrounded by 2 alternating red and blue shapes.

1316 Gold edge, Grecian, similar to 1315 but with some purple flowers.

1317 French edge, flange cup, ground band with long pattern divided by 6-petalled flower, 4 in saucer, 3 in cup, comma-like shapes inside, 16 in saucer, 10 in cup, bottom sprig.

1318 New gadroon, breakfast cup and saucer, single roses alternating with purple flowered thistles, 5 in saucer and cup, centre rose.

1319 The same as 858 only dentilled edge, Tea pattern Broseley.

1320 New gadroon dessert, 6 panels of different hatched and dotted patterns, large roses and other flowers scattered.

1321 New embossed, called Granny's Roses, large rose and bud, 3 in saucer and cup, bottom rose bud sprig.

1322 New gadroon dessert plate, 'Evan's wild flowers' sprays around border, flower centre.

1323 French edge, blue band, pattern inside of 3 dots and a hanging pink bell-like flower, 6 in saucer, 5 in cup, bottom pink flower sprig.

1324 New gadroon dessert, 4 pink panels containing flowers outlined with 'C' and 'S' scrolls and leaves, rose centre.

1325 Concave and nicked border, ground border reserving 3 long panels containing flower sprig, inside a double leafed hanging pattern, 12 in plate, large bottom group of flowers.

1326 Wellington table plate, light blue border, gold edge, reserving long panel containing a large flower, dotted small sprigs inside, 17 in border of plate, large rose centre.

1327 French edge, blue panel reserving lemon-shaped reserve alternating with similar panel containing pink, green, and blue Japan-type flower, 3 in saucer, 2 in cup, 5 groups of blue and pink flowers outside border, red and green sprig in centre, shoulder line to cup, handle to cup single comma to handle.

1328 Same as 1327, but handle with series of dots.

1329 Alternating large blue and green leaves, 3 in cup and saucer, gold edge, foot line to cup, pattern outside cup.

1330 French edge table plate, red leaves and pink Imari-style flowers.

1331 New gadroon, French edge inside cup, no foot line to cup.

1332 The printed Temple, foot line to cup and feather handle.

1333 Gadroon, blue border reserving circle motifs alternating with leaf shapes, 6 in plate. Dessert.

1334 French edge, single blue diamond alternating with 3 red and blue diamonds round edge, large panels inside alternating blue with 3 lemon-shaped pink reserves and Imari-like spray, 3 in plate. Dessert.

1335 Dessert, gold edge, blue and pale border repeated 4 times in plate, centre a large Imari-style blue tree with pink flowers and green leaves.

1336 Table plate, French edge, the same as 1318, Rose and Thistle and gold border the same exact.

1337 Table plate the same as 1319, Scallop edge.

1338 Table plate, 3 dentille borders, divided by bell sprig and inner blue band, inner sprig.

1339 Tea ware Chamberlain colours and gold balls.

1340 Table plate, dentille edge, large sprigs alternating with butterflies, 3 in plate, bottom sprig.

1341 Wellington table plate, pale blue border reserving long panel containing tulip or other flower, inside border of hanging bells, 12 in plate, bottom sprig.

1342 Wellington embossed, French edge, scrolled oblong panel containing rose and bud, flanked by bunches of small flowers, rose bud sprig centre.

1343 The enamelled French Bourbon as

was done to Allens pattern, tea ware.

1344 Pattern done by Boys in Rickhusses room, Enamelled.

1345 French edge dentelle, large roses, 2 alternating with 1, 3 in saucer, 2 in cup, leaves arranged as a star centre.

1346 No. 1 shape, French edge, jigsaw border outlining shaped ground pattern containing leaf and 3 dots, 6 in saucer, 5 in cup, centre sprig, no foot line to cup, 8 sprigs outside border to cup.

1347 New gadroon, blue border, containing leaf pattern and 3 dots, small sprigs inside, sprig centre, foot line to cup.

1348 New gadroon, large purple and yellow-centred flowers, 3 in saucer, 2 in cup, bottom sprig.

1349 New gadroon, 2 large strawberry-like flowers, strawberry centre, handle the same as 1348.

1350 Is the blue India table sett as filled in for Mortlock with gold French edge, the pattern that was done for Mortlock in London.

1351 Gold edge, 3 lines of small sprigs, the red one alternating top and bottom, 10 in saucer, no foot line.

1352 Broseley French edge inside and outside cup diamond and leaf shape trailing sprigs outlining large flower spray, 2 small sprays and scattered sprigs.

1353 Table sett white edge same as Tea ware 1343.

1355 Is Chamberlains Table Sette (? fluted) done in red and Gills (no orange).

1356 Silver edge, 3 small groups etc etc Gold border and dotted gills by Freeman, flowers by J. . . .Meigh & Norris.

1357 383 altered Lumly (pencil note 'by Lulmany')

1358 Is 1347 on Teaware, groups in bottoms of plate etc etc. (This is a Table pattern on gadroon edge.)

1359 Broseley New Blue Gills altered from the old pattern 489.

1360 Is India on Broseley, altered.

1361 Japan pattern, Gill.

1362 Japan pattern.

1363 Blue band, feather border etc etc.

1364 Enamelled pattern gills on ye Border enamelled Gills by J Rickus.

1365 (Meighs) Very rich rose colour compartments, with raised gold dots and gold sprigs compartments 4 on the saucer and 3 on ye cups, gold handle on gadroon gold border inside the cup.

1366 Ornamented gold border J Lulmans pattern 6 on gadroon, 3 urns on saucer, 3 on cup.

1367 Is same pattern as 1343, only done on gadroon with gold lines round the edges.

1368 Rose colour Dog roses, green and gold leaves painted by J Daniel, on Gadroon ware.

1369 Green border and slight gilding.

1370 Blue and gold border dentelle edge, on Nantgarrow, 28 gold nests (?) on saucer and 17 on cup Lulmans pattern.

1371 French edge, blue cornucopias and red traced flowers J Rickus, 6 in saucer, 4 in cup.

1372 French (?) altered – J R (i.e. Rickhuss).

1373 Roses as 1345 on Nantgarrow shapes.

1374 Red enamelled.

1375 Red enamelled.

1376 French Bourbon border.

1377 Mrs Whites sprigs.

1378 Mrs. Whites moss rose border green leaves.

1379 Horn (?) flute Blk border Mrs White.

1380 Blue End Border and lines on ¼ pint and stand.

1381 Blue lines and centre sprig in blue.

1382 French edge, No. 1 shape, shaped blue borders reserving panel with Imari-like pattern, pink round flowers, sprig centre, long Imari-like sprig outside border to cup.

1383 French edge, blue border reserving egg shape with rose and alternating with net shape with hatching and dots, sprig centre, No. 1 shape.

1384 French edge, blue border, the same outside border and handle as 1383, 20 in saucer, 13 in cup, small sprig centre.

1385 French edge, flange shape, blue ground, 5 oval reserves around edge containing red barbed wire, strange desert island-shaped reserve in centre containing red and green flowers.

1386 French edge, blue outside border reserving 3 scrolled diamond reserves containing pair of roses, inner ground, and centre sprig, the rest of the gilding the same as 726, outside border and handle to cup the same as 1383.

1387 Blue shaped patterns around border, the large ones containing roses, inner ground colour, centre sprig.

1388 Broseley India red grapes – by J Rickus.

1389 Gadroon 660 altered by White and in (?) cup gadroon.

1390 French edge, all-over Imari pattern, 2 blue trees, blue-green leaves, red grapes.

1391 New gadroon, blue border with cornucopia-like ends, reserves containing a 3-petalled pink flower, centre group of red flowers on a grassy bank.

1392 New gadroon, 6 blue rectangular reserves alternating with white panels containing red and blue flowers, below which hang cushion-shaped blue panels, inside border of blue and red hanging flowers, sprig centre.

1393 French edge Broseley, long sprig with 6 round-petalled flowers, 15 in saucer, bottom sprig.

1394 French edge, Paris flute, ground band, curved line and dot with

grape and vine pattern, hanging bells below, bottom sprig and outside border to cup the same as 871.

1395 Gadroon, French edge inside cup, spiralled cone pattern alternating with pumpkin shape, star-like centre. Numbered 1366 in pattern book.

1396 Dessert Gadroon, ground border, dotted and leaf hanging border inside, 8-pointed star and dot centre.

1397 Table plate, ground border and trailing dotted pattern, elaborate star or snowflake centre.

1398 Gadroon table plate, blue border, inner pattern of a bell alternating with Grecian leaf, 15 in border, large spray of flowers centre.

1399 Dessert plate gadroon, light blue border, inner sprig border, 18 in plate, large spray of flowers centre.

1400 Gadroon table plate, white edge, strawberry-like hanging border.

1401 Gadroon table plate, rose border, 3 in plate, bottom sprig of roses.

1402 Gadroon dessert, white edge, 4 flower sprigs round border, large centre group of roses and other flowers.

1403 Gadroon table plate, 3 rows of sprigs, centre sprig, one in every row the same as bottom sprig.

1405 Gadroon table plate, 2 rows of sprigs facing opposite directions, bottom sprig.

1409 Gadroon table plate, 5 flower sprays around border, large central spray.

1410 Gadroon table plate, 3 large sprays alternating with 3 tiny sprigs around border, large flower spray centre.

1411 Harris Rose Border.

1412 French edge, 106 red-tipped sprigs round the table plate.

1413 Japan Nobstick done by boy, no gold.

1414 Roses and gold dots.

1415 Gadroon, flowers the same as coffee jug.

1416 Blue border, radiating panels, alternating ones containing candlestick shape with curled base.

1417 Hanging leaf sprig border.

1418 New L shape Tea Ware Embd sprigs, same as 1405 but all the sprigs blue.

1419 Green diamonds, dentelle edge, green patterned centre, 6 diamonds in saucer and cup.

1420 Dentelle border, red leaf curls, and grapes and cornucopias, 6 curls in cup and saucer, 12 red bells in border inside.

1421 Same pattern as 1419 done on a fawn ground, dentelle and fine line on the shoulder of the cup and bottom of the saucer.

1422 Semicircle border, dots and red arrow pattern, 24 on saucer, 15 in cup, sprig centre.

1423 Gilded leaf sprays with red dots and stars, 6 in saucer, 4 in cup, sprig centre.

1424 Evans flowers done slight for Women.

1425 New L shape same pattern as 1420, blue instead of red except the dots they are red.

1426 Gadroon dessert, blue ground, Flowers in the centre, Lloyd done dessert.

1427 Col Davies's Bkfast pattern on gadroon, Rose and blue flower, the pattern done in New Book.

1428 4-petalled leaf border, all-over flowers and leaves growing out of a basket.

1429 Purple Harts Ease.

1430 Fld. Blue enamelled wreath no edge 'as was done for Thompson'.

1431 Lilac ground, 5 bells in saucer, diamond and leaf pattern, star centre. Wm Daniel done the sett.

1432 New fluted shape, Dark blue panels, square shaped panels with Mrs. Hewitt's flowers, blue band inside border.

1434 Blue border reserving octagonal panels, 3 in cup and saucer, inside snake border, flowers done by Mrs. Hewitt.

1435 Blue border, reserving scrolled panels, flowers done by Mrs. Hewitt, 3 in saucer, 2 in cup, inner border of lemons and sprigs.

1436 Blue border, reserving panels, 3 in cup and saucer, containing flowers and small group in centre 'painted by Mr. Evans', blue sprig in centre of cup.

1437 Plain gold edge, circle and 10 dots joined by line, 12 in saucer, 8 in cup, circle and bell star-like centre.

1438 Key and twisted leaf done by Lulsman G H, 12 in saucer, 9 in cup.

1439 Blue border, reserving octagonal panels, 3 in cup and saucer, X motif inside border. 'Bronze sprigs done by Mrs. Hewitt'.

1440 Plain gold edge, blue border reserving bell-like shapes, small and large, 2 in saucer and cup. 'Slight flowers done by the Women'.

1441 Gadroon edge, bell shapes upside-down above double C scrolls, 12 in dessert and dinner plates, star-like centre.

1442 Tea pattern same as 1428 Table pattern, orange work done in gold.

1443 See White, The Cover'd Pattern.

1444 See White similar to the 1443 – done slight = in the bottoms.

1445 Olbongs, arrows and red dots, 44 in saucer, 27 in cup, sprig centre.

1446 Green dragon on new low shape.

1447 Green rose and sprigs all green new low shape.

1448 Green rose and sprigs gold lines and dotted handle new low shape.

1449 Colour sprigs, Mary Harris new low shape.

1450 Purple roses new shape.

1451 Maroon ground border, bell sprigs, 6 inside border, 8-pointed star centre

1452 Slight Japan pattern done by J Rickus.

1453 Same as 1419 with blue diamond instead of green.

1454 Bronze sprigs.

1456 Gadroon, hanging sprigs, 18 in plate, above onion domes, flowers in centre.

1457 Gadroon, hanging sprigs, 12 in plate. 'Slt group in centre'.

1458 Thunder and lightning.

1460 French edge, 3 rows of scales containing weed, star in bottom.

1461 Blue scale border reserving 3 panels containing flowers and 3 dots, sprig centre, sprigs outside cup.

1462 French edge, blue and red bells, 8 in saucer, 7 in cup, bottom sprig.

1463 Border of single roses divided by leaves and blue sprigs, 7 in saucer, 4 in cup, leaf and blue sprigs, 10 outside border, rose centre.

1464 French edge, 'Union blue painted', small sprigs 'between the Blue Spriggs of The Union Blue', bottom sprig.

1465 French edge, fence border, downward sprays of leaves providing panels with 'flowers done by Margaret Roden', 6 in saucer and cup, group in centre.

1466 French edge inside and outside cup, line of 3-leaved sprigs.

1467 5 red-petalled flowers and blue leaves, enamel pattern, 6 in cup and saucer, similar centre, 16 red sprigs trailing inside border.

1468 Double shaded tulip-like flower above a butterfly gilded pattern, 3 in saucer, 2 in cup, squared star-like centre.

1469 Roses and Blue Sprigs the same as 1427 border gilt on the top of the saucer instead of the Bottom done on new low shape 24 in the border of saucer, 18 in cup with a dotted handle – 4 Roses in saucer

4 in cup with blue flowers between.

1470 Low's Sprig.

1471 Blue and Red Wreath.

1472 Blueball Japan (see Plate 99).

1473 Tea (?) Dragon Japan. Dessert ware, Essex Plain shape, Jabberwocky type.

1474 ? Sealed border.

1475 ? Japan pattern, house top centre.

1478 Dark India Thunder and Lightning.

1479 Light – do –.

1482 Rose and brown leaf.

1483 Printed Dragon filled in with green. Entry crossed out in ink.

1484 Lined 'C' shapes, flower centre.

1485 Boy Spike all round on tea ware.

1486 Butterfly shape below a tulip bell, dividing octagonal panels, 3 in saucer and cup, sprig border inside cup and bottom of saucer.

1487 Groups of flowers, on each plain part, and in bottom of Essex embossed, sprigs on the embossed part.

1488 Shield-like shapes, 18 in saucer, 13 in cup, sprig centre, trailing sprig inside border.

1489 Essex emb flowers with g line and edge.

1490 Rose and bud, divided by small sprig, around rim, centre of pattern missing from pattern book.

1491 Essex embossed shape, centre missing.

1492 5-petalled flowers around borders, flowers growing out of a pot in the centre.

1493 Whites, centre 10-petalled stylized flower, similar 8-petalled flowers around rim.

1494 Neat purple sprigs done by Mrs. Jones.

1495 Green sprigs, cups inside and out.

1496 Lulman's, barbed wire and small panels of sprigs from which hang acorns, 10 in the saucer, 8 outside the cup, star-like centre.

1497 Wm May's gold diamond and blue spots, green centre in

compartments.

1498   Wm May's green border with blue bells, gold husks and red twigging.

1499   A Low's gold purple and blue, bell-like leaves, alternating with ivy-like leaves.

1500   M Roden's Rose and Forgetmenots, a double French edge, gold and gold line.

1501   Common enamel 25/-.

1502   Bold Japan.

1503   Thos White fawn and gold, panel of large daisy-like flowers and harebells, 6 in saucer, 5 in cup.

1504   Blue compartments and dead orange, gilt with womens flowers.

1505   Blue border with India work under.

1506   Forgetmenots.

1507   Lulman oak border.

1509   Barbed wire border and scrolls, Japan flowers emerging from a cornucopia by a fence.

1510   Scroll-shaped border, alternating with stylized flowers, 6 in saucer, 5 in cup, flower centre.

1511   Horizontal and hanging stylized sprays, centre of 10-dotted sprig and 12-dotted circle.

1512   Lilac ground border, dentelle inside border, group of men's flowers in the saucer.

1513   Rose and other flower sprays, small sprigs outside.

1514   Stylized flowers and swags of leaves, border of snake motifs.

1515   Blue inside border, scrolls inside, 1 large spray of flowers, 1 smaller, and small sprigs, around the side and onto the ground.

1516   Green border, hanging C scrolls inside, centre of a 6 fleur de lys-like star.

1517   Blue border, small printed leaves inside, star-like centre.

1518   Pale ground border, dentelle inside, 'cup done in and outside', star-like centre, 'Blue daisy and green spriggs'.

1519   Pink-like border, repeated S scrolls inside, star-like centre.

1520   Pink border, tears alternating with dots outside, and bunches of dots inside, Roses and small sprigs done by Stanley Wood, star-like centre.

1521   Same as above pattern, except the ground, and that is a straw colour.

1522   Cauldron-like shape with tongues emerging, red C scrolls joined by 7 round shapes, hanging bells, below a green shape, 3 in saucer, and outside cup, bells inside border.

1523   Oval 14-lobed green-centred shapes, blue-centred diamond between, green eye centre.

1524   Is grass green sprigs painted pattern made by Mr. Wood.

1525   Union sprigs printed with purple and 3 of them gold sprigs between and 1 in centre, Gadroon dessert plate.

1526   The 391 Dark India filled up with large red leaves and 1 bunch of red grapes hanging from each compartment, Pattern made by Tom (? John) Rickuss.

1527   Is the same as 1510, with a Pink colour band above the gilding – 5 in saucer and 4 inside cup – no bottom sprig, but centre line in cup and saucer – outside of cup the same as 1510.

1528   The same as Vhaskey's (?) match.

1529   Blue and red sprigs, 28 in table plate gadroon, 6 blue sprigs inside border, large blue centre sprig.

1530   Plain notched edge table plate, Chamberlain's pattern, 3 sprigs round the plate, red and blue, Japan-style flowers, printed and filled in.

1531   Same as 1520 except the gnd and that is done with green.

1532   Same as 1512 with Blue-Green Gnd. instead of lilac – slight group in bottom of cup, 1 group outside and 2 sprigs.

1533   Same pattern as 1516 done on

Gadroon dessert plate with group of flowers in bottom painted by Mr. Evans, no line on the Gadroon next to the Gnd – 8 scallops in plate.

1535 Gadroon tea ware, border of convolvulus-type flowers, 3 in saucer each of them varied, 2 outside cup, convolvulus bud centre.

1536 Gadroon, red flowers, alternating with blue harebell-like flowers and leaves, 8 in table plate, similar centre.

1537 Running sprigs, done by Mr. May.

1538 Alternating panels of Japan-style flowers and gilded diamonds containing gold dots and red dots, gold dots inside border, 3 in plate dessert and 3 in table, red flower surrounded by blue and gold leaf centre.

1539 Large and small flowers above S scrolls, inside border of blue diamonds, group in bottom of cup and saucer.

1540 Wild roses on biscuit blue ground, gold grapes, dead gold border.

1541 Blue panels Lowe's flowers, Rickuss.

1542 Dessert hawthorn roses etc, by J. Evans from Mrs. (?) P...in.

1543 Barley ear-type stalk growing between 2 Bass Clef-type signs, alternating with an arrow, slight growth in the bottom, gilded by C. Hathaway.

1544 French edge the cup inside no lines in the saucer no footline to the cup, trailing line with 3 yellow flowers, bells and dots hanging below, bottom yellow sprig.

1545 All-over Japan pattern, red pink and a little yellow, bottom sprig in cup, 4 corner large flowers.

1546 Gadroon, double dotted wavy line enclosing red and green leaves around border, 11 similar leaves inside and 8 small gold ones.

1547 Roses inside a double scrolled border, 2 rows of running sprigs outside the cup.

1551 White and gold.

1552 Green (or yellow-green) border, star in the cup and saucer, 5-petalled sprig centre.

1556 Beige border with S scrolls, fleur-de-lys and flower alternately, wheel and star in bottom of cup.

1558 Maroon.

1559 Lelock (?).

1560 Green border, pearls either side, pattern done inside the cup and star in the centre.

1561 All-over Japan-style flowers, like 1545, bottom sprig in cup, band of similar flowers each side of cup.

1562 Dark biscuit blue reserving 3 panels and circle inside, star centre, orange border inside cup.

1563 Alternating double and single pink flowers, silver edge.

1564 3 large 3 small purple printed and enamelled sprays round border and central spray.

1565 Same as 1560, only maroon instead of green.

1566 Gadroon shape, bells suspending a blue diamond, stars below, 8 in saucer, 6 in cup.

1567 Flowers growing out of vase in India style.

1568 New gadroon, low handle, blue cornucopia of flowers, Japan building.

1569 Royal flute, blue shaped panels, reserves with 3 roses in each compartment, 1 ditto with bud adjoined in bottom.

1570 Gadroon, low handle, star-pointed flowers, blue and rose, with 3 dots, blue and rose star centre.

1571 Gadroon, low handle, blue and rose divided by diamonds, blue and rose star centre.

1572 Union sprig, printed with purple – on the New Gadroon Tea Ware low handle 3 on saucer with gold sprigs between same as Desst pattern No. 1525 – 3 small printed sprigs inside the cup, French edge in and outside cup, dotted handle.

1573 Ford's printed pattn printed with purple with gold weed – intermixed – printed in and outside the cup.

1574 New French flanged shape, rose colour ground, leaf sprig border either side.

1575 Margaret Roden's Blue sprigs – 3 large ones on saucer and outside cup – small ones in between.

1576 Margaret Roden's Dog Rose – 3 on saucer, 3 outside cup small blue bells in between.

1577 Dentelle border, Royal flute round edge not French, 3 large flowers around saucer, 2 cup centre star, large roses and dahlias with gilt leaves and buds (?) on cup. 12 gold sprigs inside border.

1578 New French flanged edge, maroon (?) border reserving C shaped scrolled panels, single flower in each by Mr. Wood, 3 lines and dot border.

1579 Blue border, half-shaded bell between shells, 4 in saucer, 3 outside cup, star centre.

1580 Pale blue ground, purple drapes hanging on chains, above upside-down bells.

1581 Same pattern as 1411 only done in Blue Royal tea ware, French edge and line.

1582 New French flanged shape, weedy leaf spray alternating with 4 groups of mens flowers.

1583 Dotted arch pattern below a blue border, star centre.

1584 Dark blue panels alternating with double C scrolled panels containing flowers done by women, 3 in saucer, 2 in cup, S scrolls inside cup and bottom of saucer.

1585 Cane ground, star centre, small bell and sprig, 48 in plate.

1586 Purple filling in . . . . work and fine line table ware.

1587 Broseley shape, blue border and red leaves, centre Indian spray from a blue cornucopia, red, blue, and green flowers, dots outside on back side of cup and in bottom.

1588 Gadroon, low handle, blue border, Japan pattern, blue leaves and scrolls, dots and red flowers.

1589 3 dots above tongues.

1590 Blue border reserving oval-like panels, slight flowers in bottom.

1591 Lemons and dots.

1592 Green ground, Wm Daniel, gilt on cup and saucer, upside-down bells, convolvulus flower centre.

1593 In the desk-common enamel pattern.

1594 In the desk.

1595 Gadroon, purple sprays, 3 on saucer, 3 on cup, outside, sprigs, purple with gold dots in the middle of the flower.

1596 (In the desk) Broseley shape, French edge, printed 3 big sprays divided by small sprig, sprig centre.

1597 In the desk.

1598 In the desk. Gadroon shape, 2 green bands, divided by 3 dots and spiked railings, flowers in between hanging bells, dog rose in centre.

1599 In the desk. Same pattern as 1598 with orange bands instead of green.

1600 In the desk. Essex embossed, dentelle border, small rose and buds round border, large rose centre by Mr. Evans.

1601 In the desk. Essex embossed, dentelle, panels of roses, rose centre, brown leaves, by George Grainger.

1602 Gadroon shape, printed 3 large sprays round border, central sprig, printed with purple.

1603 In the desk.

1604 To be finished on Monday morning by Mr. Evans, Gadroon, 3-dot border, 40 in saucer, 3 sprays of roses and other flowers, edged over the top of cup.

1605 Gadroon, semicircle and dot border, pansies, roses etc. 4 in saucer, 4

1606 In the desk. Royal Flute, small sprigs between large sprigs, sprig centre.

1607 In Rickus' book. Gadroon, diamonds and 4 dots, alternating with small groups, rose centre, stamen-like outside border.

1608 In Rickus' book. Royal Flute, hanging fleur-de-lys and dots, fleur-de-lys and dotted star centre.

1609 In Rickus' book. Old Gadroon, blue ground border, half-shaded leaves, group of flowers in centre.

1610 In Rickus' book. Low handle, blue border, half-shaded hanging bells, 2 large roses and smaller flower spray.

1611 In desk. Gadroon left white, roses by French – like blue and red sprigs, 5 in cup and saucer, bottom rose sprig.

1612 Gadroon, border of roses, 5 in plate, centre rose, small scattered rose leaves.

1613 Red and blue sprigs with roses in between, 3 in saucer, 3 outside cup, sprig centre.

1615 Groups with ground work, Roden & White (in 2nd book) Roses and sprig border, large rose centre by Mr. Roden (3rd book) Essex plain.

1616 All roses and green leaves do. (2nd book) Essex emb. roses in circles 10, 10, 6 and a centre one in plate (3rd book).

1617 One large group in bottom 6 small, all blue, White & Roden (2nd book) Gadroon, 6 sprays round border, 6 sprigs inside, large centre spray.

1618 Royal flute, 3 large and small sprigs, small sprig centre.

1619 Royal flute, dentelle, roses and trailing blue sprig, 3 of each in saucer, 3 ditto outside cup, bottom sprig.

1621 Royal flute, enamel pattn, large and small rose sprays, 3 in saucer, 3 outside cup, small rose centre.

1622 Gadroon, enamel pattn, 6 purple flowers round border, 1 in centre, leaves and stems yellow green.

1623 Enamel, blue leaves, purple chain, blue husk.

1624 Royal flute, enamel pattn. roses and trailing yellow green leaves, bottom sprig.

1625 Essex emb. French edge, roses alternating with small blue sprigs, in embossed part, rose centre.

1626 Is the same as 1602 without gilding, only shaded with purple on the dark side of the leaves.

1627 Blue band, hanging dot and spike, centre petal and bell star.

1628 Gadroon, blue border, pearls above dentelle inside, pearl star centre.

1629 Green border, French edge, hanging bells and dots, bell and dot petal centre.

1630 French edge, border with 3 dots, hanging grape-like shape, star and bell flower centre.

1631 Gadroon edged, lilac colour inside, diamonds and C scrolls and hanging bell, group of flowers in centre.

1632 Blue border, shaped panels joined by rectangular panel with leaf, slight flowers in panels, slight sprig in bottom.

1634 Royal flute, double green border, held up by upside-down shaded bell and grapes.

1635 Dentelle, hanging sprigs below wavy line, bottom sprig.

1636 Half-shaded leaves, 10 in cup, single flower in centre.

1637 Same pattern as 1533 with the blue dots done.

1638 Double archways, between dry enamel blue borders, centre 3 dotted star.

1639 Essex plain, printed sprigs around edge and large centre spray printed in purple and filled in.

1640 Essex embossed, printed with Japan-style spray border and large spray centre.

1641 Gadroon, high handle, tooth-root-like flower border, dots below ground, star centre.

1642 Gadroons, rose colour border, standing tall ovals with dot above dagger, 47 in saucer, 36 inside cup, trailing sprigs and stamens outside bar, arrow head star centre.

1643 2 green panels divided by standing tall ovals, 64 in saucer, 49 inside cup, 8 bell-star centre, low handle.

1644 Gadroon, low handle, same pattern as 1564, printed with blk. filled in with green instead of purple scollops the Gadroon – and line inside the cup. No foot line.

1645 Royal flute, enamel pattern, white edge, blue green leaf alternating with yellow green leaf, red and blue hanging sprig between, 6 of each in saucer, 3 sprigs in centre of saucer and cup.

1646 Table plate, all-over Japan, leaves yellow-green.

1647 Gadroon, low handle, white edge, hanging bell-flowered sprig and leaf, 4 dots, 7 in saucer, 6 inside cup, sprig centre.

1648 Royal flute, white edge, purple sprigs, sprig centre.

1649 Gadroon, low handle, hanging blue bells and red flowers, 11 in saucer, 10 inside cup, blue bell sprig centre, handle done with red same as 1645.

1650 Royal flute, blue border, reserved oval panels, flowers by Jno Evans, 3 in saucer, 2 inside cup, 12 blue leaves in the outside border.

1651 Royal flute same pattern as 1564 printed with black and filled in with black, no foot line.

1652 Sprigs, alternating larger and smaller, 2 rows in saucer but 1 row inside cup, low handle.

1653 Jno Daniel Dresden (?) gilt and blue with flowers.

1654 Dresden dessert light-blue ground

and gilt, slightly round compartments by Jno Lloyd, flowers in each compartment and in bottom. Evan's flowers.

1655 1562 done inside with sprig outside border.

1656 Women's flowers, 3 small sprigs inside cup and 1 in bottom, 6 around saucer and 1 in centre.

1657 Green ground, irregular gilded compartments with flowers, diamonds and 5 dotted petal inside cup.

1658 The same as 1657 with blue ground.

1659 Royal flute, trailing vine leaves and purple grapes.

1660 Royal flute, trailing green vine leaves.

1661 Royal flute, biscuit blue, hanging bells, circle of acorn-like shapes around centre, diamonds and dots in the outside border of cup.

1662 Dresden embossed, 6 panels, alternate 3 large and 3 small green flowers, rose centre.

1663 ditto. but not green, foot line is printed in blue.

1664 Gadroon, high handle, blue border above triangles and dots, Group of flowers by Jno Wood in the bottom of cup and saucer.

1665 Royal flute, flowered by women, 3 large flowers, 3 small sprigs, sprig centre, done inside the cup with 4 small sprays outside.

1666 Stalks with leaves one side and flowers the other, 6 round saucer, 4 round cup, done inside and out, centre spray.

1667 The same as 1666 only done in purple.

1668 Royal flute, breakfast, trailing large and small sprigs round border, sprig centre.

1669 Royal flute, maroon ground, lace work picked out and left white, bell and star centre.

1670 Dresden embossed, maroon ground, shaded panels containing leaves, star centre.

1671   Royal flute, blue border, alternate panels of barbed wire.

1672   Royal flute, blue border with jigsaw vermicelli, India/Japan-style centre, red fence and flowers, bottom sprig to cup.

1673   Gadroon, high handle, maroon ground, lace picked out and left white, flowers in bottom.

1675   Gadroon, high handle, Dark India filled in by May.

1677   Same as 1427 with 6 of each in table plate, 'Gadroon, line under the gadroon' by women, rose and blue flower bottom sprig.

1678   Maroon ground.

1679   New gadroon, panels shaped like clouds supported by a stemmed cup, containing flower sprays, 3 in saucer, 2 inside cup, white enamel spots on the blue.

1680   New gadroon blue border and pink reserves containing half-shaded bells and leaves.

1681   New gadroon, spray of grapes and vine leaves alternating with coloured birds in landscapes.

1682   Dresden shape with bird in each compartment and the Compt slightly gilt round with grape between, same as 1681. Bunch of grapes in centre, dentille edge, 2 birds perched on sprays inside the cup, slight landscape in each compt outside of cup done by Wm May.

1683   Plain edge, 3 gilded panels alternating with plain, each containing sprays, spray centre of Indian flowers.

1684   Leaf spray and 4 bells alternating, 6 in saucer, 4 in cup.

1685   Coloured Geranium leaf, dentille edge and plain slap down handle.

1686   Geranium leaf painted with purple. Enamel white edge.

1687   Blue band and gilt flowers in centre – Dessert pattn.

1688   India pattern.

1689   Is the same as 1654, with rose colour ground and dentille edge, gilt by Jno Lloyd and Wm Daniel.

1690   Clarendon shape, dentelle edge, single roses in 2 lines, 1 rose in bottom.

1691   Same as 1690 Roses and leaves done with blue, Clarendon shape.

1692   Dresden shape, dentille edge, roses in each compartment, rose centre, 8 roses inside cup.

1693   Clarendon shape, (gadrooned) Blue band, shaded shaped panels containing flowers, same flowers in each panel, 3 in saucer and inside cup, panels divided by weed, flower centre.

1694   Clarendon shape, blue border, arches and leaves half shaded, primrose in centre of cup, ranunculas in centre of saucer.

1695   Blue border, long panels containing flowers, sausage-like shape below left and rose-like shape below right, white enamel dots on blue, rose centre.

1696   Dresden shape, large purple sprays divided by smaller sprigs, sprig centre.

1697   Blue sprays and sprigs, sprig centre.

1698   See John Lloyd, panels divided by flowers.

1699   Chamberlains old Red prints pattern printed with purple and filled in with do. on Clarendon shape, see pattern left at home with number affixed to it.

1700   Is the 1540 done on the Clarendon shape inside cup with this outside border [2 bells joined by sprigs]. Dog rose yellow leaves, gadroon solid with a white line left between it and the pattern.

1701   Dresden shape Light blue gnd. Butterfly in each compartment. Bird in centre. See pattern left with number affixed.

1702   Clarendon shape, hanging sprigs 16 in saucer, 12 in cup, border of fleur-de-lys facing left, star centre.

1703   Clarendon shape, blue hanging

borders and dots, alternating sprig of flowers.

1704 Clarendon shape, all-over Japan-style flowers, flowers with stamens.

1705 Clarendon shape, blue border, panels containing flowers, slight group in centre, dots on the blue done with white enamel with a little yellow mixed with it.

1706 Clarendon shape, narrow band inside cup, shoulder and foot line to cup.

1707 Clarendon shape, dentelle border, blue ground, yellow ground panels containing birds done on the ground (as the Humburge's) circles below on same ground, slight landscape in centre, fleur de lys facing right.

1708 Is the same as 1707 with flowers in the compartments instead of a Bird.

1709 Blue'd same as 1680. Wreath of roses by Mrs. Hewett.

1710 Roses on Dresden ware done very nice with brown leaf.

1711 Same pattern as 1707 – no yellow ground in compartments.

1712 Green border, half-shaded oak leaf below, 12 in saucer, 10 in cup and bottom sprig, same as 1733.

1713 Same as 1712 Blue ground instead of green.

1714 Clarendon shape, blue border, fingers below and hanging small sprigs, pointed wheel-like centre.

1715 Dark green (?) border, flower sprays.

1716 Clarendon shape, blue border, vine leaves and grapes below, similar bottom sprig.

1717 Same as 1716 with Green Ground.

1718 Sames as 1716 with Rose Colour Ground.

1719 Same as 1716 with Fawn Ground.

1720 Clarendon shape, pink border, 3 large flowers around.

1721 New Shape Royal Flute, blue border reserving 3 compartments containing flowers, flower centre, flowers done by women.

1722 The same as 1712 with blue ground and Birds in the centre.

1723 The same as 1722 with Maroon Ground and flowers in the bottom.

1724 Clarendon shape, blue ground, landscapes in compartments and in centre, hanging bells around centre.

1725 The same as 1716 with Blue Ground.

1726 Maroon ground border, hanging half-shaded bells inside, landscape in the bottom of cup and saucer.

1727 Rose colour ground border, 6 compartments in saucer (3 with flower groups and 3 with blue sprigs), 5 in cup (2 groups and 3 sprigs), same bottom sprig to every piece.

1728 Green ground, 3 round compartments containing single roses, and long white spaces, blue sprig centre, the gold must not touch the green.

1729 Dresden shape, dentelle, large gold sprigs in 3 compartments, and large sprig in bottom.

1730 Dresden embossed, blue printed, gilded leaves, one large leaf spray and smaller leaves.

1731 New shaped Royal flute, blue ground, 3 compartments of flowers.

1732 Blue ground, small gilded sprigs, sprig centre.

1733 Green border, vine leaves and grapes, similar centre, same as 1712.

1734 Printed pattern, outer and inner borders of double crossed lines with 4-lobed motifs, partly gilded, in between trailing leaves and a pineapple-type shape, central sprig.

1735 Dessert plate, Royal Flute, blue festoon border, central 6 armed panels containing one main flower spray and a small flower or sprig in each arm.

1736 The same as 1735 with Green

Ground dessert.

1737 Gadrooned, Blue Ground, 6 Panels in dessert plate and a centre, S Wood's Flowers.

1738 Dresden ware, dessert plate, dentelle edge, single roses in the 6 compartments and a rose centre, Flowers by women.

1739 Jas Reaby's raised blue birds, in Dresden pannels, Dontle Edge.

1740 The same as 1737 with rose Colour Ground and edged with loops and dots.

1741 The same as 1699, filled in with red and gold, printed in red.

1742 New Dresden green printed black sprigs filled in with green.

1743 New green sprigs printed black and filled in colours.

1744 Gadroon dessert, large flower spray and 2 smaller sprays divided by sprigs.

1745 Geranium leaf and blue printed with gold twigging.

1746 As 1745 with additions of gold line, on Clarendon.

1747 Trailing grapes and vine leaves around border, star centre.

1748 Pale blue border reserving 3 compartments of landscapes, landscape centre and in bottom of cup.

1749 The same as 1657 with a bird in bottom of saucer and sprig in the other panels, the Bird inside the cup not in the bottom, all the rest are sprigs in and out etc. Dontle edge, high handle.

1750 Clarendon, biscuit blue border, trailing vine leaves and grapes, bottom sprig to cup and saucer.

1751 Blue ground, upside-down crescent moon above grapes and vine leaves, similar sprig centre.

1752 Clarendon shape, biscuit blue border, trailing vine leaves and grapes, sprig similarly in centre.

1753 Womens hair brown roses.

1754 Womens new Dresden flower sprigs printed.

1755 Green Ger^m [Geranium] printed

with gold twigging Dresden with dentelle edge Dejeur.

1756 Leafage Edge done in Black by woman 4 Black Sprigs in Saucer and cup, 3 outside cup.

1756 The same flowers as 1604, Leaf edge, Etched. This is numbered before see 1762.

1757 Roses and other flowers alternating joined in a trailing triangle with sprigs, 4 small sprigs round outside of cup, rose centre, women's flowers.

1758 Leaf edge, small sprigs, cup done inside and out.

1759 Dontle edge, low handle, fancy birds on gold twigging, scattered butterflies and sprig, birds outside cup and sprig in bottom.

1760 Leaf edge 2 groups of 2 birds on large twigging, butterfly, bug and centre sprig.

1761 Leaf edge, basket of roses and flowers and small sprigs, 23 mistletoe-like sprigs round outside of cup.

1762 Leaf edge 3 large flowers around.

1763 3 compartments of birds on twigging, green ground inside, butterfly centre.

1764 3 compartments of large roses and twigging alternating with tiny roses, blue ground inside.

1765 Solid gold leaf edge 3 rose groups with gold twigging.

1766 Broseley shape, 3 common hair brown sprigs and small central sprig, cup done inside and out.

1767 Broseley shape, hair brown colour, 1 large and 2 smaller sprigs, cup done inside and out.

1768 The same pattern as 1767 done in purple.

1769 The same pattern as 1766 done in purple.

1770 ditto as 1758 in purple.

1771 The same pattern as 1758 done in blue.

1772 Dresden, biscuit blue ground, 3 compartments of slight flowers by Jno. Evans, blue sprig centre, cup

1773 Shaded half-leaf compartments, 3 groups of flowers, fawn ground inside, single rose centre.

1774 Broseley shape, printed flowers around border and around centre, coloured.

1775 Clarendon shape, blue and red Japan-style flowers.

1776 Printed the same as 1774 with lilac flowers shaded Green instead of Colours and all the leaves solid green, [centres] gold instead of green. N.B. Printed in purple.

1777 Breakfast ware Broseley. The same pattern 1766 done in Chrome green.

1778 Gadroon, Indian-style flowers around border, cell border inside with 3 panels of flowers in baskets, large India-style centre with a blue butterfly on a flower. New India tree pattern.

1779 Gadroon, printed in red with India-style flowers same as 1780, border flowers are all filled in, all the rest finished in hair brown.

1780 As 1779, gadroon, red and gold.

1781 Printed sprays, filled in purple and orange, gold line, plain edge.

1782 The same pattern as 1781, with gold instead of orange, gadroon, the leaves done purple instead of orange, see pattern in desk. Purple India tree.

1783 The same as 1730 on Clarendon with gold line and twigging.

1784 The same as above without gold line, done on Dresden.

1785 Green geranium with twigging done on Dresden without a line.

1786 3 compartments with slight flowers, green broken ground, gold star etc.

1787 Green Dragon.

1788 Brown roses.

1789 Pink and oak leaf the same as 1712.

1790 Is 1777 altered to Table pattn, same as Mortlock & Co.

1791 New shape, two small pink flower sprig in centre of modelling in

1792 New shape, 2 gold flowers in modelling, half-shade bell and 2 leaf sprays, star centre and purple arrows.

1793 New shape, hanging festoons of leaves and flowers, 6 in saucer, 4 in cup, sprig centre.

1794 New shape, sprig centre, no line inside cup.

1795 New shape, 3 rose and flower sprays divided by yellow panels.

1796 New shape, modelled flowers coloured yellow, star centre.

1797 New Gloster shape, dontle edge, the birds and twigging done the same as 1759 with only one small butterfly in the bottom of cup, and saucer.

1798 New shape, green flowers and geranium-leaf sprigs, the cup done inside with the two small sprigs outside and the one between.

1799 New shape pineapple between barbed wire border, landscape fills the bottom of the cup and saucer.

1800 New shape, modelled flowers red, red and blue sprigs around, 3 small bits round the outside of the cup.

1801 Clarendon shape, blue border, rectangular shapes, 4 in saucer and 3 in cup, from which hang India-style flowers, Japan-style centre.

1802 New shape, fawn ground, leaf shapes inside, 8 in saucer, 6 in cup, 10 in dessert plate, leaf sprig centre.

1803 New shape, dark chrome-green border, bird and sprigging centre.

1804 New shape, blue ground border, landscape centre.

1805 New shape. The same pattern as 1803 with blue ground instead of green.

1806 The same pattern as 1804 with light chrome green instead of blue.

1807 New shape, Green printed

232

Geranium sprigs with gold twigging on the Gloster shape edged thus.

1808 New shape, small printed sprigs filled in with colours by women on the Gloster shape, edged with dots.

1809 Gloster shape dessert plate ivory border, 3 flower sprays around centre.

1810 Maroon ground gilded the same as the above with flowers all round the bottom.

1811 Rose coloured ground gilded the same as 1809 with a slight group of flowers in the centre.

1812 Dark chrome green ground gilded the same as above with gold star in the centre.

1813 Gold dentelle border, a line inside the cup and a shoulder ditto.

1814 Gloster shape Biscuit blue border outside and dry orange border, 3 compartments of birds on twigging, butterfly centre.

1815 Gloster shape, Grecian urn supporting the 2 flowers, rose sprays in 3 compartments, blue border around sprig centre.

1816 Gloster shape, blue border, 3 compartments of rose sprays.

1817 Gloster shape, Japan-style spray in 3 compartments, similar centre.

1818 Dresden shape, the same as 1657 gilt slight with lilac ground, small sprig in the bottom of the dessert plate.

1819 Clarendon shape, 3 rose sprays, small rose bud centre, cup done inside and out, by women, pretty fancy sprigs by Evans.

1820 The same as 1819 with gold.

1821 Gloster shape, large and small printed flower sprigs coloured by women.

1822 The same as 1716 with rose colour ground done on the Gloster shape, handle and outside border tadpole shapes.

1823 Dessert, 4-shell border, large star centre.

1824 The same as 1748 with green ground instead of blue.

1825 Soft chrome-green border, gold sprigs inside, star centre.

1826 Gloster shape, dentelle inside modelled flowers, star centre inside dessert ware only.

1827 The same pattern as 1781 without the border and done on the Dresden shape.

1828 The same sprig as 1800 done on the Gloster shape and edged with 3 small sprigs between and sprig in the bottom. N.B. Three large sprigs.

1829 The same sprigs as 1798 with 4 small bits between.

1830 The same as 1620 done on leaf edge and edged solid with line inside cup and saucer.

1831 Small printed sprigs coloured by women done on the leaf edge, no foot or shoulder line to the cup.

1832 The same as 1798 edged on foot line.

1833 Gloster shape, festoons, 6 in saucer, 4 in cup and can.

1834 The same pattern as 1767 done in chrome green on the shell dessert pattern without gold.

1835 Gloster shape, blue border.

1836 Royal flute B Blue panels and gold sprigs.

1837 Royal flute Biscuit Blue and oak leaf the same as 1712.

1838 Gloster shape, Green border, small hanging sprig and 2 leaves, small sprig centre.

1839 Gloster shape, blue border, 3 panels in cup and saucer of flowers, sprig centre.

1840 Gloster shape, 3 sprigs round, one in the centre.

1841 Gloster shape, 3 panels of flowers divided by winged blue panels ground with stars, single flower centre.

1842 Gloster shape, 2 green borders divided by tooth roots, 46 in saucer, 34 inside cup, star centre.

1843 The same as 1842 with maroon

ground instead of green.

1844   The same as 1842 with Blue Ground.

1845   Simple gilded lines.

1846   Gloster shape, 3 rose sprays divided by small sprigs, blue inner border, sprig centre, women's flowers.

1847   Dresden shape, line inside the cup, no foot or shoulder line.

1848   Gloster shape, biscuit blue border, long tongues around the centre, 30 in the saucer, 24 in cup.

1849   Gloster shape, dotted lines on orange ground.

1850   The same as 1848 with Maroon Ground and star instead of flower, handsomely gilt.

1851   Royal flute, 2 gold lines.

1852   Clarendon shape, gold lines, sprig in bottom of cup and saucer.

1853   Gloster shape, lilac ground, curtain like shape, 3 flower sprays by D. Evans.

1854   The same pattern as 1751 with lilac ground and the grapes all run the same way, without the half moon in the ground.

1855   Gloster shape, 3 biscuit blue triangular panels, 3 compartments, and in cup and saucer centre of birds on twigging.

1856   The same pattern as 1800 edged with gold (Gloster shape).

1857   Pink ground and gold twigging.

1858   Gloster shape, green ground, 7 small pansies.

1859   Gloster shape, 3 soft cream green panels (4 in dessert) printed coloured sprigs inside.

1860   Gloster shape, blue border, 3 compartments of 'flowers by women', small sprig centre.

1861   The same pattern as 1798 without any work on the edge.

1862   Gloster shape, 3 biscuit blue panels, printed coloured sprigs in centre.

1863   'The same printed sprig as 1662 in black'.

1864   Gloster shape, 3 fawn ground

panels, coloured printed sprig centre.

1865   Gloster shape, blue ground border, large group of flowers and 2 small in centre.

1868   The same pattern as 1712 done in maroon.

1869   The same pattern as 1832 done in blue.

1870   Gloster shape, Lulman's Green and gold edge.

1871   The same pattern as 1829 done in blue Dessert ware.

1872   The same pattern as 1798 done in blue.

1875   Dresden table plate, large and small sprigs, done in chrome green.

1876   The same as above done in blue. On the Dresden Table Plate.

1877   Shell dessert shape with 3 large flowers and small blue sprigs in bottom, gold leaf.

1878   Gloster shape, lilac ground, 3-dot hanging border, star centre.

1879   The same pattern as 1878 with maroon ground.

1880   The same as 1878 with blue ground.

1881   The same as 1878 with green ground.

1882   Leaf edge, green border grounded by W May, star centre.

1883   The same as 1882 done in blue, tea ware, leaf edge.

1884   Gloster shape, blue ground by W May, leaf shapes below, star centre.

1885   The same as 1884 done rose ground.

1886   The same pattern as 1884 done lilac ground.

1887   ditto as 1884 with Maroon ground.

1888   Dresden breakfast ware, dontail edge, leaves and blue sprigs, birds eye blue and green spray.

1889   The same as 1888 [the rest torn away], no gold.

1890   Roses and green leaves, gold dentle edge.

1891   Dresden shape, dontail edge, large blue sprigs in compartments, small sprig between and in centre, by women.

1892   The same as 1884 Nasturtion Ground, Gloster, star.

1893   Green band, border outside cup, done by W Daniel.

1895   Five blue panels, 2 birds 2 groups and flowers from a match by J Evans.

1896   Lulman's green band, gold star.

1897   Shell embossed dessert printed green geranium, gold twigging and the emboss. gilded.

1898   Gloster shape, biscuit blue, large leaves and small flowers, small star centre.

1899   Gloster shape, pink panels with hanging bell and leafage, 3 flower star centre.

1900   Gloster shape, dentelle inside border, 3 large roses divided by blue sprig (ranunculus).

1901   Gloster shape, 6 hanging balls around border, green bell star centre.

1902   Gloster shape, diamonds and leaves in chrome-green edged with black, green-centred star centre.

1903   Gloster shape, biscuit blue ground, edged by grapes and vine leaves, similar centre.

1904   Gloster shape, biscuit blue ground, 8 sprigs round the saucer and 6 in the cup, sprig centre.

1905   The same as 1712 Biscuit blue ground with a bird in the centre, 10 sprigs round outside border.

1906   Gloster border, wreaths of sprigs, 6 round the saucer, 4 in cup, sprig centre, enamel blue.

1907   Gloster border, blue lemons and double leaf sprays.

1908   Gloster shape, pink ground, blue winged panels, landscape centre.

1909   Gothic gilding with blue rose and gold.

1910   Gloster shape, edge the same as 1849.

1911   Clarendon shape, chancel arches, 8 compartments in saucer, 6 in cup.

1912   Dresden shape, dentelle border, 3 large blue roses divided by small sprigs, rose centre.

1913   The same as 1908 with the exception of the centre. Centre is a bird on twigging.

1914   Leaf shape, 3 long octagonal compartments in saucer, 2 in cup containing landscapes and birds, hanging roses around, alternating panels of fish roe, dots, and barbed wire, green ground, small landscape centre.

1915   The same pattern as 1888 done on the Gloster dessert ware.

1916   Gloster shape, printed border, small compartments of sprigs, 4 panels in dessert, 3 in tea and breakfast, sprig centre.

1917   Purple print, women's sprigs and slight gold.

1919   Blue, gold and flowers.

1920   Same as 1912 no gold (Blue roses Dresden).

1921   Rose in 3 compartments divided by small blue sprigs, rose centre.

1922   Gloster shape, sprigs round border, large and small flower sprays.

1924   The same as 1912 without dentelle, blue roses in and out.

1925   Shell dessert, fawn ground, twigging, large centre of flowers on table.

1926   The same as 1855 Maroon instead of blue.

1927   Dodd Chamberlains printed flower sprays.

1928   Red pail (?) and Gold grapes.

1929   Gloster shape, biscuit blue and green leaves, alternating with orange wheel shape, 3 compartments in cup, orange wheel and sprig centre.

1930   Hanging sprig and leaf inside border, round landscape centre.

1931   Gloster shape, biscuit blue butterfly wing compartments, 3 in cup, containing barbed wire alternating with leaves and rose diamonds star centre.

1932   Gloster shape, biscuit blue butterfly wing compartments, 3 in cup, containing weed, alternating with leaves, star centre.

1933 Gloster shape, biscuit blue ground with grapes and vine leaves inside, fine landscape centre see 1943 for flowers in the bottom.

1934 Blue border, 5-petalled flower and leaves, flower centre.

1935 The same as 1934 Maroon ground.

1936 The same as 1916, tea ware blue printed with small confin (?) group in bottom.

1937 Leaf-shape edge, chrome-green flowers and blue sprigs.

1938 Red squiggle and gold dot border, 3 compartments, small sprig border.

1939 Dentelle border, 6 chrome-green roses, rose-bud centre, 5 roses in cup.

1940 Gloster border, 3 large flowers and blue sprigs. A little fuller and better than 1900.

1941 Printed India pattern of blue tree, all the tracing in red.

1942 Gloster shape, 3 border compartments, barbed lines outlined by blue leaves, divided by sprigs, flower group centre.

1943 The same as 1933 flowers/roses in the centre. N.B. see 1948.

1944 Printed and coloured birds on twigging, blue border, gold vine leaves.

1945 6 stripes of chrome green in cup and saucer.

1946 Roses and gold leaves.

1947 Plain Gloster shape, glaze kiln blue over printed gown border, small compartments of flowers, 3 in saucer, 2 in cup.

1948 Gloster shape, grapes and vine leaves.

1949 Flowers blue, yellow dot in the centre, stems gold.

1950 Gold lines.

1951 Gloster shape, curved gold border, outside of cup same as 1950.

1952 Gloster shape, blue printed diamonds and crescent scrolls, small sprigged compartments,

group of flowers in the centre by the Men.

1953 Gloster shape, purple printed diamonds, flies in compartments, long tailed bird on tree landscape in centre.

1954 Shell edge, 4 compartments flowers in each, divided by hanging bells, sprigs in the centre.

1955 Gloster shape, chrome-green ground, dentelle and hanging bell inside, 3 coloured birds on twigging in centre.

1956 Dessert the same as 1933, landscape in the centre.

1957 The same as 1953 printed in blue, landscape in the centre, Dessert. See 1961 the right number.

1958 Gloster shape, 2 torqua green borders divided by pointed tongues, star centre.

1959 Dessert. 1952 is the pattern.

1960 Gloster shape, dark chrome green ground border, Mr. Evan's flowers.

1961 The same as 1953 printed in blue, landscape centre.

1962 Gloster shape, blue border with white enamel spots, 4 compartments with small sprig, rose centre.

1963 Gloster shape, dark maroon ground, Jessamine trailing, leaf sprigs inside, star centre.

1964 New black sprigs with urn and flowers in bottom, Dresden.

1965 The same print as above, done in purple.

1966 The same as above done in purple brown.

1967 The same as above done in hair brown.

1969 Gloster shape, maroon ground and jessamine sprigs the same as 1963, pearls inside, star centre.

1970 Green thistle border by Women.

1971 Garland border with sprigs.

1972 Green convolvulus border.

1973 The same as 1964 printed in enamel blue.

1974 Gloster shape, Maroon ground and

gilding the same as 1963, square teeth inner border, landscape centre.

1975 Dessert pattern maroon ground roses and gold leaves.

1976 The same pattern as 1855 with light blue.

1977 Gloster border, 6 chrome green roses and buds, rose centre.

1978 Gadrooned border, printed in blue, womens flowers.

1979 Gloster shape, blue butterfly wing compartments, 3 large flower sprays, blue sprig around centre.

1980 Dresden shape, dark and light blue trailing sprigs, 1 large and some smaller groups.

1981 Dessert ware on the Gloster shape 6 sprigs round and the large one in the middle, edge the same as 1916.

1982 Tableware on the Dresden shape, 6 sprigs round and the large one in the middle, edge the same as 1916.

1983 Roses and blue biscuit leaves.

1984 Leaf shape edge, torque green ground border, 2 leaf Gloster border inside, star centre. [Celeste ground]

1985 Gloster shape, torque green ground, dots inside, star centre. [Celeste]

1986 Gloster shape, Japan pattern, curling half dark biscuit blue leaf and blue panels of twigging joined by small fly, bird on twigging centre.

1987 Gloster shape, chrome green edge dotted, star centre.

1988 Gloster shape, curling half dark biscuit blue leaf and blue panels of barbs jointed by small sprigs, large flower centre.

1989 Gloster shape, chrome-green edge, dotted with orange.

1990 The same as 1989 except the fawn, i.e. fawn edge.

1991 Dessert ware, gadroon edge, printed ground pattern around border reserving oval panels of flowers, large flower spray centre.

1992 Gloster shape, dark biscuit blue border, reserved lined panels, large star centre.

1993 Gloster shape with Sparkes dark biscuit blue dotted with white enamel, reserved panels containing flies, bird in twigging centre.

1994 With Sparkes. See 2004 in the pattern G G.

1995 With Sparkes, rose and B Blue leaves. Gloster shape, 5 roses round saucer, 4 round cup, rose-bud centre.

1996 King's Japan with Sparkes, Gloster shape, dark biscuit blue reserving alternate small circles and long shapes containing Japan style buildings and flower sprays, similar centre.

1997 Gloster shape, blue border, scroll panels, flower spray centre.

1998 With Sparkes, Women flowers and dontle, flowers joined by sprig border, 4 round and 3 in the cup, rose in bottom of cup.

1999 With Sparkes, Dessert Blue ground one coat and landscapes, small squares bottom of ground, Gloster shape, edged the solid way.

2000 The same as 1712 done on Gloster shape – edged the same as 1850.

2001 Roses and brown leaves with gold on Gloucester ware done to match broken teapot.

2002 Modelled border, large spray and 2 small sprigs around, sprig centre, Women's flowers.

2003 The same as above, with the border ornamented in Green – Chrome Green.

2004 Gloster shape, large flower sprigs, 3 round outside border, inside of cup the same as saucer.

2005 The same as 1848 Torqua Green ground, rose and sprig centre, handsomely gilt. [Celeste]

2006 Dessert, Gloster shape, Torqua Green band, dentelle inside, star centre. [Celeste]

2007 Shell edge, Torqua Green shapes, a different flower in each compartment, flower centre.

2008 Dessert the same number, Flowers the same as 2002. Gloster shape.

2009 The same as above with the edge ornamented in Blue.

2010 Gloster shape, Torqua Green border, 3 gold dots, flowers in the middle. [Celeste]

2011 Leaf bordered edge, Torqua green band, scroll around centre, star centre same as 2006.

2012 'Gown pattern printed in blue under glaze' reserving '3 compartments a different sprig in each on orange ground, 2 compartments in the cup, sprigs outside the cup', sprig centre.

2013 Rich Japan pattern, blue tree with a wheel.

2014 The same pattern as 1854 done with Torqua ground used on the Gloster ware, Celeste with gold vine border.

2015 The same 1664 done on the Clarence in torqua Green. Celeste, gilt groups in bottom.

2016 'The same as 1855 . . . Blue with gold on the blue', crossed out and in its place 'See 1976'. Celeste band.

2017 The same as 2012 without orange ground in the panel.

2018 Flowers the same as 2012 printed in green on the glaze, orange in the panel, sprig centre. Gown pattern.

2019 Gloucester shape, blue winged shapes, large and small sprays, 3 small sprigs outside the cup, women's flowers.

1x Gown pattern printed under the glaze blue, reserved panels of flowers, flower spray centre, flowers by S Wood.

3x Gloster shape, twiggy sprigs and flowers printed all over, breakfast ware.

4x As 3x done in purple.

5x As 3x done in green on the plain [shape].

6x The same as 5x without twigging, plain Gloster with only the edge gold.

7x The same as 6x black [the rest torn away].

8x The same as 6x purp [the rest torn away].

9x Gown pattern printed in blue, Glaze kiln and ornamented with enamel blue, women's flowers in reserves and in centre.

10x Shell dessert, 4 roses round the border, rose spray centre.

11x The same as 9x in printed Green and ornamented in soft Croam Green.

12x The same as 9x and ornamented with Croam Green printed with Blue under the Glaze.

13x Modelled border, large flower spray and 3 small sprigs, smaller sprig centre.

15x Gown pattern printed with blue, 2 compartments in cup and 3 in saucer containing flowers, flower centre.

16x Plain ware, Torqua Green band, dots and dentelle inside, star centre.

17x Gloster shape, 3 printed sprays of flowers and spray centre.

18x Same as 1823 with rose colour by Lulman see 21x.

19x Scrolled compartments, 8 in saucer, 6 outside cup, star centre.

21x Possibly similar to 18x.

22x Gloster shape, Vine border star in the bottom Torqua Green.

23x On the Dresden, Dontail edge, large central blue and green trailing sprigs, 6 smaller ones round border.

24x The same as 1843 with Biscuit blue band.

25x Plain Gloster, Dontle edge, large rose, 2 blue trailing sprigs, small sprig centre.

26x Oxford embossed, with edge done in Chrome Green, Torqua and chrome-green sprays.

27x 1884 with light gilding, orange.

28x Table pattern, Torqua Green border,

gilded sprigs inside, star centre.

29x   Dessert, Gloster shape, Moat blue border, landscape.

30x   Torqua green band, dentelle inside, star centre.

31x   Green border, flowers and sprigs.

32x   Dark biscuit blue ball shapes, flower spray centre, men's flowers.

35x   Gloster shape, maroon ground border, scrolled inside, landscape centre.

36x   Modelled border, moat blue ground, reserving 3 compartments, in the saucer and in cup containing flowers, flower centre, men's flowers.

37x   Scroll modelled border, star centre.

38x   Fawn ground, 5-petalled flower, star centre.

39x   Dentelle edge, 3 sprays of flowers printed in green and shaded, cup printed inside and out.

40x   Printed flowers and hawthorn sprigs border, coloured torqua green, pink and yellow, similar centre.

41x   Modelled edge, torqua curtained shapes, 4 in saucer 3 outside cup, star centre.

42x   Dessert, 3 scrolled compartments containing printed flowers filled in, scrolls ornamented with torqua green, pink borders, sprigs in centre.

43x   Dessert, 3 compartments containing men's flowers, enamel blue ground, sprig centre.

45x   Table pattern the same as 42x blue ground enamel blue.

46x   Dessert Gloster shape, ground and flowers the same as 30x.

47x   . . . dark blue diamond gilded flowers 1 set done by Thos Freeman (?).

48x   Orange forgetmenot, blue ground flowers . . . by Freeman (?).

49x   Gloster shape, printed sprays in blue, hawthorne blossom.

50x   Gloster shape, printed sprays, pretty blue with gilt.

51x   Gloster shape, blue border, 3 compartments in saucer and cup containing men's flowers, sprig

centre.

52x   Gloster shape, blue border with dots in diamonds, 5 curved compartments containing flowers, the sixth spray, sprig centre.

53x   Light chrome green ground, men's flowers, 5 compartments in the saucer 4 ditto in the cup, group in the bottom of the cup.

54x   Printed blue sprigs round.

55x   Painted blue sprigs round.

56x   The same as 36x done on the Gloucester, light blue.

57x   The same as 56x Maroon ground.

58x   Biscuit blue ground with grapes and vine leaves, reserving 3 compartments of men's flowers, a different group in each, spray centre.

59x   Green roses by women on forgetmenot embosses.

60x   Modelled border, glaze kiln drab colour border, 6 roses round the border, 4 inside cup, star centre.

61x   Glaze kiln drab colour border with flowers and leaves, 3 groups round, 2 inside cup, star centre.

62x   The same as 1850 with a Chrome Green ground. The drawing actually depicts 3 printed large sprays and a small sprig centre, on Gloster shape.

63x   Gloster shape, dark blue border, 3 panels of flowers, small spray centre, men's flowers.

64x   Dessert, Gloster shape, large and small green sprigs around.

65x   Flowers painted in blue the same as 64x.

66x   Modelled border, painted in green the same as 64x.

67x   Gloster shape, outlined in green, Flowers the same as 66x.

68x   The same as 67x painted in blue.

69x   Modelled border, 4 different-sized sprigs, pretty green.

70x   Flowers and leaves, 6 compartments, 5 inside the cup, star centre.

71x   Green band, dot and dentelle inside, star centre.

72x   Gloster shape, blue curving border, 6

panels in the saucer, 4 in cup, sprig centre.

73x Gloster shape, rose border, tongue-shaped doorways, 36 round, 32 in the cup, star centre.

74x Gloster shape, rose border, leaves and hanging bells, star centre.

75x The same as 23x table pattern all done in a Croam Green, Dontail edge, Dresden.

76x Rose border, upside-down hanging bells, star centre same as 73x.

77x Breakfast pattern on the Broseley shape the same as 50x with a plain gold line.

78x The same as 66x painted in blue.

79x The same as 69x painted in blue on the plain Gloster Dentelle edge.

80x 4 dots, scroll and hanging bell, 6 panels of French sprigs around and in the cup, star centre.

81x The same as 58x Tea pattern done on the Gloster shape.

82x Dresden shape, different-sized sprigs, forget-me-nots.

83x Plain Gloster, glaze kiln drab hanging border with a bell and flowers, 3 compartments different-sized dots, star centre.

84x The same as 1980 done in Chrome Green – Dessert.

85x Same as 1865 Dark blue ground.

86x Gloster shape, ivory ground, 3 compartments, 2 in cup, containing flowers in baskets, 3 dots inside and small sprig centre.

87x Gloster shape, large centre spray of flowers.

88x Gloster shape, enamel blue through the glaze kiln, 6 compartments in the saucer, 4 do. in the cup, landscape centre.

89x Maroon ground and gilding the same as 86x, long-tailed birds on twigging, fly centre.

90x Maroon ground and gilding the same as 86x Landscapes in the panels.

91x Gloster shape, 3 panels of different weedy sprays, alternating with small coloured flower sprays.

92x The same as 86x Moat blue ground.

93x The same as 86x Dessert chrome green ground with landscapes in the Panels. Chrome green has 2 coats.

94x The same as 86x Moat blue ground, the bird done in gold and placed different ways in each panel, rose centre.

95x The same as 86x Chrome green ground, coloured birds in panels, fly centre.

96x Gloster shape, glaze kiln drab colour, 3 landscapes in panels.

97x Gloster shape, dark biscuit blue ground, panels of flowers, small flower centre.

98x Glaze kiln drab panels, flowers with leaves, 3 panels in saucer, 2 in cup, sprig centre.

99x Dessert, landscape to cover the Bottom, Torqua green band bead border around the landscape done by J. Daniel, Gloster shape, Edged the solid way.

100x Dessert, landscape to cover the bottom, moat blue band broad and fine line round the landscape done by J. Bullock, Gloster shape, edged as above.

101x Gloster shape, 3 roses and 3 tulips round, star centre.

102x The same as 1849 Maroon and enamel dots in the border.

103x The same as 1849 with light maroon instead of orange.

104x Broseley, printed in glaze kiln green, NB Dessert plain Gloster. Weed pattern.

105x Same as 104x with only the line and handle gilded, no twigging in gold.

106x The same as 104x done all blue calx and rose dots.

107x The same as 106x no gold twigging.

108x The same as 106x done with India blue.

109x Gloster shape, Glaze kiln drab, light maroon edge, feathers placed different ways in each panel, alternating with flower panels, flower centre.

110x   Glaze kiln drab band, radiating stripes and dots, star centre.

111x   Gloster shape, dessert, Chrome green border with white enamel dots, flower sprays round centre.

112x   Dessert with Maroon edge and white enamel dots, crossed out.

113x   Dessert, maroon edge with enamel dots, Basket of flowers in the bottom of the plate.

115x   Leaf edge shape, large sprigs in green, gold twiging round each of the sprigs.

116x   Gloster shape, edged with Chrome Green and Gold, sprigs the same as above with no gold twigging, filled in in colours.

117x   Sprigs, gold twigging round each sprig.

118x   Plain Gloster Dessert, scattered sprigs and twigging.

119x   The same as 118x in colours plain Gloster.

120x   Chrome green Jessamine border, border inside the cup, 3 sprigs outside, see White's pattern.

121x   Purple brown border, border outside the cup, see White's pattern.

122x   Jessamine sprigs, Oxford embossed, see White's pattern (purple jessamine).

124x   Flower sprays by the men, large hanging bunch of grapes and vine leaves. The other 3 compartments the same as 91x.

125x   Gloster shape, maroon and white enamel border, star centre.

127x   Oxford embossed, dresden coloured sprigs and gold edge.

128x   Oxford embossed, dresden green sprigs – Gold edge.

129x   Leaf edge shape, painted in shiny black, 3 sprigs around and small sprig in centre.

130x   Coloured sprigs the same as 1754 with gold twigging and a fine line.

131x   The same as 130x only Green sprigs.

132x   Blue, purple, and gold with women's flowers.

133x   Gloster shape, dark blue panels, the same printed sprigs as 1862.

134x   Printed sprig on the Broseley shape, large leaves and groups of flowers.

135x   Modelled edge, chrome green leaves, alternating with flowered stars, flowered star centre.

136x   Gloster shape, biscuit blue ground panels, 3 compartments of slight flowers, sprig centre.

137x   Glaze kiln lilac border, 3 large panels of flowers, flower centre.

138x   Gloster shape, Torqua green ground, hanging scrolls and a bell, star centre.

139x   Shell dessert shape, Torqua green and gold edged, large star centre.

140x   The same as 104x green weed, red dots, no gold.

141x   Oxford embossed, 4 sprigs round, each of them the same, 3 sprigs inside the cup and a small sprig in the centre (forgetmenots).

142x   Oxford embossed, 3 sprigs in the inside of the cup a small one in the centre.

143x   Gloster shape, embossed 2 flowers, glaze kiln lilac, 8 branches of grapes round the saucer 6 do. in the cup, large spray of flowers and 2 small sprigs in the centre.

144x   Gloster shape, glaze kiln lilac, hanging leaves, star centre.

145x   Gloster shape, dark biscuit blue border, vine leaves, small sprigs in panels, large flower spray in centre, flowers outside as well.

146x   Table ware, gown pattern blue printed, small sprigs in border panels, large spray of flowers centre.

147x   Green wreath.

148x   Japan Bird by W Evans.

149x   Plain Gloster, blue dots each side of wavy line.

150x   Oxford embossed dark blue weed red dots and French line.

151x   The same as 135x done all in gold.

152x   Blue and gold with 2 panels of flowers, and one in bottom.

153x Squat shape, dentelle, dark biscuit blue wavy panels with weed sprigs, 5 compartments of flowers, small sprig centre.

154x Squat shape, dark biscuit blue ground wavy panels, 8 compartments in saucer and outside cup, different flower in each panel, 3 sprigs round inside of cup, sprig, centre, dontelle edge outside cup.

155x Biscuit blue ground, sprigs of weed round, small weed sprig centre.

156x Broseley light blue weed and red dots.

157x Squat shape, biscuit blue panel, trailing sprigs each side, small sprigg centre.

158x Squat shape, biscuit blue leaves and weed, 3 compartments round, round weed centre.

159x Dessert, green and white bands and leaves, large star centre.

161x Biscuit blue panels, 3 and 4 dots, feathered-edged compartments of flowers, 3 in saucer, 2 in cup, flower sprig centre.

162x Biscuit blue ground border, leaves and flowers around, central spray of flowers, flowers around inside of cup.

163x Gloster shape, glaze kiln lilac border, weed and hanging leaves, star centre.

164x Gloster shape, glaze kiln lilac border, leaf and weed, bird on twigging centre.

165x Gloster shape, hanging bell and dots, flower spray centre.

166x Squat shape, thick and thin gold line.

167x Dessert, glaze kiln green bands and leaves, 2 compartments of flowers, landscape in the middle.

168x The same as 173x done all in lilac.

169x Squat shape, biscuit blue ground border, hanging bell and leaf sprigs, sprig centre.

170x Squat shape, 3 green roses and 3 small sprigs, rose bud sprig centre.

171x Dessert, blue stripes and leaf sprays, 2 panels of flowers, flower spray and sprig centre.

172x Squat shape, Breakfast, French edge, myrtle weed sprigs printed in Mouse colour with gold dots, sprig centre.

173x Breakfast ware, French edge, lilac ground, leaf sprays, sprig centre.

174x Dessert, large sprig and scattered smaller ones.

175x Squat shape, breakfast, French edge, 4 long coloured sprigs around, small sprig centre.

176x The same as 175x with no gold.

177x Table ware, Dresden, large central rose spray and scattered sprigs.

178x Oxford embossed, Mulberry twigging in compartments.

179x The same as 178x in green.

180x The same as 165x with a landscape in the centre.

181x Oxford embossed 2 thistle sprays round saucer in each panel, 1 in each panel round cup, 3 round inside and one in the middle.

182x Gloster shape, blue printed roses, ornamented with gold.

183x The same as 182x printed in mouse colour.

184x Printed currant border, filled in with blue green on the squat shape.

185x Squat shape, large sprig and small sprigs, small sprig centre.

186x The same as 187x with gold edge.

187x Oxford embossed, a sprig in each panel round the outside of the cup and saucer, sprig centre.

188x Squat shape, 3 large sprigs and central sprig painted in purple.

189x Squat shape, French edge, Japan-style flowers and leaves.

191x Dessert, blue border and twigging, large bird in centre.

192x The same as 102x done in the new Dresden plate with Dresden pattern done prettily in gold.

193x The same as 86x with enamel Blue ground and landscapes, line round the middle landscape.

194x Gloster shape, glaze kiln blue border, hanging curtain shapes, large bird in tree centre.

195x Gloster shape, biscuit blue ground with white enamel dots, 3 compartments containing flowers.

196x Glaze kiln lilac ground, orange leaves and orange edge the same as 109x.

197x Siamese youth India pattern.

198x Hawthorn blossom border in blue with flowers and gilt to be put in.

199x Gloster shape, ivory (straw) ground and green, 42 scallops round saucer and 30 round cup.

201x Table, Blue printed Japan (pattern as 189x) lustre edge.

202x Torque enamelled prettily, gilt on Gloster ware.

203x Dessert printed flowers.

204x New shape dessert ware, blue sprigs etc, Gloster edge.

205x 3 panels of flowers in saucer, 2 in cup, weed and green dots, flower centre, pretty Dresden pattern.

206x Gloster shape, light glaze kiln blue ground, gilding same as 165x, star centre.

207x Japan-style pattern, hollow blue rocks in 2 shades, twigging, centre of 3-storied Japan house and blue rock.

208x Gloster shape, maroon ground, hanging bell-like leaves, star centre.

209x Dentelle, green stripe and gold sprigs, 18 bars round saucer, 14 round cup, sprig centre.

210x The same as 172x, squat shape.

211x Dessert, 4 compartments a sprig in each, flower centre.

212x Dessert, ? New Dresden, alternate panels of hanging bell grapes and vines, 2 of each, large flower centre.

213x Biscuit blue ground and ornamental gilding the same as 191x, groups of flowers in the middle.

214x Table ware, 3 small groups of flowers printed and coloured.

215x Dessert, pink border and green edging, floral centre.

216x Gloster shape, 4 compartments, a sprig in each, landscape centre.

217x Bronze sprigs.

218x Dontelle edge, small sprigs, cups painted inside and out.

222x Blue glaze kiln printed rose dontail edge and foot line.

223x Same as 222x in mouse colour.

224x Same as 183x the rose and buds done in yellow.

225x Same as 224x rose colour instead of yellow.

226x Same as 22x in mouse colour.

227x New Dresden Dessert etched with blue green and golds.

228x Gloster shape, grey printed flowers around border, flowers in the bottom by Freeman. This pattern done again in 1940.

229x Table ware Chrome green ground and flowers, gilded by Lucas.

230x Blue printed ground – and gold by Freeman.

231x Gloster shape, glaze kiln green border, leaf gilding, sprig centre. Cup not yet done.

232x Gloster shape, hard kiln blue border, gilding and centre as 231x, the pattern saucer not done.

233x The same as 1712 on the Gloster shape with flowers.

234x The same as 199x with flowers in the middle instead of a line, Gloster shape.

235x Gloster shape, hard kiln maroon ground, leaf and dot gilding, landscape centre.

236x Gloster shape, hawthorn blossom border, landscape centre.

237x Plain Gloster, dontail edge, green and gold vine leaves, vine leaf sprig centre.

238x Gloster shape, glaze kiln ground, hanging weed, flower centre. Salmony pink – a rather muddy pink border.

239x Dessert, ? New Dresden, flowers done slight in 4 compartments and in centre.

240x Dessert, plain Gloster, dentelle

edge, green seaweed with rose colour dots, 4 sprays and centre.

241x   Mouse coloured ground, hawthorne blossom pattern, gilded vine leaves and grapes around centre.

242x   The same as 241x with no gilding in the bottom sprig, blue ground.

243x   Gilding the same as 241x, vine leaf sprig in bottom, Blue printed ground (Hick).

244x   Same as 240x the ware done with fine line instead of dentelle.

245x   New printed pattern with new blue rose intermixed and gilt on Gloster shape as Teaset Hick had.

247x   Gloster shape, pink ground, leaf and weed gilding, landscape centre.

248x   Gloster shape, pink ground with thin bars, dot and arrow around, star centre.

254x   Gold and Birds done by Rickhuss.

255x   Blue-Gold and flowers by Rickhuss.

256x   Gloster shape, 3 large sprigs and 3 small ones round, 2 of each inside the cup, outlined in gold, vine leaf and grape gilding around centre.

257x   Same as 1745 geranium printed in mouse color.

258x   Gloster shape, dark biscuit blue ground, landscape in centre.

259x   Green weedy twigs.

260x   Dessert, lilac, hawthorn blossom, flower centre.

261x   Blue printed hawthorn – Dessert the same as 260x with star instead of flowers.

262x   Gloster shape, torqua green border, star centre.

263x   'Roses green leaf and sprig', 3 round the border and centre.

264x   Blue and fine gold with star in the centre.

265x   Gloster shape, lilac ground, 3 compartments in saucer, 2 inside cup, with flowers, small rose centre.

266x   The same as 265x chrome green ground with light rose colour

leaves and edge.

267x   Enamel blue ground with orange leaves and edge the same as 265x.

268x   The same as 265x maroon ground with pink leaf and edge.

269x   Light maroon edge, leaf gilding and 8-petalled flower.

270x   Gloster shape, light maroon ground, leaf spray gilding and sprig centre.

271x   Light fawn ground, 3 compartments of sprigs, sprig centre.

272x   Feather leaf edged border, dark maroon (?) ground, 8-petalled leaf and sprig centre.

273x   Three flower sprigs, small blue sprig centre.

274x   Hawthorn blossom on ground, leaves inside, sprig centre.

275x   Gloster shape, light maroon panels with barbed wire, star centre.

276x   Gloster shape, Lee's emb[d], large and small sprigs.

277x   Three compartments of flowers, outlined with green, inside saucer and outside cup.

278x   The same as 277x ornamented with rose colour instead of green.

279x   Hawthorn blossom on ground, dentelle border and twigging, large and 2 small flower sprigs.

280x   The same as 1745, mouse colour.

281x   Table pattern geranium leaf under glaze green, gold twigging – Dresden shape.

282x   Dessert, torqua ground and star, New Dessert plate.

283x   Same as 265x in rose colour.

284x   Shell dessert, glaze kiln geranium green, vine leaves and grapes.

285x   Dessert new Dresden shape, large and small green and blue sprigs.

286x   The same as 27x without flowers, printed sprigs in the bottom, Flang[d] shape.

287x   Mr. Lee's shape. Torqua green edge.

288x   Gilding and ground as 282x, flower centre.

289x   Gloster shape, 3 compartments in

saucer, 2 in cup of glaze kiln green, grapes and leaves, star centre.

290x The same as 289x, stone colour ground and the upper half of the white compartment as a wash of dry orange.

291x Gloster shape, stone colour ground, G G's Painted glaze kiln green, green leaves and sprig centre.

292x Gloster shape, green leaves, grape gilding star centre, slightest 3^d gilding.

293x The same as 294x mouse colour ground.

294x Light maroon ground.

295x The same as 312x enamel lilac ground, Lee's embossed shape (see 312x).

296x Dessert, glaze kiln lilac ground, flower centre.

297x The same as 292x done slight.

298x The same as 312x Chrome green ground Lee's embossed shape.

299x Gloster shape, glaze kiln stone colour, large leaves and grapes.

300x Lee's embossed shape, a bird in each compartment, twigging around, fly centre.

307x Dessert, ornamented with torqua green, 4 compartments . . . 2 birds and 2 flies in the compartments, a bird and nest in the centre.

308x The same as 299x with dark glaze kiln green leaves.

309x The same as 289x with a flower in the centre instead of a star.

310x Dessert, 6 compartments with a sprig in each, 3 sprigs around centre.

311x Gloucester shape, 3 compartments in saucer and saucer containing flowers outlined with leaves, flower sprig centre.

312x 'See next to 295x put there in a mistake, this is the right number G G': under the old 296x is 'Lee's embossed shape, rose colour ground, 3 compartments round saucer, 3 outside cup', with

flowers, flower sprig centre.

313x G Green shells with gold twigging.

314x Gloster shape, glaze kiln green leaves and grapes.

316x The same as 145x with dark glaze kiln green ground.

317x The same flowers as 285x but no gilding and this is done on the old Dresden plate.

318x Mouse colour, thistle and gold.

319x Green thistle and gold.

320x Dessert, 3 torqua green panels alternating with flower panels, flower centre.

321x Gloster shape, blue border, sprig centre.

322x Dessert, torqua green panels, alternating with flower panels, flower sprig centre.

323x The same as 314x with drab leaves.

324x Mouse col. thistle and gold no edge.

325x The same as 321x Chrome green ground.

326x Blue border, leaves, lemon shapes inside border, spinning star border.

327x Gloster shape, maroon ground, long leaves, star centre.

328x The same as 329x light chrome green ground.

329x Gloster shape, blue ground and weed twigging, twig sprig centre.

330x Lilac ground, 3 compartments, 3 flower swags, sprig centre.

331x Dentelle edge, panels of small sprigs, sprig centre.

332x Gloster shape, lilac ground, grapes and vine leaves inside ground and in centre.

333x Gown pattern border printed in glaze kiln green, either upright flute shape, or Broseley shape.

334x The same as 333x in mouse colour.

335x Gown pattern printed in glaze kiln green, weedy twigs, either upright flute shape or Broseley shape.

336x The same as above in mouse colour.

337x The same as 334x with no line.

338x See 355x.

339x Dentelle edge, Lee's embossed shape, 3 flower sprigs around, small sprig centre.

340x Torqua green ground, female figures inside border, star centre. ? Siamese. [Someone has painted in graffiti of male and female figures in the hanging shapes.]

341x The same as 330x, Dessert, Lee's embossed, lilac ground.

342x Gloster shape, 4 compartments printed diamond shapes, small panels, flower centre.

343x Same as 327x Blue Ground – maroon.

344x Dessert, Lee's embossed, dontail edge, flowers alternating with small sprigs, sprig centre.

345x Same as 330x blue ground – 3 lilac.

346x Biscuit blue, flowers and leaves, star centre.

347x Mouse coloured printed diamond pattern, 3 compartments with small sprigs, flower sprig centre.

348x Table pattern, mouse coloured gown pattern and mouse coloured flowers – Dresden.

349x The same as 144x on a biscuit blue ground.

350x The same as 1807 mouse col. leaves.

351x The same as 289x, dark biscuit blue ground.

352x Mouse col. seaweed.

354x Gloster edge, coloured sprigs around and in centre.

355x Same as 271x, dark blue ground.

356x Green thistle and gold, Lee's embossed shape.

357x The same as 356x mouse colour.

358x The same as 96x, light blue ground.

359x The same as 1807 with the green printed under the glaze.

360x The same as 359x mouse colour under the glaze.

361x Blue and gold, to be put in the book. Blue band to be put on Gloster dessert, gold grape border, half on the blue and half off, flowers in the centre.

362x Gloster shape, blue ground, leaves and lobster-like shapes.

369x Same as 348x Bk pattern.

370x Same as 328x green gown instead of mouse & mouse roses Bk pattern.

371x The same as 250x Enamel blue ground.

372x Gloster shape, large leaves & flowers, 3 compartments in cup.

373x Salmon ground, 3 varied sprigs round saucer, 2 round inside of cup, small sprigs centre.

374x Gloster shape, Salmon ground, 2 birds on twigging, 3 compartments in saucer 2 in cup, fly centre.

375x The same as 374x with birds & fly done entirely in green.

380x Table pattern. 4 sprigs, of thistles, thistle centre.

381x The same as 380x, breakfast pattern, 3 sprigs round the saucer & inside cup & 3 sprigs and 2 gold sprigs outside.

382x Salmon colour ground, trailing gold sprigs.

383x Mouse colour gown pattern, grapes and vines, twigging sprigs in the bottom.

384x Gloster shape, dark glaze kiln green large leaves and flowers, 3 compartments inside cup.

385x Gloster shape, diamond shape pattern printed in mouse colour, flower centre.

386x 2 dot & 4 leaf modelled border, large vine leaves & grapes printed in green.

387x Gloster shape, blue ground, 3 compartments inside the cup.

388x Gloster shape, diamond shape pattern printed in mouse colour, sprigs centre.

389x Salmon col. ground, 3 gold sprigs the same all round the bird varied a little.

390x Lee's pattern with the star.

391x The same as 389x New grass green ground, the beading left white – the bird in the centre only done green – Gloster shape.

392x New Imperial green ground, bird on large twigging & flies on twigging centre.

393x Chrome green & gold with blue flower sprigs . . . altered by Rickuss – Table.

394x Cell pattern inner ring, outside sprigs of Japan flowers, inside a full centre of Japan tree and flowers, printed in mouse col. filled in with glaze kiln blue & red.

395x Mouse colour band, gown pattern, 3 birds & 3 butterflies round the border.

397x Plain Gloster, dessert & teaware, green and gold leaf shapes with pansies or hearts ease between.

399x Gloster shape, dessert Lee's pattern printed in glaze kiln green, diamond printed pattern, flower centre.

400x Gloster shape, harebell-type flower sprigs.

401x The same as 400x Lee's embossed shape.

402x Gloster shape, mouse col. grass.

403x Same as 402x with line, no foot line.

404x Same as 403x dessert – Dresden shape.

405x Same as 402x Green.

406x Same as 403x Green.

407x Dessert, Imperial chrome green, double and single bars leaves on single, dontelle edge, flower spray centre.

408x Same as 403x Printed in Blue.

409x New Gentian (?) Embd dessert 185x sprigs Gilt Gentians (?) & gold line as 378x.

410x Breakfast pattern same sprigs as 218x on the Gloster shape – no gold.

411x Gloster shape. Imperial chrome green, grasses & leaves.

412x Shell & leaf moulded border, Imperial blue ground border, shell shape gilding, star centre.

413x Same shape as above, mauve

ground border, grapes in compartments, star centre.

414x Gold & green leaves, see (Rickuss?).

415x Gloster shape, the same as 416x.

416x Glaze kiln stone colour, bars of leaves, star centre.

417x Glaze kiln stone colour, compartments of grapes, 5 in saucer, 4 in cup.

418x Pale ground, dots & leaves inside, 3 compartments in saucer, 2 in cup, small sprig centre.

419x Gloster shape, Imperial chrome green edge, grass-like leaves, & similar small centre.

420x Dessert hearts ease . . . gold leaves & green sprigs of . . . R for . . . (R = Rickuss).

421x Dessert (11 shape), printed mouse colour anthemian (?) blossom gilt.

422x Dessert Salmon ground with green birds & gold sprigs & fly on a gold sprig in the middle, dentelle edge.

423x Dessert (11 shape), Imperial blue ground, 2 leaves leaning one way and 2 the other, star centre.

424x Green printed gown pattern, scrolled panels, outlined with green, crest of an elephant in the centre of the plate.

425x The same as 332x only Imperial chrome green.

426x The same as 415x Imperial chrome green, no gold wreath upon the green and white stripe, gold by the side of the green stripe.

427x Same as 415x only Imperial chrome green, and the fine work upon the ground left white, also the parts of the gold wreath that join'd it.

428x Shell & leaf shape edge.

429x Same as 394x green instead of blue and mouse.

430x Dessert patterns, blue leaves in each flute of New Gentians emboss'd ware on fawn ground gold star pattern altogether neat and well gilt.

431x Table pattern similar to 424 with

GRAINGER'S WORCESTER PORCELAIN

Blue Green x gold – ground, printed flowers colour'd. See T Freeman.

432x Tea pattern, blue band, the border done inside the cup of the middle outside, large wheel-like & grapes shape.

433x The same as 404x printed in Biscuit blue on Gloster shape plain gold line on the edge – no foot line.

434x Gloster shape, green edge, landscape centre.

435x The same as 434x without any green in the border.

436x Gloster shape, landscape inside the cup same as the saucer.

437x 2 scrolled edge shape, gown pattern border, printed in mouse colour, sprigs of weed in centre.

438x Gloster shape, 2 different coloured cornucopia-like shapes, flower centre.

439x Gloster shape, rose col'd edge and feathers, a group of flowers in each compartment & in the middle, 2 compartments inside the cup, crossed feathers round the ground.

440x Same as 439x ground done in Imperial new chrome green.

441x Same as 440x birds on gold sprigs, no flowers.

442x Dessert, large & 4 small arches of small vine leaves on blue ground, wheel star centre.

443x India flowers printed & colour'd gilt.

444x Table pattern, 1 large & 2 small sprays of printed flowers coloured in red yellow & orange.

445x Same pattern as above ungilt.

452x The same as 451x with landscape in the centre.

453x Dark green border, panels containing a fly, bird on nest & twigging in centre.

454x Bright Imperial chrome green leaf sprays, 3 large & 3 small, small leaf centre.

455x Gloster shape, new soft Imperial

chrome green border, scroll gilding, star centre.

456x Dessert (shape 11) New hard chrome green, Imperial green, Imperial green for gilding on, green border with flowers, star centre.

457x New soft green Imperial border, compartments of green flowers, grapes & shell gilding, star centre.

458x Leaf edge, green border with coloured bird, new hard Imperial chrome green for gilding on, star centre.

459x Gloster shape, green border, leaves in new hard Imperial chrome green, star centre.

460x 2 dot & 4 leaf shaped edge, mouse colour border, landscape centre.

461x Dessert (shape 11) sprays of leaves, washed in with the new soft chrome green, & cut up with black.

462x Panels of leaves & flowers & in cup, small sprigs in bottom.

463x Dresden, chrome (?) Gown & rose gilt & torqua as (Morley).

475x Sprigs enamel as 310x gilt edge as 462x.

476x Leaf edge, rose ground done close up to the gilding, flower centre.

477x Dessert, leaf edged panels, the embossed flowers done with the same new soft chrome green.

479x Gloster shape, G G's Celeste, Celeste ground, star centre.

480x Gloster shape, printed green weed & blue dot, 4 around border & in centre.

481x The same as 480x mouse colour & green dots.

482x Gloster shape, printed vase of flowers in centre, 3 flower sprigs around, 2 outside cup.

483x Green & orange/red sprigs. 3 large & small.

484x Gloster shape, glaze kiln drab ground border, panels of small flowers, sprig centre, 2 compartments inside cup, G G's

248

485x Gloster shape, hard pea green ground, leaf gilding, star centre.
486x Gilded, maize colour compartments, Gloster shape.
489x Gloster shape, stone colour ground, scroll & twig gilding, star centre.
490x Stone colour ground, triangular shaped panels, printed and coloured sprigs.
491x The same as 250x with stone colour ground.
492x Pink large & small spiral panels, 3 compartments of flowers, gold circle in the bottom of the cup instead of sprigs about an inch in diameter.
493x Upright flute, breakfast pattern, 16 spears of Imperial chrome green round, gold sprigs in centre.
494x Squat flute, pattern as 493x rose instead of green.
495x The same as 494x painted with maroon colour instead of rose, squat flute shape.
496x Same as 444x breakfast ware.
497x Gloster shape, stone colour border, gold half shaded leaves, flower centre.
498x Dot & 4-leaf edge, flower sprigs.
499x Breakfast pattern, green stripes, 29 round saucer, 19 cup.
500x Gold scrolled edge.
501x Gloster shape, blossoms mouse colour & leaves No. 1 glaze kiln green, green leaf sprigs.
502x Stone ground, gold sprigging & scrolls.
503x Gloster shape, painted panels of glaze kiln stone drab No. 1, landscape in centre.
504x The same as 250x New glaze kiln blue ground instead of green.
505x Gloster shape, glaze kiln chocolate ground No. 1, sprigging and red flowers, star centre.
506x The same as 500x, biscuit blue ground, gilding the same as 500x.
507x Gloster shape, glaze kiln Imperial blue, gold leaves, flowers & twigging, sprigs centre.

508x Gloster shape, glaze kiln stone drab No. 1, large flower & twigging, sprigs centre.
514x Blue border, panels of butterfly, bird on nest centre.
515x The same as 514x, maroon ground.
516x The same as 514x, celeste ground, small groups of flowers in each compartment & sprig in centre.
517x Imperial soft chrome green ground, same as 514x, a simple flower crossed by a small sprig in each compartment & in the centre.
518x Imperial hard chrome green border, scrolls, star centre.
519x 5 waves round, trailing rose bud garland, rose bud centre.
520x Maroon Gd, landscape in bottom, c'd sprigs in compartments.
521x Same as above only light blue.
522x Laurustinus printed, chocolate colour, leaves & flowers.
523x The same as 522x no edge, Gloster shape.
524x The same as 522x Broseley shape, no edge or footline, slap down handle.
525x Dessert, the same as 522x notched edge line on the edge.
526x Large & small green sprigs.
527x Large & small trailing green sprigs.
528x Imperial chrome green flying arrow-like shapes.
529x Modelled border, star centre.
530x Thistle sprig & thistle leaf, 3 of each round & thistle centre.
531x Green Lauristinus Table pattern, printed.
532x Light glaze kiln blue border, grapes & vine leaves 8 round saucer, 6 inside cup, 10 bunches of leaves round the dessert plate, grape centre.
533x The same as 532x with stone colour ground.
534x New Dresden shape, stone colour ground.
536x 3 coloured sprigs round, sprigs centre.
537x A fine foot line round the outside of cup, 2 tadpoles curl border.

grounding drab No. 1.

538x   Lee's embost, blue printed ¼/s stand, 3 sprigs outside cup (Laurustinus leaf and flowers).

539x   Gilding the same as 538x with new edge & painted in green, no foot line, Gloster shape.

540x   Ground border with trailing flower & leaf sprigs, flower spray centre.

541x   Mauve print, Indian tree-type pattern with 8-pointed star centre & pattern outside border.

542x   Ground border & grapes & vine leaves, flower spray centre.

543x   The same as 542x with grape sprigs in bottom, on Gloster shape.

544x   Gloster shape, ground border, swags of leaves, star centre.

545x   Trailing weed & leaves, hanging from a bell, sprig centre.

546x   Dessert plate, flower in each compartment, sprig centre.

547x   Table plate, gilding the same as 538x, printed in green.

548x   New Dresden shape dessert, treble clef-like shapes, sprig centre.

549x   3 celeste bars alternating with double spray of vine leaves, large group of flowers in centre.

550x   The same shape as 549x, egg-like shapes around triangular blue border, sprays of twigging with flies, bird on twigging centre.

551x   All over twigging, bird in centre, 3 flies around.

552x   Large & small sprigs, small sprig centre.

553x   New shape dessert, honeysuckle & gilt dessert.

554x   Like 545x, sprig centre.

555x   As . . . see Lulman. . .

557x   Blue buds & dot & gold wreath, New Gloster edge.

558x   Flower, leaf festoons & small sprigs round border, large flower centre.

559x   3-petalled coloured flowers joined by 3-leaved sprigs, small landscape in bottom.

560x   Gilding the same as 559x, colourful sprigs centre.

561x   Biscuit blue ground, 3 compartments of landscapes, 2 inside cup, small landscape centre.

562x   Shells in centre.

563x   Vase of flowers centre, blue harebells around, gilding the same as 558x.

564x   Green flowers with black centres, pairs of horn cornucopias, green flower sprig centre.

565x   Biscuit blue ground, 3 compartments of Indian flowers (2 in cup), Indian sprig centre, pink flowers.

566x   Gloster edge, 12 compartments (8 inside cup), Imperial chrome green twigging.

567x   All over Japan-style with some gold decoration.

569x   Dessert, biscuit blue ground, compartments of oriental flowers printed in mouse colour, all over centre of 3 orientals with baskets, a yellow table & a large vase, coloured with rose colour, red, purple, yellow-green, blue-green, blue & yellow and gilding.

570x   Hard chrome green ground with 3 half flowers, 3 compartments of Indian-style sprigs, centre the same as 569x printed in dark green.

571x   The same as 436x border done with Imperial chrome green & star instead of landscape.

572x   4 red & green sprigs, 3 round inside & outside of cup.

573x   The same as 506x except being green instead of blue.

574x   Ground border, twigging inside, coloured shell centre.

575x   The same as 562x with fruit instead of shells.

576x   Gloster edge shape, maroon ground border, hanging sprigs, bird on twigging centre.

577x   Dessert, wavy edge, hard chrome green border, with twigging & white enamel dots, vine leaf star centre.

578x   Gloster shape, hard chrome green ground border, gold leaf

579x sprigging, group of coloured shells centre.

579x The same shaped sprigs as 527 done with purple.

580x the same as 506x drab ground stone colour.

581x Rose colour border, pencil celeste, tadpoles inside and star centre.

582x C scroll shapes, with flower sprigging, similar centre, ornamented with pencil celeste.

583x Green border, leaf edging inside, star centre.

584x 3 large & 3 small sprigs & sprig centre, blue & green.

585x Table pattern, Dresden shape, 3 large & 3 small printed & coloured in sprigs, 2 inside cup.

586x Narrow green border, 5 small sprigs, 3 in cup, and a central one.

587x Maroon band, gold edge & line & star with firm line upon the outside of cup.

588x Table pattern gadroon edge, chrome green band, scollop'd edge, dentelle next the centre, star in bottom.

589x The same as 540x with landscape instead of flowers.

590x Imperial chrome border, panels of green tadpoles, large & 2 small groups of flowers.

591x 3 larger and 3 small sprigs around, small sprigs centre.

592x Wavy trailing line with yellow flowers, twiggy star centre.

593x Green border, flower group centre.

594x The same as 593x with single sprigs instead of group.

595x Festoon of flowers, 9 in festoon & 3 small ones, 3 small flower sprigs centre.

596x Green all over except for star centre, overlapping déjeuner tray-like shape.

597x Table pattern Dresden shape, 2 groups & 2 sprigs inside the cup (details crossed out).

598x Grey green printed pattern, gilt by Yarwood.

599x Imperial chrome green ground, pencil celeste tadpoles in 4 compartments (3 inside cup) & a yellow leaf.

600x The same as 546x new printed coloured flowers instead of green sprigs.

601x The same as 600x, all green instead of gold.

602x Same as 584x green line instead of blue & gold edge, slap down handle, no foot line.

603x Pink ground, compartments with pencil celeste tadpoles, 4 in saucer, 3 in cup, star centre.

604x Same as 2019 new gilding, green instead of blue ground.

606x Japan.

607x Flowers the same as 585x with a small sprig in the centre, dentelle edge.

608x Flowers the same as 588x with a small sprig in the centre, trailing sprigging around border.

609x Pencil celeste tadpoles & dots, 3-leaf clover twigging & similar sprig centre.

610x Fawn ground border, dot & twigging inside, large spray of apple blossom centre.

611x The same as above, pink ground.

612x Thistle the same as 530x with no gold on.

613x Thistle printed in mouse colour.

614x Sea weed printed in mouse colour with edge the same as 613x.

615x Grass printed in blue with edge the same as 613x.

616x 3 apple blossom sprigs.

617x The same as 585x with a small additional sprig in the centre.

618x Grey ground border, twigging either side of a wavy inner line, landscape centre.

619x Green curving panels, 3 flowers & hanging spray of leaves, leaf sprig centre.

620x The same as 619x on stone colour ground.

621x Dessert, hawthorn blossom printed border, star centre.

622x Dessert, 6 groups of printed & coloured flower sprigs around.

623x Dessert, trailing spriggy edge, 4 sprigs of printed apple blossoms, coloured in.

624x Printed & coloured flower, 3 trailing sprigs round the rim, large group round centre, shaded strong with rose colour & the new *Imperial*!!! chrome red.

625x As above, ornamented with chrome red.

626x Mouse coloured Fountain Birds & gilt, no edge. The Fountain pattern.

627x Is green fountain, gilt as 626x.

628x

629x Narrow green bars, 24 round saucer 18 inside cup, small green sprig centre.

630x The same as 629x in the green only, no gold.

631x The same as 610x, glaze kiln blue instead of fawn ground.

632x The same as 610x impl. chrome green for. . .

633x The same as 610x stone colour for. . .

634x The same as 633x but sprig in bottom as 500x instead of flowers.

635x Green & gold alternating zig-zags, 32 in saucer, 24 in cup, very small sprig centre.

636x The same as 635x in Imperial chrome red instead of green.

637x Dessert, the same as 635x done in rose colour instead of green, 48 round.

638x Blue border, twigging either side, twigging star centre.

639x Maroon border, leaf gilding, bird on twigging in centre.

640x New col'd Slows (?) flowers, blue border coloured flowers & leaves.

641x Pale border panels outlined with leaves & honeysuckle-like flowers containing birds on nest, butterfly centre.

642x Green Fountain Gilt.

643x 3 compartments, a different

butterfly in each, 2 compartments inside the cup, butterfly centre.

644x 3 compartments, different flowers in each, 2 compartments inside the cup.

645x Stone colour ground, hanging leaf twigging.

646x Barbed wire border Fountain pattern printed in green.

647x Dark blue border, hanging leafage with pencil celeste leaves, flower spray centre.

648x Edge the same as 612x, star in the bottom.

649x Dessert, col. printed flowers.

650x Table pattern per Mr. May. Note pattern on dish 1462 in Dyson Perrins museum.

651x As 565x only celeste instead of blue.

652x The same as 538x printed in mouse colour, new edge & no foot line.

653x The same as 538x with new edge on Gloster shape.

654x Dark biscuit blue, 8 bunches of grapes & vine leaves round, 6 inside cup, landscape centre.

655x Dark biscuit blue border, panels of barbed wire, & flying twigs, flower spray centre.

656x Ground border, edged with yellow flowers, flower centre.

657x Flying twigs and double shaded leaves, red dots.

658x Strawberries (blue) and leaves, twiggy star centre.

659x The same as 650x with gold on the edge only.

660x Mouse col. thistle, gilt, with a line on the edge of the same colour, instead of gold.

661x Leaf edge, maroon leaves, twiggy star centre with some maroon leaves.

662x Yellow leaves edging maroon ground, small sprig centre.

663x Imperial chrome green leaf edge, 3 roses & 3 sprigs round, sprig centre.

664x Printed & coloured flowers round border & centre, purple blue &

665x   yellow.

665x   Alternating panels of biscuit blue and straw with twigging, star centre.

666x   As 664x, rose, green & yellow.

667x   Straw coloured edge, maroon zig-zag panels, small sprig centre.

668x   Pale ground 3 birds on twigging round saucer, 2 in cup, butterfly centre.

669x   The same as 670x with flowers in the centre instead of gold butterfly, in dark blue.

670x   Vine leaves and grapes on mouse border, twigging inside, butterfly centre.

671x   Green border with twigging & fawn flower, flower spray centre.

672x   Green border, grapes & half-shaded leaves, butterfly on twigging centre.

673x   Thistle the same as 530x painted with purple & green instead of blue & green, gold edge only.

674x   Printed roses in mouse colour with edge the same as 673x, no foot line.

675x   Printed pattern gilded by Yarwood, stripe & wavy line border.

676x   3 coloured sprigs round, small sprig centre.

677x   Notched edge, mouse colour printed flowers round, large printed flower centre.

678x   The same as 610x, soft blue ground.

679x   The same as 610x, stone colour ground.

680x   Double row of flowers round, single flower centre.

681x   The same as 675x, no edge & no gilding.

682x   The same as 680x, no gold.

683x   The same as 676x, no gold.

684x   Dark blue Laurustinus, edge as 612x.

685x   The same as 676x, no gold.

686x   The same as 680x, no gold.

687x   Mouse coloured print of whorls, circle of coloured-in flowers round rim, similar centre, with trees.

688x   As 687, no gold, all in colour.

689x   As above, blue ground.

690x   As 689x, all colour.

691x   Same as 689x, green ground instead of blue.

692x   Same as 691x, all colour, no gold.

693x   Twigging round & in centre.

694x   Blue printed whorls & flowers round border, flowers & tree, twigging centre.

695x   Dessert, edge the same as 661x large & small sprays of snowdrops.

696x   Same as 629x in blue.

697x   Same as 624x, no gold, old red instead of orange red.

698x   Same as 665x in stone.

699x   Compartments of twigging and butterflies, butterfly centre.

700x   Outside border same as 699x, flower spray centre.

701x   Pencil celeste stripes, 20 round saucer, 15 in cup, sprig centre.

702x   Groups of weed twigging & bells (pattern crossed out).

703x   Leafy twigging with butterflies, sprig centre.

704x   Imperial chrome green border, panels of twigging, coloured sprig centre.

705x   Printed & coloured flowers round, centre of printed & coloured Chinese house & flowers.

706x   Dessert, edge the same as 661x done with torque green in place of the maroon, 3 apple blossom sprigs coloured in the centre.

707x   Gilding the same as 700x, sprig centre.

708x   Gloster edge, green dotted border, pattern like 705x.

709x   Mouse coloured gown pattern, leaves inside, sprig centre.

710x   3 green triangular panels, twigging, butterfly centre.

711x   Enamel blue crossed stripes border, small sprig centre.

712x   The same as 711x painted in chrome green.

713x   Stone ground, outside border same

as 699x, leaf & twigging inside, small sprig centre.

714x   Compartments of blue & flowers, vine leaves & grapes inside, butterfly centre.

715x   Horn shaped panels, twigging, small flower spray centre.

716x   All over flowers printed with maroon, dry orange & gilding.

717x   The same as 716x with no colour in the compartments round the edge.

718x   Small blue flowers with gold sprigs, gilt by Jones.

719x   The same as 710x painted with Victoria (?) blue instead of green & sprig in centre.

720x   Radiating stripes in No. 1 Salmon ground glaze kiln colour, twigging inside.

721x   Compartments outlined in Victoria blue underglaze containing leaf spray, small sprig centre.

722x   3 blue outlined rectangular panels of 2 sizes, containing blue green and red sprigs, similar centre, colours under the glaze.

723x   Plant dessert, grounding blue done on the glaze.

724x   Glaze kiln colours, Victoria blue & yellow green, sprigs.

725x   Large & small sprigs, blue green & red underglaze colours.

726x   Same as 722x no gold.

727x   Same as 724x no gold.

728x   Gloster shape, Victoria blue underglaze around border, hanging sprigs inside, sprig centre.

729x   Radiating stripes in Original Lilac glaze kiln colour for ground, see 720x for other parts of the gilding.

730x   Victoria blue underglaze, vine leaves & grapes in panels & centre.

731x   3 compartments of barbed wire, No. 2 Salmon glaze kiln colour, landscape centre.

732x   Blue crossing lines & dots, maroon border inside, sprig centre.

733x   Gloster shape, panels of flowers alternating with thistles, Victoria blue under the glaze, coloured sprig centre.

734x   Pale panels with vine leaves & grapes, alternating with coloured flowers, grapes and vine leaves centre.

735x   Glaze kiln lilac No. 2 panels with birds on twigging, 3 compartments of single flowers, sprig centre.

736x   Glaze kiln Salmon No. 2 ground borders with birds on twigging varied, compartments of flowers, sprig centre.

737x   Embossed edge, Brunswick Emb'd, edging in blue, revolving star centre.

738x   Blue green border, printed apple blossom sprays coloured in.

739x   Green band (?) lines &c.

740x   Brunswick (?) Emb'd, small sprigs round, large flower spray centre.

741x   Dessert see White.

742x   Dessert, hanging vine leaves and blue & green sprigs round.

743x   Double green stripe & gold.

744x   Meandering shaded border in blue, done by dusting.

745x   The same as 744x, no gold.

747x   Like 744x ultramarine, and small sprigs.

748x   The same as 742x, barbed wire border.

749x   Lilac No. 2 border, panels of sprigging, twigging inside, coloured bird on sprigging centre.

750x   Gloster shape, glaze kiln ultramarine blue border, hanging leaf sprigs inside, flower centre.

751x   Wavy panels in Victoria blue, containing printed and coloured flowers, sprig centre.

752x   Breakfast pattern, ultramarine blue wheel spoke pattern, 50 spokes round saucer, 40 inside cup, star centre.

753x   The same as 723x with landscape instead of plants (words crossed out)

754x   As 744x, panels of printed and

coloured sprigs, ultramarine blue.

755x Ultramarine the same as 754x with no gold except on the edge, coloured printed sprigs.

756x Table pattern, the same as 754x with the blue only touched, barbed wire border.

757x Outer & inner ultramarine borders, flower sprigs & leaves in between, sprig centre.

758x Gloster shape, lilac ground with flowers and leaves, compartments of coloured sprigs.

759x Large & small sprays of printed & coloured flowers & butterflies, with gold.

760x The same as 758x with ultramarine ground and single line done over the edge on plain suss. . . (?).

761x Inner & outer ultramarine with trailing sprigs, single roses in panels in between, sprig centre.

762x Modelled border edge with green, No. 2 Salmon ground panels with sprigging alternating with flowers, star centre.

763x Table plate, 100 double green stripes round, printed & coloured flower sprigs inside.

764x Same pattern as 723x only with landscape instead of plants.

765x Same pattern as 728x only flowers in bottom instead of star.

766x Gold & Ultramarine blue stripes crossing on border, 24 round saucer, 18 inside cup (breakfast shape has 26 and 20 respectively), sprig centre.

767x Dessert by Yarwood.

768x Is 758x with salmon No. 2 instead of lilac.

769x Rose ground, raspberries & leaves & bees, insect & sprig centre.

770x The same as 769x no ground & no inner border Bronze.

771x Blackberry border & butterfly in the middle, no gilding except the edge, mouse colour.

772x Antwerp blue 18 stripes with arches in between, star centre.

773x Antwerp blue leaf shaped panels,

gilded sprigs a little varied in each, compartments of flowers, star centre.

774x Modelled edge, almost same as 772x.

775x Gloster shape, as 774x but with sprigging, flower spray centre by Stan Wood.

776x The same as 769x, no ground & no edge.

777x Bourbon sprig done in green, flowers dark green & leaves light green (French Sprig ?).

778x Same as 771x in Bronze

779x Same as 771x in blue

780x Same as 771x green

781x Same as 770x in mouse

782x Same as 770x in green

783x Same as 770x in blue

784x Same as 783x, no edge, blue

785x Same as 784x in green

786x Same as 785x in mouse

787x Same as 786x in Bronze

788x No. 2 Salmon ground glaze kiln colour, 16 trellis stripes round saucer, 12 inside cup, sprigging inside.

789x Imperial green & gold, trellis & sprigging, star centre.

790x The same as 789x with biscuit blue ground.

791x No. 2 Salmon ground, trellis & sprigging, sprig centre.

792x Same as 549x in dark blue ground.

793x Same as 792x, star as 1850, no flowers.

794x Large & small sprigs alternating, small sprig centre.

795x Same as 794x edges as 612x.

796x Edge the same as 612x with star in the bottom.

797x The same as 743x without gold.

798x The same as 549x biscuit blue ground (crossed out).

799x Enamel, lilac flower, chrome green leaf, geranium.

800x Biscuit blue & green, thistle, no gold.

801x The same as 752x no gold.

802x Blue stripes & gold, coloured printed sprigs.

803x Flowers, gold edge, lightly gilt sprigs.

804x The same as 1849, maroon edge instead of orange.

805x Gloster shape, Antwerp blue ground, leaves & sprigs, flower centre.

806x Same as 805x with No. 5 green ground instead of blue.

807x Blue convolvulus, edge gilded the same as blackberry, no foot line.

808x Modelled edge, convolvulus printed in Antwerp blue.

809x The same as 808x, no edge.

810x Brous (?) print, whorls & flowers, No. 5 green, Antwerp blue, chrome green, yellow green & yellow, done by Mrs. May.

811x Brouse ground, inner & outer borders of trefoils, coloured in printed flowers & pineapple pattern, Antwerp blue, rose colour, green & yellow green.

812x The same as 811x, printed in Antwerp blue, the flowers in the outside & inner ornamental rings painted with No. 5 green instead of Antwerp blue.

813x Gloster shape, Antwerp blue stripes & arches, sprig centre.

814x Gloster shape, Antwerp blue borders reserving large double leaf & small flower heads, flower centre.

815x Wild flowers, dessert.

816x Same as 815x no gold.

817x Whorl & flowers border, flowers & tree centre, printed in Bronze & coloured in.

818x The same as 817x, no gilt, except gold line on the edge.

819x Table pattern printed chintz-bronze, gilt etc.

820x 3 harebell-like sprigs round & 1 in centre.

821x The same as 670x biscuit blue ground & flower in the bottom instead of the fly.

822x The same as 610x biscuit blue ground.

823x Printed & coloured flowers scattered all over, Antwerp blue, azure blue, green, pink & yellow. (Large version of Challie pattern.)

824x Gloster, mouse weed, edge same as blackberry 778-779-780x, gold.

826x Blue vine, Broseley shape, gilt.

827x Antwerp blue stripes & arches with sprigging, bird on sprigging in centre.

828x Wild flower, printed in Antwerp blue with rose colour & edge, the same as 774x.

829x The same as 828x printed in Bronze.

830x Wild flower in Antwerp blue, only the edge gilt.

831x Wild flower printed in bronze, blossom in Antwerp blue, edge as 774x.

832x Same as 280x in Antwerp blue.

833x As 827x, no orange, flower spray in centre.

834x Challie pattern printed in Antwerp blue.

836x Large version of Challie pattern printed in Antwerp blue.

837x The same as 813x, flowers in the centre instead of gold sprig.

838x Antwerp blue radiating bars, large ragged leaf & sprigging, star centre.

839x Jigsaw border, non-interlocking, leaves around & in centre.

840x The same as 808x printed in bronze.

841x The same as 808x printed in mouse.

842x The same as 808x printed in green.

843x Biscuit blue ground, gilt foliage and three gold scroll pads, jigsaw border.

844x Gold scrollwork border hung with leafage & weed sprigs in gold.

846x Gold scrollwork and trailing flower border, 3 compartments of flower sprays in colour and Imperial chrome green.

847x Border as 846x but without coloured sprigs.

848x Biscuit blue ground, cream & gold

rim, gilt foliate and weed, painted botanical centre and inside cups.

849x Biscuit blue ground reserving 4 border flower panels, painted coloured flower centre.

850x Same pattern as 876x without any ground (white and gold only).

851x Scroll edge in blue & gold, centre botanical sprays.

852x K. Salmon ground No. 2, gold scrollwork border as 846x, flowers in the centre.

853x Stone drab ground, gold scrollwork & foliage, jigsaw rim, flower centres.

854x The same as 853x, no flowers but gold sprigs.

855x Azure blue flowerheads and gold scrollwork border as 846x.

856x Bronze vase printed pattern with edge the same as 771x.

857x Printed all over wild flowers & leaves in bronze.

858x Bronze printed convolvulus, the edge only gilt the same as 808x.

859x Mouse Convolvulus edge only, same as 807x.

860x Green Convolvulus edge only, as 807x.

861x The same as 758x Dark biscuit blue ground & simple line done over the edge.

862x Green printed wild flowers with gold edge the same as 774x.

863x Antwerp blue and cream striped ground, gold scrollwork & flower panels, star centres.

864x The same as 769x inner gold border no ground, printed in biscuit blue ground.

865x Azure blue cornucopia panels with fawn & gold leaves and gilt foliage, central coloured bouquets and flower sprays in purple & pink.

866x The same as 855x dark biscuit blue stars with orange leaves.

867x Fawn ground, gilt shell edging and vine sprigs, star centre.

868x Fawn ground, gilt with vines, 3 border panels and centre colour printed flowers.

869x As 865x, flower sprigs in blue.

870x The same as 869x with orange instead of blue and no orange on the leaves.

871x As 869x without flowers and with landscape centre.

872x The same as 871x no orange on the leaves, with gold leaf sprigs in the centre instead of landscapes.

873x Fawn colour ground gilt scrollwork and views, 3 panels, col. printed flowers.

874x The same as 853x dark biscuit blue ground with sprigs in centre.

875x Fawn colour ground, gilt whorl scrolls and vines, vine centres.

876x Same as 853x with No. 2 Salmon colour ground & leaf sprigs in centre instead of flowers.

877x Orange ground cornucopia compartments, gold leaves and foliage.

878x Fawn colour stripes, 24 round the saucer, 18 inside the cup, gold scroll edge, vine centre.

879x Antwerp blue and fawn stripes, gilt foliage and shell edging, flower painted panels, star centre.

880x Gold whorl scrolls & foliage, sprigs with matt blue & imperial green.

881x Dessert, the same as 878x, spring green, 22 round.

882x Convolvulus printed in dark blue all over.

883x The same as 882x printed in mouse colour, no edge.

884x Fawn leaves and gold whorl scrollwork, ground of Azure blue and bronze trellis, flower centre.

885x As 884x, trellis with star patterns printed in bronze and Azure blue, flower centres and sprigs.

886x Azure blue stripes with flowers and gilt.

887x Fawn band & star centre, gold scroll edge.

888x Challie in Impl. Blue, edge as 808x.

889x Challie printed in bronze and filled in.

890x Hawthorn enamel 352x edge.

891x Gilding same as 700x with views.
892x Gold edge on white same as 778x.
893x Same as 854x white & gold.
894x Gilding same as 669x Dark blue ground instead of stone & bird instead of flowers.
895x Blue bradd (?) border (later crossed out and written 'error').
896x Biscuit blue ground gold festooned grape, grape centre.
897x Challie filled in on Gloster, shaped edge as 807x.
899x French marigold & gold sprig.
900x Biscuit blue ground, dessert, the same as 670x, bird with landscape in the centre.
901x New Dresden shape biscuit blue ground, white panels, printed Dresden sprigs, fill'd in in colours, bald & flute gilt slight.
902x No. 2 Salmon colour ground glaze kiln, gilt grape and weed, colour printed sprigs, see 905x.
905x Azure blue ground on the shell edge, gold whorl, scrolls, colour printed flower sprigs & insects.
906x Edge the same as 905x, colour printed flowers insects and blue and gilt weed.
908x Edge the same as 905x with additions of flower festoons, colour printed flowers.
909x Queen's plain shape, lilac No. 2 ground, gilt whorl scrolls and foliage, colour printed flowers, flies & festoons.
910x Queen's plain colour printed sprigs & insects, gold scroll border and gilt weed.
911x Lilac No. 2 border with gilt jigsaw, scrollwork & weed, colour printed flowers and flies and panels.
912x Bronze hawthorn ground gold whorl scrolls and leafage, flower sprays.
913x Azure blue and gold stripes, jigsaw border, colour printed flower centre, Sussex shape.
914x Colour printed sprigs and insects, single gold edge 2 large sprigs and 5 small ones inside the cup.
916x Printed colour sprigs as 910x, dark

biscuit blue vine and scroll border.
917x Brown printed foliage and diaper borders filled in in colours, azure blue rim.
918x Colour printed flowers and insects all over, single line edge.
919x Stone coloured dessert pattern, stone colour ground, gadroon and leaf edging, colour printed flowers and festoons.
920x Same as 919x only Salmon ground.
921x Green and gold by Thos. White, whorl scroll and leaf border.
922x Bronze hawthorn ground and flowers, gilt scrolls, weed and flowerheads, colour printed flowers, insects and weed. The table plate has one large sprig.
923x Same pattern as 909x, Salmon ground instead of lilac.
924x Table pattern see Stephens.
925x Dark blue Challie & gold, see J S.
926x Same pattern as 909x Dark blue ground instead of lilac.
927x Bronze hawthorn ground, border panels & sprigs.
928x Challie pattern printed in dark blue filled in in colours.
929x Azure blue stripes, stone ground, flower centre.
931x Challie printed in mouse colour & coloured with red, purple etc.
932x Green and gold whorl scroll and foliate border, weed centre.
933x Lilac ground gilt with vines and weed, panels of fancy birds, insects and weeds.
934x Blue and grey stripes gilt with foliate festoons, leaf and weed centre.
934x Blue and grey stripes gilt with foliate festoons, leaf and weed centre.
935x Gold gadroon edge with whorl scrolls, leaves and vines, weed centre.
936x As 935x but with pale blue ground, landscape panels and centre.
937x Pale blue-grey ground, gilt C scrolls, fawn leaves, inner jigsaw

border and weed centre.

938x   Same border as 935x in pale blue and gold, colour printed flowers, insects and weed.

939x   Same pattern as 937x only salmon ground and no orange on the leaves.

940x   Same as 909x Dark Calx blue ground.

941x   C scroll and leaf border with fawn and two-tone blue grounds, flower panels & weed centre.

942x   Bronze blackberry ground, bronze line with gold stripe.

943x   Simple gadroon edging and central weed.

944x   Blue-printed convolvulus in Antwerp blue with gilt edge & handle as 943x.

945x   As 936x with fawn and biscuit grounds, flower panels.

946x   Azure blue stripes and gold bars, alternate printed coloured sprigs and insects, 12 stripes on saucers.

948x   Brown line edge with gold stripes, printed coloured sprigs, Kent fluted shape.

949x   Cobalt blue convolvulus in Queen's plain, edge & handle same as 943x.

950x   C scroll and leaf border edging, colour printed sprigs & festoons, gilt insects and weed outside.

951x   Kent fluted shape, dark biscuit blue sprigs with leaves and tendrils, gold line edge.

952x   Mouse vase, edge same as 774x.

953x   Queen shape, azure blue stain edge with two gold lines and gold weed sprig in bottom.

954x   Colbalt blue blackberry on Queen's plain, edge & handle same as 943x.

955x   Antwerp blue blackberry on Queen's Plain, dessert pattern edge same as 943x.

956x   Gold C scrolls and leafy tendrils, three sections with 12 balls in azure blue.

957x   Stone colour ground with gilt C scrolls, leaves and grapes,

coloured flower prints and insects in panels.

958x   G.K. Salmon ground, gold C scrolls, leaves and weed, Jigsaw inner border, weed centre.

959x   Gilding the same as 958x, lilac ground flower painted centre.

960x   The same as 958x, Dark biscuit blue ground, the leaves orange, landscape in the bottom.

961x   G.K. Salmon ground, blue enamel convolvulus sprays, black leaves.

962x   The same as 951x mouse colour.

963x   The same as 951x, bronze-printed.

964x   The same as 921x with plants instead of sprigs in the centre.

965x   Azure blue stripes with orange leaves and gold whorl scrolls and foliage, central painted specimen.

966x   The same as 905x with shell edging in gold.

967x   Biscuit blue and Azure blue checker ground & enamel-kiln fawn border, landscape panels, gold weed centre.

968x   Gilding the same as 967x, checker ground in stone colour and Antwerp blue, flower panels.

969x   Biscuit blue border with fawn and gold leaves, colour printed sprigs and insects with gold weed.

970x   Deep blue border with fawn leaves & gold shell edging, gold foliate festoons and centre.

971x   The same as 970x with the blue plain, no leaves on.

972x   Gold scroll edge and vines, bat- printed landscape panels filled in in colour.

973x   Elaborate design with biscuit blue, azure blue and salmon grounds, paeony and rock panels in bronze and puce.

974x   Printed vase in mouse colour, the highlights done in gold, centre sprays.

975x   'The same as 951x printed in bronze' crossed out and replaced by 'Gilt border of shell and scroll motifs hung with foliage, central star'.

976x   Scattered flower sprays in mauves & Imperial Chrome Green, gold edge.

977x   Scattered sprays of hanging flowers in pink and green, no edge.

978x   Challie in grey with blue and puce wash.

979x   Scattered green and mauve sprays, edge same as 944x.

980x   Border fawn & gold leaf & C scrolls, coloured flower prints, central weed.

981x   Same as 921x. Plants instead of gold sprig in bottom.

982x   Green sprig, Lee's Embossed, see C. Richards, same as 976x no gold.

983x   Same pattern as 970x only stone instead of blue.

984x   Same pattern as 970x only Salmon instead of blue.

985x   Mouse convolvulus gilt as 808x, gold line, on New Punch shape.

986x   Mouse convolvulus on Queen's Plain, edge only as 943x commonly called dessert edge.

987x   Bronze convolvulus on Queen's Plain, edge as 943x.

988x   The same as 951x, Mouse colour, no edge.

989x   Antwerp leaf ground, gold scroll edging to panels, painted sprig centre, the gilding slighter altogether than this is given J E.

990x   Printed leaf Ground in blue, blue leaf diaper, Gentian (?) leaf new blue, gold edge, central coral wreath in gold, coloured flower centre.

991x   The same as 990x with landscape in the centre to 1″ of gold.

992x   Gold edge and central wreath of weed, weed centre.

993x   As 992x but with blue leaf ground border, flower centre same as centre of 989x.

994x   The same as 951x and the gilding but without the gold edge and printed in bronze.

995x   The same as 909x with the ground done with glaze kiln grey.

996x   The same as 937x glaze kiln grey ground.

997x   The same as 945x glaze kiln grey ground.

998x   Same as 951x but printed in bronze.

999x   Antwerp ground leaf on Kent shape gt. by Mrs. Donnel (? Daniel).

1000x   Antwerp ground leaf gilt as 999x only on French shape.

1001x   Same as 1000x only bronze.

1002x   Queen's Emboss'd Dessert white ware gilt edge only as 944x.

1003x   Azure blue ground with bronze leaf, gilt feather edge and vines with scroll panels, vines round outside of cup.

1004x   Same pattern as 1003x bronze ground, G.K. (glaze kiln) Orange Leaf.

1005x   Azure blue ground gilt vines with G.K. Orange leaves, white panels with gold foliage.

1006x   Same pattern as 1005x bronze pale instead of blue.

1007x   Feather-like leaf whorls with panels of flowers and weed, fox glove on front of cup, pale bronze ground.

1008x   Same as 1007x with Azure blue ground instead of pale bronze.

1009x   Pale bronze whorl panels and orange leaves, gilt with trailing vines.

1011x   Azure blue ground with leaves and flowers.

1012x   Same as 1011x Mouse colour GK orange blossom and landscape.

1013x   Same as 1012x blue printed GK orange blossom and group of slight flowers.

1014x   Antwerp blue and gold leaf border with gold leaf sprigs.

1015x   Same as 1014x in Imperial Chrome green.

1016x   Fine double stripes in Imperial Chrome green, 48 round saucer 36 round cup.

1017x   Same as 944x in white.

1018x   Antwerp blue grass edge only as 807x.

1019x   No. 4. Antwerp blue printed leaf –

slight gold sprays underneath – French edge.

1020x   Dark blue sprig with gold edge the same as 990x.

1021x   The same as 989x printed in mouse colour.

1022x   Border of green band edged with gold lines.

1023x   As 1019x bronze.

1024x   As 1019x mouse.

1026x   Green ground wide border edged gold weed, centre painted flower spray.

1027x   Pale cream or fawn ground, gilt trailing weed and starlike flowerheads, feather edge.

1028x   Weed with blue green dots.

1029x   . . .k (? dark) blue, blackberry edg'd as 990x

1030x   All over leaf and weed pattern, vermilion edged

1031x   Azure blue band and line with foot line.

1032x   Azure blue edge, coloured print flower sprigs and dotted all over pattern.

1033x   Antwerp blue printed leaf all over the saucer and outside the cup, 2 lines inside the cup.

1034x   Weed(?) border, hanging weed, weed and berry centre.

1035x   Coloured printed sprigs in panels, vine leaf and weed pattern.

1036x   Wide border, hanging weed inner border and outside cup, weed centre.

1037x   Weed border, flowers and red sprigs, flower centre and weed sprig.

1038x   Hanging weed and leaf border, weeds surrounding centre of Men's Flowers.

1039x   Brown and azure blue leaf and weed border, weed centre.

1040x   Azure blue weed and leaf border, weed outside.

1041x   Weed and coloured flowers border, flower centre.

1042x   The same as 951x without the edge.

1043x   Green printed vine gilt.

1044x   Tea pattern, maroon ground, spotted with gold.

1051x   Blue border as 1052x, vase of flowers centre surrounded by weed, weed outside cup.

1052x   G K Primrose, dark biscuit blue ground, 5 large compartments around rim with weed, central leafage star.

1053x   Antwerp blue printed Kent sprigs, Queen's embossed.

1054x   Japan pattern, dark biscuit blue, G K bronze, yellow, green blue, green and red, 3 compartments in the saucer, 2 inside the cup.

1056x   Japan dessert as 1054x.

1057x   Printed flowers in mouse colour, the same as 1070x.

1058x   Ground surrounded by weed, 3 compartments of flowers, 2 inside cup.

1059x   20 dark blue biscuit sprigs, 16 inside the cup, weed in centre, shoulder line, no foot line.

1060x   The same flower a little raised in each of 6 compartments, 6 pointed star shaped centre surrounding flower.

1061x   Dark biscuit blue stripes, a flower sprig and a fly alternately printed and coloured, weed centre.

1062x   5 flower sprigs alternating with weed, large flower centre, printed in Antwerp blue, touched in red.

1063x   4 flower sprigs round saucer, 3 in cup, small sprig centre printed in mouse colour, dot and berry edge.

1064x   Same as 1063x printed in bronze but not gilt.

1065x   Same as 1063x printed in Antwerp blue edge and gold sprigs.

1066x   Same as 990x printed in mouse colour.

1067x   3 large sprigs of flowers and small sprig centre, edge same as 1063x.

1068x   Same as 1067x edged as 1053x.

1069x   Same as 1071x dark biscuit blue

band.

1070x Printed flowers same as 1063x, flowers not gilt, border printed in bronze.

1071x Blue band on border, scattered flower sprigs, outside cup same as saucer.

1072x Printed flowers in bronze, the same as 1063x, no gold.

1073x Fawn ground, gadrooned edge, flowers sprigs and weed.

1074x Large numbers of scattered flowers, printed and coloured in, Red and rose colour G K (glaze kiln), Antwerp G K, printed in dark blue.

1075x Flower sprays and sprigs printed in Antwerp blue, slight gilding.

1076x Gadroon edge with gilt dashes, azure blue border with gilt vines, painted with pink flower sprays.

1077x Azure blue arcaded border with panels of pink flowers and gilt foliage, gilt festoons and flowers centre.

1078x Convolvulus printed in mouse colour with puce high-lights.

1079x Antwerp blue stripes with gilt dashes and gold vine centre.

1080x Azure blue panels as 1077x, grey leaves and gold vines instead of painted flowers.

1082x Dark biscuit blue border edged in gold printed insects and sprigs.

1083x The same as 1070x printed in G K (glaze kiln) Green.

1084x The same as 1070 printed in mouse. (This entry crossed out.)

1085x The same as 1080x dark biscuit instead of Antwerp blue.

1086x Convolvulus printed in Antwerp blue, gold scroll border, Table pattern.

1087x Dark biscuit blue alternating panels, the same convolvulus like flower a little raised in each, similar in each.

1088x Printed weed in mouse colour, edged as 1070x.

1089x Large and small sprigs of

convolvulus, Imperial Chrome and the yellow green is Imperial mixed with common yellow, 2 sprigs inside the cup.

1090x Antwerp blue underglaze and primrose ditto, leaves and weed, 8 round saucer, 6 inside cup.

1091x Queen's plain, primrose ground, 3 compartments of landscapes (or flowers) round saucer, 2 inside cup.

1092x Glaze kiln grey ground and primrose, 3 compartments of flies, 2 inside the cup and a hare in the bottom (or may be game birds).

1093x Queen embossed, primrose ground with leaves and weed, landscape in centre.

1094x Border pattern of cross hatching, crossed out.

1095x Same as 1061x Antwerp blue stripe without the printed coloured sprigs, gold only.

1096x Queen's Plain, pink band (for dessert brown), 3 compartments, same coloured flower in each, same gilding as 1076x.

1097x Same as 1060x on the Kent shape and the pattern done outside.

1098x Blue scalloped border and slight gilding.

1099x Printed in Antwerp blue the same as 1062x, scratched edge, the edge only gilt.

1100x Same as 1063x the printed sprigs not gilt.

1101x Large primrose coloured leaves forming 3 panels with flies and blue and gold weed.

1102x Same as 1063x printed in slate colour, the printed sprigs not gilt, scrat (?) edge.

1103x Printed sprigs in Antwerp blue the same as 1063x no gilding.

1104x Same as 1019x printed in slate colour.

1105x Same as dessert 1062x in slate.

1106x Same as 836x not filled in with blue.

1107x Same as 1076x with plants in centre.

1108x Tea pattern sprigs, same as 1063x with the difference of scratched edge, printed in slate colour.

1109x Leaf ground mouse, 6 flower headed sprigs, 4 of each round.

1110x All over leaves and dotted trailing stems printed in Antwerp blue.

1111x Same as 921x done with the same blue as in Plant dessert instead of green.

1112x Flowers and weed sprigs, edged the same as 1111x.

1113x Same as 1091, slight landscapes.

1114x Azure blue panels with vine leaves, 4 of each.

1115x 7 compartments of flowers, dark biscuit blue centre shape surrounding weed, colouring of the flowers as 1087x.

1116x Gadroon edge, large flowers and leaves in dark biscuit blue and bronze, yellow green, jet black and red.

1117x Same as 1027x with slight landscapes.

1118x Same as 1116x Table pattern edged only with lustre.

1119x Same as 1101x, 2 compartments in the saucer and 2 inside cup.

1120x Slate colour Kent sprigs (hanging weed) 10 round.

1121x Painted with blue the same as 946x with gold edge and no flowers.

1122x Plain Sussex shape, 9 stylised green flower heads round saucer, 8 round outside and inside of cup, green star centre.

1123x Same as 1063x printed in slate colour with gold sprigs the same but printed sprigs, gilt slighter, scrat edge.

1124x Queen's shape, dark blue fibre 2 drag line edge.

1125x Same as 976x (on table ware with small sprigs extra).

1126x Same as 882x printed in Antwerp blue and edged as 1070x.

1127x Grey border with weed, landscape centre.

1128x Yellow ground between 2 blue bands, blue leaves 3 groups round, flower group centre.

1129x Drab and cane panels, 8 compartments, weed centre.

1130x Shell surrounded by weed on yellow ground, weed star centre same as 1129x.

1131x Same as 1127, no ground and leaf with trailing vine in centre instead of landscape.

1132x Not drawn.

1133x 8 compartments alternating blue and pale with weed, large plant centre (passion flower shown in book).

1134x Same as 1128x but weedy leaf centre.

1135x 8 compartments round saucer, 6 in cup, slight weed, weed and leaf centre, drab.

1136x Slate coloured vine leaves, 4 round saucer, 4 inside cup.

1137x Slate and primrose panels with slight weed, 8 in saucer, 6 inside cup, weed right round outside.

1138x Grey and primrose border with vine leaves, vine and sprig centre.

1139x Grey shell on primrose ground and weed.

1140x Weed and berry sprig, 8 large round saucer, 7 inside cup.

1141x Dessert pattern, slate flowers.

1142x Same as 1135x grey instead of drab, sprigs in bottom, same as 1129x.

1143x 20 green stripes alternating with weed, weed centre.

1144x Queen's shape slate coloured weed same as 1141x.

1147x Large hanging weed over pale ground, fly centre.

1148x Queen's Plain, 2 large and 2 small flowers sprigs inside the cup with small in the bottom, 2 large and 1 small outside the cup.

1149x 3 large coloured sprigs and 3 small, small sprig centre, 3 sprigs outside cup.

1150x 3 sprigs round saucer and inside cup, one of them being heartsease, small sprig outside.

1151x Large and small red, green and yellow sprigs.

1152x Printed weed in slate and inside cup.

1153x Same as 1152x, printed in bronze, gold edge only.

1154x 3 compartments, a different flower in each, red berried weed over a ground.

1155x Grounded as 1133x and gilt as 1135x.

1156x Pink border and berried weed.

1157x Yellow border, flower springs alternating with berried weed.

1158x Blue border 3 sprays of roses, 2 inside cup, berried weed, weed outside border.

1159x Yellow border, berried weed, 3 compartments of flowers in saucer and 2 in cup, outside border same as 1158x.

1160x Stone colour ground, gilt the same as 1159x.

1161x Pink ground, hanging weed, 6 compartments round saucer and inside cup, weed outside.

1162x Same as 1161x with stone ground.

1163x Same as dessert 1157 without sprigs in bottom, 3 sprigs in saucer and 2 in•cup, outside border as 1158x.

1164x Same gilding and ground as dessert 1127x, group of flowers instead of landscape.

1165x Yellow ground, 13 sprigs of weed round, landscape centre.

1166x Wild flower dessert, gilt and line, Queen's Plain, 3 small sprigs round.

1167x Scrolled leaf on yellow ground with weed, floral centre.

1168x Weed and leaves all over printed in slate colour, cup outside and inside.

1169x Same as 1127x only no ground, white and gold.

1170x Mouse, fountain pattern, blackberry

edge.

1171x Same gilding as 1168x, printed in mouse colour on Queen's Plain.

1172x Same as 1168x, gilt only Scratched.

1173x Same gilding as 1091x, flowers in panel.

1174x Antwerp fibre on Queen's.

1175x Slate fibre on Queen's, edge as 1174x.

1176x Bronze fibre on Queen's, scratch edge as 944x.

1177x Same as 1063 in slate colour, no gilding on the sprigs.

1178x The same as 1148x with gold sprig in place of the small sprig, ring handle.

1179x Same as 1178x, leaf ring.

1180x Dark biscuit blue ground, panels of landscape, tulip and weed centre.

1181x Same as 1127x, dark biscuit blue ground and flowers.

1182x Same as 1032x, dessert green ground on Queen's Plain edged wavy gold.

1183x Dark biscuit blue ground and large leaves.

1184x Dark biscuit blue trees with red flowers.

1185x Dark biscuit blue border and centre, 20 sprigs of weed round rim irregular and 16 round centre.

1186x Same as 1090x with dark biscuit blue ground.

1187x Blue stripes alternating weed and leaves, 8 compartments, 4 of each, 3 of each inside cup, Glaze kiln torqua blue and yellow, dessert plate 8 round, no yellow in bottom sprig.

1188x Same gilding as 1168x, printed in Antwerp blue, edged as 1207x.

1189x Dark biscuit blue border, 3 compartments of flowers, 2 in cup, star centre, vine weed outside.

1190x Green stripes, alternating weed and flowers, 8 in saucer, 6 in cup, 3 coloured flies and sprig in bottom of cup.

1191x   Dark biscuit blue ground and fibre, flower sprigs and flies, 3 compartments in saucer, 2 in cup, coloured printed sprigs.

1192x   Coloured flower in panel of fibre, exact size of the ground and gilding same as 1189x.

1193x   Same gilding as 1140x done in dark blue.

1194x   Same pattern as 1032x green instead of Antwerp.

1195x   Same as 1142x in dark blue instead of grey and bottom sprigs of leaf and fibre instead of as 1142x.

1196x   Japan pattern, same as 1184x tea pattern, fibre outside cup.

1197x   Same as 1168x printed in Antwerp blue, teaware, edge as 1207x.

1198x   Coloured and edged same as 1199x, no gold sprigs.

1199x   Sprigs same as 1151x, the flowers in matt blue, green leaves, red seed in flowers, 3 coloured sprigs and inside cup, no gold sprigs outside.

1200x   Dessert pattern, 3 sprigs coloured same as 1199x and edged as 1174x Queen's shape.

1201x   Moss fibre printed in Bronze, edged same as 1174x, same number for dessert and tea pattern.

1202x   3 compartments round saucer, 2 inside cup, 3 single roses outside the cup, no foot line.

1203x   Glaze celeste stripes same as 1187x with printed coloured sprigs instead of the yellow and gold ones, gold sprig in bottom and outside border same as 1187x.

1204x   Blossom print in Antwerp blue, gold dots in blossom, 3 compartments in dessert plate, small plant in bottom by Jno. Wood.

1205x   Same as 1204x, star in gold instead of plant.

1206x   Same as 1204x, 3 compartments in saucer and 2 in cup, sprig inside.

1207x   Same as 1168x with dragged edge border, slate fibre.

1208x   Same as 1168x with edge as 1207x in Antwerp blue.

1209x   Same as 1159x in green slate.

1210x   Same as 1148x on Gloster shape instead of Queen Edge as 352x.

1211x   Painted as 410x on Queen's Plain edge as 1202x.

1212x   Dessert, Queen's Plain, Antwerp, blossom border and fibre centre.

1213x   Dessert, Queen's, Antwerp blossom border, large plant centre.

1214x   Queen's Plain, Antwerp, wide blossom border, line inside cup and saucer.

1215x   Queen's, Antwerp, blossom border and fibre, fibre centre, no foot line.

1216x   Deep blue border, fibre in panels, large flower group in centre.

1217x   Kent shape, Antwerp, blossom border, 3 sprigs inside.

1218x   Queen's Antwerp, blossom border, plant centre, scratch edge inside at top, 3 sprig outside ¼ pint.

1219x   Same as 1218x, dark instead of Antwerp.

1220x   Gilt spray work as 808x edge as 944x, Antwerp convolvulus on Queen's Plain dessert.

1221x   Yellow border and fibre sprigs, 6 round cup and down, flowers around centre.

1222x   Same print as 1065x gilt on edge only as 1063x, Antwerp.

1223x   Slate fibre on Queen's, Scratch edge as 944x.

1224x   Dark blue fibre, Queen's Shape, gilt as 1207x edge only.

1225x   Antwerp blue fibre, Scratch edge, Queen's shape.

1226x   Dark blue sprigs, Queen's shape, gilt as 1065x.

1227x   Dark blue large sprigs and gilt.

1228x   Gloster shape, bronze convolvulus, edge only as 771x coloured blackberry edge.

1229x   As 1221x in new blue or silver grey.

1230x   Hawthorn ground in Antwerp

blue, gilt weed, flower sprays and wreath in colours.

1231x Queen's rim, elaborate gold weed, central coloured flower wreaths, G K (glaze kiln) cane ground.

1232x Biscuit Blue and G K cane stripes, gilt leaves and weed.

1233x Dark blue ground gilt red, border of G K cane leaves, heightened in gold.

1234x G K cane shaped border, gilt weed, panels of coloured flowers, Queen's rim.

1235x Trailing gold border, alternate coloured flowers and gold weed, central wreath, gilt on leaves.

1236x Same as 1235 no gold on pointed leaves.

1237x Same as 1232 with cane ground instead of dark blue.

1238x Stone coloured flowers and gold foliage, stone border.

1239x G K (glaze kiln) cane ground, gold weed, star centre.

1240x G K cane ground, gilt weed, alternate pink roses and blue flowers, rose centre.

1241x Roses painted in biscuit in Antwerp blue, linked by gold weed, 8 roses in each row.

1242x Roses painted in G K Antwerp blue for grounds in the bisque, 5 or 6 in each row.

1243x Roses in biscuit Antwerp blue and in pink, gilt weed.

1244x Antwerp blue and red and green roses, 6 of each round saucer, 5 round cup, blue rose bottom of cup, 2 roses of each outside.

1245x Cane ground, notched edge, 6 sprigs of flowers round border and in centre.

1246x Cane Glost Kiln colour, dark blue calx and fibre, 3 compartments in dessert plate, leaf and fibre centre.

1247x Antwerp blue hawthorn border, panels of sprigs, in strong bronze and part filled in, copper number 25 (has a mark of crossed swords and G W

engraved).

1248x Dark blue calx inside a cane edge, 25 round saucer and 20 round cup.

1249x Antwerp hawthorn print on glaze and dipped, 3 sprigs in bronze and part filled in.

1250x Dark blue calx and cane edge, 3 compartments in saucer and 2 in cup, same outside border as 1248x.

1251x Printed in slate, flowers rose colour, large sprigs of flowers and fibre.

1252x Same as 1251x flowers in Antwerp blue, for grounds slate fibre.

1253x Cane border, inner border of 30 Vandyke shapes in Hill's Grey, star shaped centre.

1254x Cane ground, panels of flowers, 1 spray in each compartment and 3 in bottom of plate.

1255x All over fibre in slate, Queen's Plain shape.

1256x Same pattern as 1248x, but with lilac No. 2 G K instead of dark blue.

1257x Same pattern as 1238x, but with dark blue flowers instead of slate.

1258x Same pattern as 1207x but with dark fibre instead of slate.

1259x Table pattern same as dessert 1212x with line instead of scratch edge.

1260x Vase painted in bronze; coloured flowers – weed edge.

1261x Same as dessert 1241x, 10 roses in cup, in bottom, 5 roses outside cup with gold sprig between, 12 roses in saucer, 1 in bottom.

1262x Same as 1242x, Gloster edge as 352x.

1263x Same as 1293x with silver grey band instead of blue.

1264x Same as 1192x silver grey instead of cane and printed flowers in compartments instead of flowers done by men.

1265x Same as 1159x, silver grey instead of cane.

1266x	Dark blue fibre, scratch edge.
1267x	Dark blue border 3 groups of 3 flowers and scrolls in saucer, 2 in cup, no foot line.
1268x	Same as 1267x silver grey instead of blue, line outside.
1269x	Same as 1268x in stone colour, line outside cup instead of border, as 1267x.
1270x	Silver grey border and vine sprigs, 3 compartments of red and yellow flowers in plate.
1271x	Silver grey border, 3 flower heads and gilt weed, landscape centre.
1272x	Silver grey and green chevron border, gilt weed, landscape centre, Vandyke edge.
1273x	Silver grey band border, gold flowerhead and leaf centre.
1274x	As 1273x but with gold weed centre.
1275x	Same pattern as 1216x in Russet brown instead of dark blue grounds.
1276x	Same pattern as 1292x in silver grey, Russet brown border.
1277x	Silver grey border gold flower and weed centre, same as 1263x.
1278x	See 1292x G G (i.e. George Grainger).
1279x	Same gilding as 1270x grounded in cane and convolvulus in blue instead of pink.
1280x	Antwerp blue vine, Blackberry edge.
1281x	Same pattern as 1240x, stone ground instead of cane.
1282x	Same gilding as 1240x with gold star centre, no flowers, dark blue ground instead of cane.
1283x	Same gilding as 1267x, cane ground.
1284x	Child's Brown weed gilt Bos's Shape (i.e. Broseley).
1285x	Gilt Hathorn blossom on Antwerp blue ground, centre blue spray.
1286x	Cane and dark blue cobalt grounds, gilt scrolls and two flowerheads, centre gold star.
1287x	Cane ground, 5 roses in colours and gilt trailing foliage, gold

	flowerheads on edge.
1288x	Silver grey ground, gilt scrolls and flowerheads, gold foliage centre.
1289x	Russet brown ground, gilt scrolls, leaves and fine foliage, leafy centre in gold.
1290x	White and gold flowerhead border and central sprig.
1291x	Cane ground gilt with trailing foliage, flowerhead edge.
1292x	Silver grey ground gilt scrolls and leaves, cane leaves and fine foliage, Queen's shape.
1293x	Large leaves in Russet brown and silver grey, painted coloured flower sprays, gilt weed, Queen's.
1294x	Silver grey and cane leaves alternating with gold leaves and flowers (see Mr. Grainger before doing any).
1295x	Dark blue and cane grounds, gilt scrolls, foliage and vines, centres painted coloured flowers, ring handle.
1296x	Antwerp blue ground, white panels gilt foliage and diaper, centre fine flower sprays.
1297x	Printed flower sprays in brown, leaves heightened in red, dark blue rim; Oak Leaf.
1298x	As 1297x in Bronze.
1299x	As 1297x in Antwerp Blue.
1300x	As 1297x in Mouse.
1301x	Gilt as 1297x in Antwerp blue, Queen's edge gilt.
1302x	As 1301, Bronze, Queen's.
1303x	As 1301x dark blue.
1304x	As 1301x Mouse.
1305x	Oak leaf in dark blue edge only, as 1301x Queen's
1306x	Oak leaf bronze, as 1301x.
1307x	do. Antwerp blue do. do.
1308x	do. Mouse do. do.
1309x	Oak leaf, Brown, heightened in red, dark blue rim.
1310x	As 1309x in Antwerp blue, Queen's.
1311x	As 1309x in Bronze, Queen's.
1312x	As 1309x in Mouse, Queen's.
1313x	As 1284x on Gloster, edged.

1314x   As 1312x, Gloster, no edge.

1315x   Fawn ground gilt flowers and
foliage, cane and white leaves,
coloured flower sprays printed
and filled in.

1316x   Queen's edge in gold, coloured
flower sprigs.

1317x   No. 65 copper ground gilt weed,
printed dragons and scrolls
filled in colours, centre fence,
paeony and flowers in coloured
print.

1318x   As 1317x except cane ground, no
gold except on edges.

1319x   Copper No. 65 ground, bronze
print coloured, flowers and
sprigs and gold weed, centre 3
Chinese figures by vase.

1320x   Moss fibre, ? in bronze.

1321x   As 1319x, printed in dark blue, no
gold except on edge.

1322x   Dark blue oak leaf, Queen's edge.

1323x   As 1295x Russet brown instead of
dark blue.

1324x   As 1271x, group of flowers instead
of landscape.

1325x   Groups of 3 flowers and blue small
sprigs, C scroll and weed
borders.

1326x   Brown ground with white arcade,
gold scrolls and weed edge, star
centre.

1327x   Same as 1326x with silver grey
ground.

1328x   Dark biscuit blue ground, cane and
gold leaf scrolls and foliage, star
centre.

1329x   Dark biscuit blue ground reserved
with cane leaves and branches,
gilt weed, centre coloured
flowers.

1330x   Biscuit blue ground reserved with
white and gold arcade, cane and
gold scrolls, central coloured
flowers.

1331x   Dark biscuit blue ground reserved
with cane leaves and branches,
gold foliage, scrollwork and
weed.

1332x   Russet brown ground, see 1339x,
Wales shape.

1333x   Same as 1332x in silver grey,
Prince of Wales shape, see
1340x dessert ware.

1334x   Dark biscuit blue ground reserved
with pink flowerheads and gold
foliage, centre blue and pink
rock and foliage.

1335x   Same as 1326x dark biscuit blue
ground.

1336x   See 1339x biscuit blue ground,
should have been 1339x.

1337x   Apple green ground, gold
flowerheads and line edge, gilt
leaves and trailing branch.

1338x   Same as 1337x Rose colour
ground.

1339x   Dark biscuit blue ground, reserved
with white and gold arcade,
gold sprig inside and central
coloured flowers.

1340x   As 1339x but dessert.

1341x   Moss fibre in Antwerp blue, gold
dots and some gold twigging,
Queen's.

1342x   Moss fibre in slate, gilt as 1341x.

1343x   Dark blue vine, blackberry edge
and sprigs in gold.

1344x   Same pattern as 1292x in Russet
Brown on Gloster shape.

1345x   Mouse oak leaf on Queen's,
scratch edge.

1346x   Stone coloured ground, cane leaves
and blue vines heightened in
gold.

1347x   Russet brown ground, gilt foliage
and scroll work, painted pink
roses, centre gold foliage.

1348x   Russet brown ground with white
and brown leaves and gilt
foliage, central coloured flower
sprig.

1349x   Same as 1348x in stone colour,
flowers same.

1350x   Alternate silver grey and white
stripes, gilt and brown weed,
gilt foliage centre, 13 round
plates.

1351x   Silver grey ground gilt with trailing
foliage, reserved pink roses, rose
centre with gold leaves.

1352x   Russet brown ground reserved

	with white branches and gilt weed, fruiting branch centre.
1353x	Same as 1352x in silver grey.
1354x	Inside and outer border of wave bands in silver grey, white and gold, gold leafage between.
1355x	Russet brown with darker brown and gold feather-like leafage, gold weed and foliage centre.
1356x	Brown line edge sprays of forget-me-nots in colours.
1357x	As 1352x, silver grey ground and dark blue highlights to branches, Queen's shape.
1358x	As 1355x on Teawares.
1359x	(Same as 1358x, cane ground shade in Russet brown) crossed out and replaced by Russet brown ground with blue vines and gilt and white leaves.
1360x	Same as 1359x dark blue instead of Russet brown.
1361x	Silver grey ground reserved groups of 3 white leaves, blue and gold foliage, Queen's.
1362x	Same as 1361x Russet brown instead of silver grey.
1363x	Silver grey ground reserving panels edged with scrolls.
1364x	Silver grey ground reserved with white branches, three gold scroll framed panels and central panels of coloured landscapes, Queen's shape.
1365x	Queen's, silver grey ground, 10 white chain-stripes and gold foliage.
1366x	Russet brown ground with darker brown and white leaves, gold foliage centres.
1367x	As 1366x in silver grey.
1368x	As 1366x in stone colour.
1369x	Silver grey ground reserving panels of single pink roses, gilt foliage and weed, Queen's.
1370x	Same as 1369x in Russet brown.
1371x	Pink roses and blue forget-me-nots, green weed, roses outside cups.
1372x	Spiral stripes in silver grey and white, gold and Russet brown weed, Queen's shape.

1373x	Queen's. As pattern 1371x, gilt weed, also small gold sprigs.
1374x	Same as 1358x cane ground, shade in Russet brown.
1375x	Same pattern as 887x done in dark blue.
1376x	Antwerp blue small sprigs, Queen's shape, edge as 1322x.
1377x	French shape, French edge and fine line, vine outside cup.
1378x	Gold edging, green called match green for grounds.
1379x	French shape, green band and line border, gold French edge.
1380x	Malvern shape gold foliage edge, green ground with feather-like leaves, central gold foliage.
1381x	Malvern shape, gold highlights to foliage edge, single gold line centre.
1382x	Malvern shape, 3 Antwerp blue leaves and weed (Moss fibre) 3 painted sprays in saucer, gold edge.
1383x	Malvern shape, gold edging and foliage between chain stripes.
1384x	Weed mouse, Malvern shape, gilt edge as 1382x.
1385x	As 1365 in stone colour instead of silver grey, groups of flowers instead of gold sprigs, Queen's, no white chain work.
1386x	Antwerp blue vein leaf, gilt weed, gold edging.
1387x	Malvern shape, silver grey ground gilt scrolls and barley sprigs.
1388x	Malvern; silver grey ground reserved white feathers and gilt weed, foliage centre.
1389x	3 panels of Russet brown, gilt scroll work and leafage, Malvern shape.
1390x	Antwerp blue Hawthorn ground, gilt foliage inside border.
1391x	Large vine leaves printed in Antwerp blue, gold edging, Malvern.
1392x	As 1391x, Antwerp blue.
1393x	The same as 1392x Mouse
1394x	do. Bronze.
1395x	do. Dark blue.

1396x   The same as 1391x Mouse

1397x   do.   Bronze

1398x   do.   Dark blue

1400x   Same pattern as 1387x, Russet brown instead of silver grey, no orange on the edge.

1401x   Cane ground, gold scrolls, vines and barley, centre coloured flowers, Malvern shape.

1402x   Dark blue ground, cane edge, gilt vine leaves, three panels on saucer and 2 in coffee, centre painted landscapes.

1403x   As 1387x, dark blue instead of silver grey.

1404x   As 1389x, dark blue instead of Russet brown, the edge same as 1402x.

1405x   As 1388, in dark blue instead of silver grey.

1406x   As 1388x, in Russet brown instead of silver grey.

1407x   Gilt edge, green ground with white feather-like leaves, centre gold scrollwork, Dessert.

1408x   Same pattern as 1382x mouse colour fibre, Malvern shape.

1409x   Same pattern as 1384x, green weed on bisque, edge as 1382x, Malvern.

1410x   Antwerp Hawthorn border on Malvern, edge only as 1382x.

1411x   Silver grey ground gilt with plants and barley and scrollwork, coloured flower centres, Malvern dessert.

1412x   As 1411x, Russet brown instead of silver grey, sprig in bottom instead of flowers.

1413x   Mouse colour Hawthorn ground gilt scroll edging and gilt foliage, centre painted Men's flowers, Queen's Plate shape.

1414x   Antwerp blue Hawthorn, gilt as 1413x, gold sprigs instead of flowers.

1415x   Same as 1411x with biscuit blue ground.

1416x   Mouse oak leaf print on Baden shape gold edge.

1417x   Large vine leaves, printed in slate, filled in in cane.

1418x   Large vine leaves, printed in Bronze filled in in match green, no edge.

1419x   do.   printed in slate, filled in in cane, highlights.

1420x   do.   printed in Bronze, filled in in match green, gold edge.

1421x   Antwerp blue Hawthorn, gold scroll edges, no sprigs or line centre.

1422x   Antwerp blue Hawthorn, gold scroll edge, sprig centre and line, Malvern.

1423x   Same pattern as 1402x, flowers instead of vines.

1424x   Petal shaped lobed design in dark blue, French shape.

1425x   Same as 1424x, in Antwerp blue.

1426x   Same as 1392x in slate.

1427x   1980 on Malvern shape, edge as 1422x.

1428x   Sprays and sprigs of forget-me-nots, gold edges, Malvern.

1429x   Gold scroll edge on Malvern, large gilt leaves and weed.

1430x   Sprigs of bell flowers in pink, blue and green, gold rim.

1431x   Same as 1411x, dark blue instead of silver grey, gold sprig in bottom.

1432x   Dark blue lace dessert ware on Queen's, green leaves same as 1420x.

1433x   Malvern shape, white edged same as 1382x.

1434x   Dark blue ground with cane rim, reserved white leaves and gilt barley, central printed landscapes.

1435x   As 1434x, Men's flowers instead of landscapes.

1436x   Malvern; cane rim gilt with scrolls, all over trailing small blue flowers.

1437x   As 1436x Dessert instead of Bte (? Breakfast) Malvern.

1438x   Malvern shape, Match green and gold edge, centre sprig.

1439x   Same as 1438x in matt blue instead of green, Malvern.

1440x Same as 1438x in maroon instead of green.

1441x Maroon ground, yellow and gold edge, gold foliage wreath and sprig centre.

1442x Same as 1441x in Match green instead of maroon, no yellow on edge.

1443x Oak leaf as 1297x in chocolate, Malvern shape, edge as 1422x.

1444x Blue ground with gilt shapes and scrolls, yellow rim, coloured flower sprays printed and filled in.

1445x Same edge as 1382x printed on the glaze with green weed.

1446x Green fibre on glaze, Queen's shape edge as 1373x.

1447x Same as 1324x dark blue instead of silver grey

1448x French shape, hair brown stripes, sprig in centre.

1449x Same as 1448x in Match green instead of hair brown.

1450x Silver grey spiral stripes alternating with flowers and hair brown leaves, blue flower heads in centre, wavy edge.

1451x As 1450x with plain edge, outside border to cup as 1389x.

1452x Wavy edge in gold, weed pattern in match green.

1453x Bristle border, 4-petalled flower border, spray flower spray centre.

1454x Russet brown ground, hair brown leafy weed sprigs, 6 compartments in saucer, outlined in red.

1455x Russet brown panels like 1454x alternating with flower sprays, 3 in saucer, 2 in cup.

1456x As 1455x but with cane ground.

1457x Silver grey border, centre flower spray surrounded by hair brown sprigs.

1458x Same gilding as 1140x views instead of bottom sprig.

1459x Same pattern as 1402x Lilac Ground instead of blue.

1460x Dessert pattern cocoa leaf on Queen's shape plain, same edge only as No. 1413x.

1461x Malvern shape Bk (? Breakfast) ware, cocoa oak leaf, edge only as 1382x.

1462x Same pattern as 1247x, Dark blue Hawthorn instead of Antwerp.

1463x Same pattern as 989x done with cane on the embossed part.

1464x Same pattern as 1021x Maroon ground instead of mouse leaf.

1465x Same pattern as 1438x hair brown instead of green.

1466x Dessert pattern as 1454x with group flowers in bottom instead of sprig, 7 compartments in plate.

1467x Dark R/Blue ground with wreaths, landscape in centre.

1468x Crossed out as Error – as 1467x gold sprig instead of landscape.

1469x Same as 1467x in silver edge sprig in bottom (this seems to replace 1468x).

1470x As 1469x in Albert, drab instead of silver grey.

1471x Russet brown ground, panels of flower sprigs and butterflies.

1472x As 1471x in Albert new drab.

1473x As 1468 in cane instead of stone.

1474x As 1467 Albert drab instead of dark blue.

1475x Dessert as 1467, no landscape, in Albert new drab, 4 leaves round dessert plate, gold border in bottom.

1476x Same as 1402x primrose ground.

1477x Same pattern as 1467x gold sprig in bottom instead of blue.

1478x Same pattern as 1471x in dark blue instead of Russet brown.

1483x Blue edge, leafy weed sprig border inside and in bottom.

1484x Same as 1483x except dotted shape inside border.

1485x Cane ground between two blue and gilt long leaves, centre flower group.

1486x As 1485x small landscape instead of flowers.

1487x As 1405x, yellow ground and

roses, star centre.

1488x   Dark blue ground with oval gilded shapes, centre flower group.

1489x   As 1488x Albert drab instead of dark blue, landscape instead of flowers.

1490x   Same as 1485x Dark blue instead of cane and cane leaves instead of Antwerp blue. As Bradley & Co.

1491x   Same pattern as 1436x stain edge as 1483x.

1492x   Same pattern as 1436x no cane on edge.

1493x   Same pattern as 1436x no gold on cane on edge.

1494x   Same pattern as 1422x Maroon ground instead of Hawthorn.

1495x   Same pattern as 1422x Green ground instead of Hawthorn.

1496x   Same pattern as 1422x Dark blue ground instead of Hawthorn.

1497x   Malvern shape flow blue coral shapes, dark blue flowers.

1498x   As 1497x in Bronze instead of flowing blue.

1499x   As 1497x in Antwerp blue.

1500x   As 1497x in Mouse.

1501x   Antwerp blue Coral shapes, Malvern shape, no foot line.

1502x   As 1501 in dark blue instead of Antwerp blue.

1503x   As 1501x in Bronze instead of Antwerp blue.

1504x   As 1501x in Mouse.

1505x   As 1471x in Silver grey instead of Russet, 4 compartments in dessert plate on Queen's shape.

1506x   As 1505x in dark blue and coloured flowers.

1507x   Queen's shape printed in Antwerp blue, elaborate print with 3 shaped panels and central flowers.

1508x   S & T flowering blue as Baileys, French shape, gold edge.

1509x   Malvern shape blue panels and gilt sprigs, 2 in cup and 3 in saucer.

1510x   As 1509x in Albert drab instead of dark blue and landscape in bottom, Queen's shape as

Rhodes.

1511x   Dark blue and cane alternating stripes, landscape centre.

1512x   As 1511x flowers instead of landscapes.

1513x   As 1512x Antwerp blue instead of dark blue.

1514x   Green striped border flowers in centre.

1515x   Flow blue and cane stripes, landscapes in centre.

1516x   White and gold stripes with trailing sprig, 6-star centre.

1517x   French round edge panels of dark flowing blue 12 in saucer 9 in cup.

1518x   As 1517x on Malvern shape.

1519x   French round edge, dark flowing blue, somewhat like 1517x.

1520x   As 1517x Antwerp blue on French shape.

1521x   Same as 1518x edge and line only, no gilding on blue.

1522x   Same as 1518x in Antwerp blue instead of flowing blue.

1523x   Same as 1521x in Antwerp blue instead of flowing blue.

1524x   Large and small sprigs of flowers alternating.

1525x   French shape, Antwerp blue square shaded shapes, pattern done inside cup.

1526x   Same as 1525x maroon instead of Antwerp blue.

1527x   Flowing blue zig zag shapes, centre sprig.

1528x   Edge, line and sprig as 1527x but straight blue stripes in flow blue.

1529x   Malvern shape flowing blue zig zag shapes.

1530x   Gilded and yellow rim, large flower spray centre.

1531x   As 1527x in maroon instead of dark blue, French shape instead of Malvern.

1532x   French shape, blue and gold trellis-like shapes round border.

1533x   As 953x flowing blue instead of Antwerp blue stain.

1534x   Alternate hair brown and gold

concentric lines.

1535x As 1534x French shape, done in green.

1536x As 1535x in maroon.

1537x As 1536x in blue.

1538x Chinese print flowing blue and gold edge, French shape.

1539x See Parry. Cane ground with trellis, landscape centre.

1540x As 1539x with flowers instead of landscape.

1541x Same edge as 953x, sprig in bottom as 1453x.

1542x As 1541x in flowing blue.

1543x French shape blue and gold flowers round.

1544x Trellis shapes round border, sprig in centre.

1545x Malvern shape, silver grey panels, weedy twigs, butterfly centre.

1546x Russet brown panels, trailing twigs, sprig centre.

1547x Mouse weed table wares, gold dots and French line, Mouse sprig in bottom of plate as Allsup.

1548x As 1532x Blue only instead of blue and gold, French shape.

1549x French shape, flowing blue stripes.

1550x Flowing blue stripes, edge as 1384x.

1551x Cane ground, flowers in panels and in centre painted in bronze and colours.

1552x Same sprig as 1551x in rose colour instead of cane.

1553x Match green border, no star nor spray in centre but 2 inch diam. ring centre.

1554x As 1553x Maroon instead of green.

1555x Stripes of dark blue alternating with cane, 13 of each round plate, rich plant in centre.

1556x As 1512x, glaze kiln yellow green instead of dark blue, plant in bottom, instead of group.

1557x As 1540x cane ground all over plate.

1558x As 1247x match green instead of Antwerp blue, Hawthorn ground.

1559x Same as 1402x flowers instead of

views, glaze kiln Victoria green ground.

1560x Malvern shape, Antwerp blue, shaded edge Winchester Lee Gibbon, sprig centre.

1561x Antwerp coral Malvern edge only, as 1382x.

1562x Silver grey and cane ground, twig sprig centre and on ground.

1563x As 1562x Dark blue instead of silver grey.

1564x As 1562x G K (glaze kiln) Green instead of silver grey.

1565x Dark blue border with leaves, gilded sprigs.

1566x As 1565x in silver grey instead of dark blue.

1567x Silver grey border and trellis type shapes, star centre.

1568x Green border, trellis type shapes, sprig centre.

1569x Alsup with rose colour sprigs in centre of cup and saucer, 3 leaf shapes round border.

1570x Cane and Antwerp blue leaves divided by ground round border and centre.

1571x As 1570x, leaf centre.

1572x Glaze kiln green border, trellis shapes, 26 round plate, 8 star centre.

1573x French shape, Match green and gold zig zag shapes round border, 24 in breakfast stand, 16 in breakfast cup and tea and saucer.

1574x As 1573x Vandyke green, instead of gold and green.

1575x As 1573x Hair brown and gold.

1576x As 1573 in Matt blue and gold.

1577x As 1573x Vandyke all Matt blue zig zag.

1578x French shape, Matt blue concentric circles.

1579x As 1578x Imperial chrome green instead of Blue.

1581x Matt blue and brown ties over 2 concentric lines, 16 in breakfast saucer, 10 in cup.

1582x As 1581x in match green instead of Matt blue.

1583x Matt blue zig zags, 24 in saucer and cup.

1584x As 1583x Match green and gold instead of matt blue.

1585x As 1483x in G K Victoria green.

1586x G K Victoria green and cane ground with twig gilding border, trellis inside, flower centre.

1587x As 1586x silver grey instead of green, 5-star centre.

1588x Antwerp blue and cane ground reserving ovals, 14 round plate, fancy bird and leafy weed in gold centre.

1589x As 1588x G K Green instead of Antwerp blue, flower centre.

1590x As 1571x in G K Green instead of blue, the green not shaded.

1591x Silver grey and cane border, chains holding up trellis 3-starred centre.

1592x Cane ground and shaded Antwerp blue leaves, 6 in saucer, 4 in cup, leafy twig centre.

1593x As 1592x Dark blue ground instead of cane, leaf cane instead of blue.

1594x Russet brown and cane leaves shaded in Antwerp blue, leafy twig centre.

1595x As 1594x in Antwerp blue instead of Russet brown.

1596x As 1594x Albert drab instead of Antwerp blue.

1597x As 1562x in G K Green instead of Antwerp blue and group of flowers in bottom in lieu of gold sprigs.

1598x Antwerp blue and gold edge.

1599x As 1598x in Victoria green instead of blue.

1600x As 1598x in Antwerp blue – crossed out Error.

1601x As 1569 G K Green instead of Antwerp blue, leaves cane, Malvern shape, Allsups with rose colour sprig in bottom of cup and saucer, as 1453x. For the white and gold see 2/306.

1602x Same pattern as 1570x all cane instead of cane and blue edge.

1603x Same pattern as 1483x G K Green instead of Antwerp edge, line instead of border inside cup and saucer.

1604x Blue stripes and cane leaves, large plant centre.

1605x Same as 1485x green leaves instead of blue.

1606x Same as 1467x in Victoria green instead of dark blue, gold sprig in bottom, no views.

1607x Same as 1402x green ground and flowers.

1608x As 506x in Victoria G K green instead of dark blue.

1609x As 1485x leaf shaded in Victoria green instead of blue. This is in twice see 1605x.

1610x As 1467x in Victoria green, group of flowers bottom – Men's flowers.

1611x Is 1467x in Albert drab, dessert pattern on Queen's shape, slight group of flowers in bottom.

1612x Cane border and twigs, leaves inside shaded in blue, sprig centre.

1613x See 1610x – crossed out details.

1614x As 1592x in Victoria green instead of cane, leaf cut up in cane instead of blue.

1615x As 1592x in silver grey instead of green, leaf cut up in cane.

1616x Victoria green panels with leaves, cane leaves each side, bottom sprig in cup and saucer.

1617x As 1616x in silver grey instead of green.

1618x As 1435x dessert in Victoria green instead of dark blue, flowers the same.

1619x Pink and gold concentric lines, French shape.

1620x Green and cane stripes in leafy panels, flower panels and flower centres.

1621x Gold line with trailing green spriggy shape.

1622x As 1621x in blue line, same pattern Globe shape see 1682x.

1623x As 1621x in Antwerp blue.

1624x Wreath as 1621 in Antwerp blue instead of green, gold edge only and coloured spray in bottom.

1625x French shape, flowing blue and gold swags, for same pattern Globe see 1681x.

1626x Victoria green and birds, see Jno Goodman's pattern sold at shop.

1627x See 1614x.

1628x Same pattern as 1571x Dark blue instead of Antwerp blue.

1629x Same pattern as 1560x Glaze kiln green edge instead of blue.

1630x Same pattern as 1612x dark blue instead of cane and cane leaf.

1631x Same pattern as 1610x printed group in bottom instead of painted.

1632x Same pattern as 723x Imperial chrome green instead of blue.

1633x Same pattern as 506x Russet brown instead of dark blue.

1634x Same as 953x G K green edge instead of blue.

1635x White and gold printed flowers filled in, 6 in saucer, 5 in cup, sprig centre.

1636x Flowing blue and gold, trailing sprigs and sprig centre.

1637x Flowing blue trellising on Queen's shape, sprig centre.

1638x Gold and flowing blue stripes, 12 of each, star centre.

1639x As 1471x in Victoria G K green instead of Russet brown.

1640x Flowing blue fleur de lys type shapes, 16 in saucer, 12 in cup, star centre, Malvern shape.

1641x Same as 1640x Globe shape instead of Malvern.

1642x Flowing blue hanging fleur de lys type shapes across blue line, star centre.

1643x Flowing blue, blue and gold stripes.

1644x One flowing blue line, entwining twiggy shape and double dashes, twig centre.

1645x Dark blue and silver grey entwining semicircles filled in with cane colour, sprig centre.

1646x Dark blue and cane panels and C scroll gilding, 3 in plate, 6 star centre.

1647x Panels of blue and barbed wire on white with shell shape, star centre.

1648x As 1644x, 2 flowing blue lines instead of one.

1649x Albert drab ground, bronze print, 1 large and 2 small flower sprigs.

1650x As 1649x in Russet brown instead of Albert drab.

1651x As 1649x in Russet brown instead of stone, no gilding on wreath.

1652x As 1651x fawn ground, no gilding on wreath.

1653x As 1649x, no gold on wreath, same ground.

1654x Same as 1651x in green instead of russet brown.

1655x Silver grey ground, enamelled wreath printed in bronze, no gold on ground.

1656x Same print as 1655x but Albert drab, green and gilt as 1649x.

1657x Same as 1656x ? green ground.

1658x Same as 1651x in dark blue instead of russet brown.

1659x Same as 1551x dark blue ground.

1660x As 1625x on globe shape, done outside instead of in.

1661x Victoria G K green ground, printed and coloured flowers.

1662x Same as 1661x in Albert drab instead of green, printed in bronze.

1663x Same as 1661x in Russet brown instead of green.

1664x Same as 1651x Russet brown ground.

1665x Dark blue ground, painted in dark blue, printed and coloured in flowers.

1666x Malvern shape, russet ground border and flowers printed in bronze and coloured, sprig centre.

1667x As 1666x printed flowers filled in as 1649x centre.

1668x   As 1667x Victoria G K green instead of fawn ground, printed sprigs filled in, Malvern shape.

1669x   French shape, painted in flowing blue with roses.

1670x   French shape, flowing blue rose as 1669x not gilt on flowers, fine gold line and blue edge.

1671x   French shape, as 1670x gold edge only, no gold on sprigs.

1672x   French shape, flowing blue rose as 1669x blue edge and line, no gold.

1673x   As 1671x on Globe shape.

1674x   Regular Malvern edge, flowing blue wreath on Malvern shape.

1675x   Flow blue wavy lines and dotted twig, gilt as 1140x.

1676x   Flow blue C scrolls and twigs with gilt leaves.

1677x   Dark blue ground, dark blue wreath, twiggy centre; Malvern shape.

1678x   As 1640x on French shape instead of Malvern.

1679x   Single flowing wreath on Globe shape, gold edge.

1680x   Error, see 1622x.

1681x   Flowing wreaths as 1625x done outside cup on Globe shape, for same pattern French shape see 1625x.

1682x   As 1621x flowing blue instead of green on Globe shape.

1683x   Not to be done G G (gold edge and blue lines).

1684x   Flowing blue, small Kent sprig, gold edge, Malvern shape.

1685x   Berkeley shape printed in flowing blue, coloured regular way, Malvern.

1686x   Same as 1643x on French shape instead of Malvern round edge to cup.

1687x   Victoria green top border, spriggy pattern top and centre.

1688x   French shape, fawn ground, flowing blue wreath and centre, no gilding on ground.

1689x   Same as 1688x orange ground instead of fawn, hair brown edge, French shape.

1690x   Same as 1688x in enamel orange ground.

1691x   Same as 1688x blue green ground, blue edge and handle no gold, French shape.

1692x   Malvern shape, flowing blue trellis, star centre.

1693x   Same as 1692x on Globe shape.

1694x   Malvern shape, flowing blue trellis and centre sprig.

1695x   Same as 1471x in green, dessert pattern, Queen's shape.

1696x   Enamel blue green ground, no gold printed and coloured sprigs.

1697x   As 1691x enamel silver grey instead of blue green, French shape, no gold, blue edge.

1698x   Russet brown ground, compartments of orange flowers, Men's flowers done well in centre (also later 2/466 fruit and flowers).

1699x   Witley shape, russet brown ground with coloured birds and flowers, 6-star centre.

1700x   Dark blue ground with orange leaf, slight plant in bottom.

1701x   Russet border, birds in landscape centre (on Victoria green, see 1739x).

1702x   Flowing blue scales, sprigs in compartments, Men's flowers in bottom.

1703x   Fawn leaves and flow blue, 3 printed sprigs in bottom filled in as 1704x.

1704x   Shaded in Victoria Green underglaze, orange flowers, 3 large printed sprigs coloured, 1 small fly between each sprig, small sprig in bottom.

1705x   Dark blue ground, wheatsheaf-like shape part orange painted sprig in each compartment, painted rose in centre of plate.

1706x   As 1586x dark blue instead of Victoria green.

1707x   Lee's embossed, flowing blue traced and painted sprig.

1708x   Same as 1668x, dark blue ground, instead of Victoria green.

1709x   Dark blue ground and cane compartments, centre group of Men's flowers done well.

1710x   Orange edge, match green ground, centre flowers by Parry.

1711x   Same as 1710x maroon instead of green, some flowers.

1712x   Same as 1710x pink ground instead of green, flowers same.

1714x   Malvern shape, wreath painted in bronze, 1 large 2 small printed and coloured sprigs.

1715x   As 1714x no printed sprigs, small sprig in bottom of cup and saucer.

1716x   Victoria green ground, 3 compartments, Parry's.

1719x   Malvern edge only, Malvern Antwerp vase as 1392x.

1720x   As 1371x blue edge French shape.

1721x   As 1720x gold edge, French shape.

1722x   Coloured convolvulus flowers.

1723x   Dark blue and cane ground, C scrolls and twiggy shapes.

1724x   Green ground, blue thistles and bottom sprig.

1725x   Flowing blue leaf and twig around fawn strip, gold on leaf.

1726x   As 1725x, orange on blue leaf instead of gold.

1727x   As 1725x no gold, blue edge line and foot line.

1728x   As 1725x silver grey stripe instead of fawn, blue edge.

1729x   As 1725x printed in Antwerp blue, filled in stripes in silver grey, blue edge.

1730x   As 1725x printed in bronze, shaded in maroon, maroon stripe, no gold on leaves.

1731x   As 1725x printed in bronze, shaded in maroon, gold stripe.

1733x   Same as 1441x Dark blue instead of Maroon.

1734x   Same as 1661x in dark blue.

1735x   Same as 1661x stone colour instead of green ground.

1736x   Double flowing wreath, blue edge, French shape, as G T Rollason.

1737x   Malvern shape, dark blue and cane ground, leaves and hanging bells.

1738x   As 1737x in Victoria green instead of dark blue.

1739x   Same as 1701x Victoria green instead of Russet.

1740x   Same as 1698x Victoria green instead of russet, birds in panels.

1741x   Same as 1698x with birds in bottom as 1701x instead of flowers.

1742x   French shape, blue ground enamel, outside border as 1697x.

1743x   As 1742x in green ground instead of blue.

1744x   Match green stripe, printed in bronze, shaded in rose, French shape, gold toffee apples in centre.

1745x   As 1744x shaded in enamel blue instead of rose.

1746x   As 1744x not shaded in rose but a touch of rose in each leaf.

1747x   Leaf printed in bronze shaded in rose, joined up twig around centre.

1748x   As 1744x in flowing blue, maroon stripe instead of match green.

1749x   Round, gold edged, pink concentric lines.

1750x   As 1479x with gold and blue lines instead of pink.

1751x   Gold blue and gold lines, the blue thicker than others.

1752x   As 1698 with 2 birds, fly, landscape and tree in bottom by T Dovey.

1753x   Blue edge, blue green ground and wreaths, 1 large and 3 small sprigs in bottom.

1754x   As 1753x wreath painted on flowing blue, maroon ground instead of green, large sprig in bottom, blue edge.

1755x   Red and blue coloured border modelling, red centre line to saucer.

1756x   As 1755x with centre line to cup and saucer.

1757x   As 1756x with sprig in cup and saucer.

1758x   As 1755x on French shape.

1759x   As 1661x gold wiggle in bottom instead of printed flowers in dark blue ground, as Rollason.

1760x   As 1759x in russet brown instead of dark blue.

1761x   Witley shape, blue and gold scrolls and wreaths, flowers in centre by Parry.

1762x   Dark blue ground and scrolls, Men's flowers in centre.

1763x   Green ground and roses, panels of printed shells coloured in, 6-star centre.

1764x   Yellow or fawn (?) ground, shell scroll and twigs, coloured shell in bottom.

1765x   Green ground and flower sprigs, 3-star centre.

1766x   Trailing blue and fawn leaves on rim, Men's flowers in centre.

1767x   Russet brown and gilding flower centre (for bl ground and landscape see 1789x).

1768x   Dark blue, compartments of flowers, star centre as 1762x.

1769x   Russet ground, roses, 3 in saucer 2 in cup.

1770x   Green ground, 2 flower heads in panels, 1 in centre.

1771x   Russet ground and gilded scrolls, C scroll centre.

1772x   Russet brown and gilding, flower head and sprig centre.

1773x   Weedy gilding, printed flower sprays filled in.

1774x   Leaf festoons coloured and gold.

1775x   Coloured sprigs and gold sprigs.

1776x   Gold sprigs and long wreath of flowers.

1777x   Gilt as dessert 1766x gold wreath on edge.

1779x   Same as 1701x dark blue ground instead of russet.

1780x   Same as 1688x in blue green instead of fawn.

1781x   Same as 1688x in enamel silver grey instead of fawn.

1782x   Chailie coloured (flowing flowers) and French line as Brameld & Co printed in orange and filled in.

1783x   Matt blue, blue and gold entwining sprigs.

1784x   Queen's shape, sprigs as 1448x.

1785x   Witley edge, sprigs as Glos. 982x.

1786x   French shape, gold dentelle and inner matt blue wiggly line.

1787x   As 1786x rose coloured instead of matt blue.

1788x   Dark blue stripes, crossed by sprigs.

1789x   Dark blue ground, same pattern as 1767x blue ground.

1790x   As 1789x russet ground instead of dark blue, Witley shape.

1791x   As 1796x landscape instead of flowers and orange, in compartments, same star in bottom.

1792x   Witley shape, blue and gold rim, large landscape centre.

1793x   As 1762x in Victoria green instead of dark blue, landscape same size as 1792x.

1794x   As 1709x slighter, landscape instead of flowers, for same plant see 1857x.

1795x   Gilt as 1768x, slight landscape in compartments, star centre.

1796x   Blue border, blue and gold spray.

1797x   Green border, centre line in gold, no flowers.

1798x   As 1797x dark blue, printed flowers filled in.

1799x   Russet brown ground, shell coloured in each compartment.

1800x   As 1753x gold edge instead of blue.

1801x   As 1797x 3 large and small sprigs.

1802x   Blue green ground, flowing blue inside.

1803x   As 1802x in silver grey instead of blue green.

1804x   As 1802x Victoria green, painted in bronze instead of flowing blue.

1806x   Gilded C scrolls, landscape centre.

1807x   As 1789x plants instead of landscape as Du Cro, dark blue band.

1808x   Underglaze green ground, bird and gold sprigs in compartments, star in bottom.

1809x   Victoria green, bird and flies in compartments.

1810x   As 1791x birds and small landscape instead of landscape.

1811x   Green underglaze and cane ground, small landscape in bottom.

1812x   Same as 1767x group of flowers in bottom by S Wood, instead of roses and birds.

1813x   Same as 1793x Group of flowers in bottom instead of view.

1814x   Same as 1767x views instead of birds etc.

1815x   Antwerp coral on Malvern shape.

1816x   Same as 1802x Match green instead of blue green.

1817x   Same as 1749x Match green instead of pink.

1818x   Leaf, mouse ground on Dresden, Victoria green on leaves as Winchester MacGibbon – last set.

1819x   Leaf pattern painted in mouse, notched edge leaves touched here and there with Victoria green, large printed sprig in bottom of plate filled in, as Child's.

1820x   As 1818x blue green on leaves, Table ware Dresden.

1821x   Dark blue calx ground, large plant centre.

1822x   Dark blue and cane ground, groups in 2 compartments, sprig in other.

1823x   Dark blue and cane, large landscape in bottom.

1824x   Dark blue and cane, landscape large as above, 3 compartments in plate.

1825x   Dark blue ground, large curls, flowers in bottom.

1826x   3 sprigs round each plate, dessert, sprig centre.

1827x   Green on glaze ground and outlined gilding.

1828x   Flowing blue C scrolls and gold hanging bells.

1829x   Flow blue concentric band.

1830x   As 1829x Enamel kiln matt blue ground instead of flowing blue.

1831x   Malvern shape Victoria green and cane ground, small landscape in compartments.

1832x   As 1831x Russet brown instead of green, no cane, small groups of flowers in compartments, sprays in bottom.

1833x   Malvern shape, Victoria green glaze kiln, gilded sprigs.

1834x   Dark blue ground, C scroll compartments, sprig centre.

1835x   Russet brown and white, C scrolls, sprig centre.

1836x   Gold sprigs in arabesque panels.

1837x   Landscapes in arabesque panels, star centre.

1838x   Malvern shape, dark blue and cane, gold spray in bottom.

1839x   As 1838x Victoria green instead of dark blue.

1840x   Chinese pattern washed over in Victoria and green around border.

1841x   As 1840x printed in dove instead of orange, silver grey, grey ground instead of green.

1842x   Victoria green underglaze printed flowers from rockwork coloured in famille rose colours.

1843x   Flowing blue single wreath, Victoria green ground, blue edge, as 1691x.

1844x   Gilt as 1853x Malvern shape.

1845x   Same ground and gilding as 1799x with 1021x flowers coloured.

1846x   Same as 1838x dark blue.

1847x   Same as 1831x in dark blue instead of green.

1848x   French shape, dark blue jigsaw pattern and cane, dentelle edge.

1849x   As 1848x with hanging twigs.

1850x   As 1848x with gold wiggle.

1851x   As 1850x russet and cane instead of dark blue, sprig centre.

1852x   As 1850x, leafy centre.

1853x   Victoria green, entwining spriggy leaves.

1854x   Same as 1853x dark blue flowing

band instead of green.

1855x   Leafy twigs in gold and C scrolls.

1856x   Same as 1757x hair brown instead of green.

1857x   As 1709x, slighter and plant instead of group.

1858x   Dark blue jigsaw and cane, landscape centre.

1859x   Dark blue border and gilding, gilded centre sprig.

1860x   As 1840x printed in bronze and Maroon band instead of green.

1861x   Border band and wiggle inside, shoulder and foot line outside cup.

1862x   3 large 3 small flowers inside and outside cup.

1863x   Minton in bronze and coloured, hair brown edge (scrolling border with flowers and leaves, Oriental plant and grass in centre).

1864x   As 1863x breakfast ware on Malvern shape.

1865x   As 1864x breakfast ware on French.

1866x   Tea pattern gilt by Parry, dark blue and beige, small landscapes, Malvern.

1867x   Dark blue border and wiggle.

1868x   As 1840x printed in flowing blue instead of bronze, maroon instead of green.

1869x   Folowing blue and gold zig zags.

1870x   Dark blue and cane jigsaw, landscape in bottom.

1871x   As 1870x flowers in lieu of view in bottom.

1872x   Chinese border printed in flowing blue.

1873x   As 1730x maroon edge lines instead of gold.

1874x   As 1838x Victoria green instead of dark blue.

1875x   As 1636x maroon instead of dark flowing blue – as Allsups.

1876x   As 1636x Glaze kiln green instead of dark flowing blue on Malvern shape.

1877x   Blue edge, centre line to saucer, not cup. Malvern shape.

1878x   As 1877x, all blue, no gold.

1879x   Blue C scrolls in Grecian style inside rim.

1880x   As 1879x around rim.

1881x   French, blue edge, 3 large 3 small printed and coloured flowers.

1882x   Malvern, modelling gilded and with small twigs.

1883x   As 1882x without twigs.

1884x   Gilded and leaved border, Queen's fine footline as A-P (? Apsley Pellatt).

1885x   As 1569x in dark blue and cane leaves.

1886x   Gilded modelling round rim and with leaf and twig.

1887x   As 1838x with view in bottom, Malvern shape.

1888x   As 1886x, fine line outside cup and foot line.

1889x   As 1821x, russet brown ground instead of dark blue.

1890x   As 1569x in russet brown.

1891x   As 1764x plant in bottom in lieu of shell.

1892x   As 1867x Malvern instead of French, Winchester MacGibbon.

1893x   Pink ground and white between ground and gold, landscape done well by Beard.

1894x   As 1850x flowers in bottom instead of gold sprig.

1895x   French, leaves shaded green and yellow.

1896x   As 1569x done in maroon (instead of blue) cane leaves.

1897x   Blue, cane and maroon leaves, spiral spriggy centre.

1898x   3 compartments of grey and cane, spiral gilded centre.

1899x   As 1898x, small women's flowers in panels, star centre.

1900x   Cane outside blue border, sprig centre.

1901x   Green border and gilding, plain centre.

1902x   Dark green and cane border, gilded flower centre.

1903x   Green ground with pansy type flowers.

1904x	Pale green and cane border, gilded twiggy flower centre.		birds in bottom.
1905x	Pale green and cane panels and squiggle gilding, small flowers in colour.	*1931x*	Not tea pattern J G, stone ground rich gold Windsor.
1907x	Light green border, reserving small flowers, plain centre.	*1932x*	Dark blue jigsaw inside cane and gold border, 6-star centre.
1908x	Trailing flowers, inside border.	*1933x*	Same ground and gilding as 1898x, no orange.
1909x	Malvern, gilded on modelling, bird in landscape centre.	*1934x*	Green and gold wavy snake and 3-leaved shape.
1910x	Gilded C scrolls and leaves, 6-star centre.	*1935x*	Green shaded U shapes in gold.
1911x	As 1596x green instead of blue, French shape.	*1936x*	Matt blue diamonds and gold C scrolls, French.
1912x	French, enamel kiln green (pale), Antwerp blue flowers shaded in silver grey.	*1937x*	Matt green diamonds in gold arabesques.
1913x	As 1912x, no gold on leaves, gold edge only.	*1938x*	As 1937x, blue instead of green.
1914x	As 1912x printed in bronze, silver grey ground instead of green.	*1939x*	Pink band through gold hoops.
		1940x	As 1939x in matt blue.
1915x	As 1914x, gold edge and slap down handle only.	*1941x*	As 1939x in match green.
1916x	French zig zag wiggle in blue between gold.	*1942x*	Match green shaded 3-leafed shapes within gold bands.
1917x	Large gilded leaves and gold vine leaves and grapes.	*1943x*	As 1942x silver grey instead of match green.
1918x	As 1651x in dark blue ground.	*1944x*	As 1916x done in red, blue and green instead of blue and gold (green top, blue centre, red bottom).
1919x	As 1651x in pink ground.		
1920x	As 1651x in maroon ground.		
1921x	As 1704x in russet instead of green.		
		1945x	Same gilding as 1826x new coloured flowers instead of painted flower.
1922x	Windsor (New shape) white and gold barbed wire round edge.		
1923x	Windsor, matt blue border, small lacy sprigs inside and in bottom.	*1946x*	Kent shape, 3 blue and gold arabesque lines and dragged blue in inside line.
1924x	Windsor, maroon and cane, large and small sprigs.	*1947x*	As 1946x rose coloured instead of blue.
1925x	Windsor, Russet border, gilded on modelling.	*1948x*	Match green large band, squiggly gold and dragged blue, 8-star centre.
1926x	Windsor, blue and gold on modelling and similar squiggles inside rim.	*1949x*	Dark blue and red compartments, large flower shaded in rose, small in purple, similar centre.
1927x	Windsor, maroon and gold, maroon line inside border.	*1950x*	Silver grey crossed lines inside rim.
1928x	As 1927x blue instead of maroon.	*1951x*	As 1950x in dark blue instead of silver grey.
1929x	Silver grey border, scales and flowing blue inside, 8-star centre.	*1952x*	As 1950x in glaze kiln green.
		1954x	Silver grey spiral lines inside rim joined with gold twigs.
1930x	As 1909x dessert on Witley, 2	*1955x*	Dark blue shading on modelled leaves.
		1956x	As 1931x in dark blue instead of stone.
		1957x	As 1931x in green underglaze

instead of stone.

1958x   French, Match green and gold spikey twigs, large and small.

1959x   As 1939x in dark blue.

1960x   As 1959x in silver grey.

1961x   Thistle-like flower heads in purple on rose colour shaded gold leaves and twig, similar centre.

19862   French, dark blue thorny twig with rose and yellow flower heads.

1963x   Table pattern as 1948x pink ground instead of green.

1964x   As 1948x enamel blue ground.

1965x   Table pattern as 1962x without the flower, only gilt as 1958x.

1966x   Cane ground, red and rose coloured flowers, purple balls in compartments.

1967x   French, dark blue and gold, large thorny sprigs.

1968x   As 1929x enamel blue green instead of silver grey, stencilled gold butterfly wings in rim.

1969x   As 1963x maroon instead of matt blue.

1970x   As 1925x dark blue instead of russet.

1971x   As 1925x Victoria green instead of russet.

1972x   As 1931x russet brown (for this with view see 2/110).

1973x   As 1923x printed sprigs filled in instead of painted as Brameld.

1974x   As 1925x with inside border same as 1922x.

1975x   As 1807x birds and view instead of plant.

1976x   Malvern, gilded grapes and leaves, twiggy centre.

1977x   As 1925x in stone.

1978x   As 1926x match green instead of blue.

1979x   Blue dots inside edge and blue scrolls.

1980x   Silver grey C scrolls and gold.

1981x   As 1980x in dark blue instead of silver grey.

1982x   As 1980x in cane instead of silver grey

1983x   Silver grey spots in and out of gold C scrolls.

1984x   Green ground, scrolled panels and twiggy leaves in gold.

1985x   As 1984x, no ground, white and gold only.

1986x   C scrolls and dots in gold, landscape centre.

1987x   Blue and gold alternating lines and C scrolls.

1988x   Blue and rose trellising on rim, gold C scrolls and sprigs.

1989x   Match green border, gold C scrolls and sprigs.

1990x   As 1989x in enamel silver grey.

1991x   Dark blue border, gilt leaf and twiggy centre.

1992x   As 1991x, no ground, white and gold only.

1993x   Russet brown and gilt C scrolls and hanging twigs

1994x   As 1993x no ground, white and gold only.

1995x   Match green and squiggly gold arond rim, green and gold C scrolls.

1996x   Blue and gold leafy C scrolls.

1997x   Rose and gold and scrolls.

1998x   Blue and gold scrolls.

1999x   Silver grey large band, gold trellising.

2000x   Silver grey large band, gold trellising ending in 3 leaves.

2001x   As 1998x rose colour instead of blue – deleted.

2002x   As 1881x hair brown edge line instead of blue as Townsend.

2003x   As 1993x in Victoria green.

2004x   As 1909x landscape instead of bird.

2005x   As 1989x pink instead of green.

2006x   As 1801x (?), matt blue ground, no gold.

2007x   As 1989x dark blue instead of green.

2008x   As 1991x silver grey instead of dark blue.

2/1   New version, Pink ground border, landscape.

2/2   As 1896x Dresden flowers instead of landscape.

2/3   Inner panel of Vermicelli in dark blue.

2/4	As 2/3 glaze kiln green instead of dark blue.		line.
2/5	As 1930x landscape in bottom instead of 2 birds.	2/32	As 2/31, printed in mouse, line in mouse.
2/6	Leaves painted in enamel kiln black filled in match green, sprig in bottom, green edge.	2/33	Hawthorn print in Antwerp blue and gold.
		2/34	As 2/33 in mouse.
2/7	New shape, as 2/6, larger sprig in bottom.	2/35	Antwerp blue and gold 6-star centre.
2/8	As 2/6 gold edge instead of green, same shape.	2/36	Witley, Antwerp blue and gold zig zag, coloured fly centre.
2/9	As 2/7 Imperial shape, gold edge.	2/37	Matt blue, single palm frond in gold ovules.
2/10	Windsor, inner thick and thin lines of No. 1 Imperial chrome green.	2/38	Antwerp blue and gold jigsaw border.
2/11	Enamel silver grey border, gold sprigs and scrolls.	2/39	As 2/38 in dark blue.
2/12	Thick and thin blue line, Imperial shape.	2/40	As 2/36 dark blue instead of Antwerp blue, 4-star centre instead of bird and gold sprig.
2/13	As 2/23 in Match green.	2/41	Matt blue treble clef like signs over 2 gold lines.
2/14	French, Pale green band and gold line.	2/42	Malvern, as 2/41 same matt blue.
2/15	Victoria green ground, panels with 2 flower heads and gold.	2/43	As 723x birds in bottom instead of plants, Brunswick.
2/16	As 1980x no blue, white and gold only.	2/44	As 1931x white and gold with landscape in bottom, Windsor.
2/17	Is 2/6 on the Imperial shape.	2/45	As 1931x white and gold, no landscape in bottom, Windsor.
2/18	Is 2/13 in Matt blue 2 coats.	2/46	Victoria green and cane ground, landscape in centre.
2/19	Is 2/23 in matt blue 2 coats.		
2/20	Is 1976x on the Windsor shape, pattern outside cup.	2/47	Blue curling inner border.
		2/48	Blue and gold lines.
2/21	Is 1910x on Windsor, pattern outside cup.	2/49	Matt blue and gold broken diamonds, Windsor.
2/22	Is 1871x on Windsor, pattern outside cup.	2/50	Blue balls with 2 gold curves each side.
2/23	Maroon Imperial, very thick and a thin maroon band.	2/51	Imperial, gold slap downs in small panels.
2/24	This was done for Mr. Barry as 2/13 only that the grounded bands were ⅓rd narrower than the regular pattern 2/13.	2/52	Dark blue ground and gold bells, 6-star centre, Windsor.
		2/53	Gold dentelles, celeste ground, one coat and Grecian gilding inside.
2/25	Same gilding and shape as 1984x dark blue instead of green.	2/54	Malvern, pink ground, hanging flower head sprigs, 6-star centre.
2/26	Blue green border, flowing blue line and scroll below, Imperial.	2/55	Green border, 3 dots gold panels.
2/27	Imperial, printed dark blue jigsaw filled with fawn.	2/56	Russet ground with jigsaw compartments.
2/28	Imperial, printed dark blue jigsaw.	2/57	Gilded hanging bells in ovules, painted birds in bottom.
2/29	Imperial, Antwerp blue jigsaw and red, red border.	2/58	Matt blue border and gold sprigging.
2/30	As 2/29 red outlining jigsaws.		
2/31	As 2/29, no red except on rim and	2/59	Blue, green and gold leaves and

flowers, dotted border.

2/60 Concentric gold lines broken by scrolls, floral centre.

2/61 Round edge, 4 compartments in saucer 3 in cup, flower centre by S Wood, group flowers in bottom of cup.

2/62 Round edge, dragged blue, 3 compartments in saucer, 2 in cup.

2/63 Green edged compartments with flies, sprigs between, flower centre.

2/64 Hawthorn print in Antwerp blue.

2/65 Matt blue in panels, 6 in plate, 6-star centre.

2/66 Matt blue band inside gilded eyes.

2/67 Pink band around rim with gilded tadpole inside.

2/68 As 2/67 but no ground.

2/69 As 2/67 but celeste ground.

2/70 Silver grey ground printed with flowing blue and bit of gold in long trailing sprig, similar sprig in bottom.

2/71 As 2/61 no flowers, Imperial shape.

2/72 Match green ground inside gold diamonds, with dentelles, 8-star centre.

2/73 As 2/72 but with Matt blue.

2/74 As 2/73 celeste ground and 4-star centre.

2/75 Dark blue and cane border, dentelles, 6-star centre.

2/76 Chrome green border, 6-star centre.

2/77 Dark blue border to edge of plate, dentelles and 6-star centre.

2/78 Blue green ground with C scrolls and dragged blue.

2/79 As 2/70 Pink ground.

2/80 As 2/70 in blue green ground.

2/81 As 2/70 in match green ground.

2/82 As 1838x on the Imperial shape done outside and sprig in bottom.

2/83 As 2/30 but done in Victoria green.

2/84 As 2/36 but done in dark blue.

2/85 As 2/36 done in Victoria green.

2/86 As 2/14 matt blue 2 coats.

2/87 Cane with gold ovals outside dark blue and silver grey inside.

2/88 Russet shaded in silver grey outside.

2/89 Gold U shaded in underglaze green.

2/90 As 2/87 white and gold, Imperial shape.

2/91 Fine French edge, green and gilt oak leaves.

2/92 Dark blue and cane thistle heads and leaves.

2/93 Dark blue top and bottom of a band of figure of 8 shapes.

2/94 Cane filled U shapes outside dark blue ground.

2/95 Dark blue reserving panels of small flowers, gilded line and tadpoles.

2/96 Dark blue outside cane bat wings and ovals.

2/97 Matt blue band cutting shanked thick and thin gold lines.

2/98 Fine French line pale blue squiggles and trailing sprig.

2/99 As 2/98 without squiggles.

2/100 Alternating blue and gilt hanging leaf sprigs, snakey wiggles.

2/101 As 1821x in match green 2 coats, no gilding on ground.

2/102 Underglaze green and cane border with gilding, large plant centre by brock.

2/103 As 1441x in matt blue on Malvern shape.

2/104 As 1441x in pink on Malvern shape.

2/105 Russet ground either side of twisted napkin ring shapes shaded in silver blue, dentelles, landscape centre.

2/106 As 2/105 in dark blue instead of russet ? no landscape.

2/107 As 1930x with plant instead of bird.

2/108 Jigsaw pattern printed in Victoria green, elaborate star centre.

2/109 As 1442x pink instead of match green.

2/110 As 1972x with views.

2/111 As 2/40 in Antwerp blue instead of dark blue.

2/112 French green band and green lines, Brameld, very fine line outside.

2/113 As 2/112 in maroon as Brameld.

2/114 As 2/112 in matt blue as Brameld.

2/115 As 1930x but elaborate 3-star centre instead of birds.

2/116 As 1863x Minton, printed in bronze and coloured, no orange on leaves or coloured edge, done for Wiley, Wolverhampton.

2/117 As 2/66 in pink.

2/118 White and gold, elaborate gilding on modelled edge, star centre.

2/119 Brameld on Windsor shape, dark blue band outside as 2007x with gold lines.

2/120 As 2/119 in pink.

2/121 Dark blue and cane border, 5-star centre.

2/122 As 2/121 in green, no cane.

2/123 As 2/121 in russet brown and silver grey.

2/124 Russet and silver grey border, star centre.

2/125 Russet brown border, flowers in centre by Brock.

2/126 Green and cane border, 4-star centre.

2/127 Glasgow shape, blue lines and gilded border, plant centre and bottom by Brock.

2/128 Cane and silver grey border, plant by Brock.

2/129 Glasgow shape, gold border, large and small sprig panels and centre flowers by Brock.

2/130 Stone border, gilt as 2/126, star centre same.

2/131 Gilt as 1651x silver grey instead of russet, flowers same, on Malvern shape.

2/132 Match green border, large flower centre.

2/133 As 2/92 on Malvern, dark blue and cane, edge as Brameld.

2/134 As 2/133 in green on Malvern.

2/135 Gloster shape green ground and gold, gold sprig in centre.

2/136 As 2/135, sprig in cup and saucer.

2/137 As 2/136 pink instead of green, on Malvern.

2/138 As 2/136 enamel kiln silver grey on Malvern.

2/139 As 2/135 in pink, Gloster shape.

2/140 Malvern shape, Victoria green ground, printed in bronze with flowers filled in by women.

2/142 Red border, gold C scrolls, vine leaves and grapes.

2/143 Green border outside pink and gilded sprigs, large plant centre.

2/144 Jigsaw printed in Victoria green, brown lines.

2/145 As 2/135 maroon ground instead of green on Malvern shape.

2/146 Antwerp blue, dark leaf, scratch edge, Queen's.

2/147 Same pattern and gilding as 1930x with group of flowers instead of birds, Witley dessert ware.

2/148 Glaze kiln green outside pink border, small plant in centre.

2/149 As 2/122 in maroon, no cane.

2/150 As 2/123 in maroon but no silver grey.

2/151 As 2/135 in enamel russet on Malvern shape.

2/152 Cane and dark blue, gilding as 1930x plant in bottom by S Wood.

2/153 Mat blue bits in gilt arch shapes, fine line inside.

2/154 As 2/153, rose coloured instead of matt blue.

2/155 Malvern, Gold stripe each side of blue shape, cane leaves, 6-star centre.

2/156 Russet ground, petals shaded in silver grey, no star centre.

2/157 Blue band and thin gold and blue band inside.

2/158 As 2/157 in maroon.

2/159 As 2/157 in green.

2/160 V-shaped gilded rim vine leaf and grape sprigs and in centre.

2/161 Onion domes, 8 in saucer, 6 in cup, rose and forget-me-not centre.

2/162 As 2/161 rose shape in gold, gold star centre.

2/163 As 2/162 dark blue and cane above domes.

2/164 Gold star shapes arranged in triangular form round border, star centre.

2/165 As 2/164 but stars in blue and gold.

2/166 As 500x in maroon by Jones.

2/167 French edge, 2 blue and 2 gold
slaps alternating round rim.

2/168 Cane edge with dragged gold rim,
blue line inside, flower printed
in purple and filled in by
women in centre.

2/169 Hawthorn printed in Antwerp blue
and dark blue scrolls, 6-star
centre.

2/170 2 bands of chrome green 1 coat,
with flower sprigs between,
flower sprig centre.

2/171 Large and small Bourbon sprigs in
green, red and blue, 6 round
saucer, 5 outside cup.

2/172 Trailing blue and rose coloured
flowers.

2/173 Wild dog rose on French round,
gold edge and fine line inside
cup.

2/175 Arabesque panel and shanked gold
lines above blue squiggly line.

2/176 Gold and blue Arabesque panels
filled with flowers printed in
purple and filled in in colours.

2/177 Brown border, gilt and gold edge,
French shape.

2/178 Error, see 2/185.

2/179 Dessert Witley shape, plant in
centre and gold edge only.

2/180 Matt blue and gold thin stripes.

2/181 As 2/180 in chrome green,
Imperial.

2/182 As 2/180 in pink.

2/183 As 2/180 in maroon.

2/185 Imperial, chrome green leaf border,
gilded sprigs.

2/186 As 2/185 in silver grey G K.

2/187 As 2/185 in dark blue.

2/188 As 2/185 in russet brown.

2/189 Blue green ground, Greek snaky
meander ribbon printed in
bronze.

2/190 Is 2/189 in chrome green.

2/191 Is 2/189 in silver grey, enamel kiln.

2/192 Is 2/189 printed in Antwerp blue
grounded bluegreen, enamel
blue edge and line (no gold) but
done all blue as the gold in
2/189.

2/195 Mellon shape, as 2/189 in pink

ground.

2/196 As 2/195 celeste ground one coat.

2/197 As 2/196 Imperial chrome green
ground.

2/200 French shape breakfast, Antwerp
blue moss fibre, blue edge.

2/201 Windsor shape and gold line, fine
line inside cup.

2/202 Cane border outside jigsaw shapes
printed in glaze kiln green,
trailing gilt sprigs.

2/203 As 2/202 but printed in Antwerp
blue.

2/204 Dark blue stripes, thin gold stripes.

2/205 As 2/204 in silver grey on biscuit.

2/206 Glaze kiln green straps and pink
lines.

2/207 Dark blue scrolling fronds and half
flowers with gold.

2/208 Cleest border inside gold
diamonds, dentelles, 4-star
centre.

2/209 Blue ground, cane coloured leaf
panels with sprigs.

2/210 Dark blue leaf shapes, silver grey
flower heads.

2/211 Dark blue and cane ground,
landscape centre.

2/212 Dark blue leaves, russet panels
with gilded flowers, 6-star
centre.

2/213 Russet panels, stripes shaded in
silver grey, cane leaf heads,
elaborate 3-star centre.

2/214 Scrolls shaped in silver grey, russet
ground reserving sprigs various,
sprig in centre.

2/215 Cane and gold leaves, dark blue
ground, 8-star centre, inside
dentelles.

2/216 Russet ground with cane coloured
flower head, leaves shaded in
silver grey, plant centre by
Copson.

2/217 Glaze kiln green border outside
cane panels, gilt C scrolls,
landscape centre.

2/218 Blue and gold scrolled border.

2/219 As 2/218 in maroon.

2/220 As 2/218 in green.

2/221 Gilt leaf scrolls inside border.

2/222	Kent sprigs filled in in colours, large and small, fly centre.	2/245	Is 189x done outside Argyle shape with sprigs outside.
2/223	Maroon and gold fronds inside rim.	2/246	As 2/209 in Victoria green G K.
2/224	As 2/223 in blue.	2/247	As 2/207 white and gold.
2/225	Gilt double lines and half Greek key frets.	2/248	3 lines printed in Antwerp blue, gold either side.
2/226	Elaborately gilded panelled border with hanging flower heads, 12 star centre but not inside cup.	2/249	Russet leaves shaded under in dark blue, plant centre by Copson.
		2/250	As 2/10 but done upon Argyle shape.
2/227	As 2/207 but scrolls in glaze kiln green.	2/251	As 2/10 but done upon Argyle shape in pink.
2/228	Russet ground, cane panels with silver grey shaded flowers.	2/252	As 500x on Argyle shape, line inside and gold edge.
2/229	Gilded leaf and scrolled edge, square star shaped centre.	2/253	As 2/187 on Argyle, border outside cup.
2/230	Blue drags inside gilded leafshapes.	2/254	As 1847x in russet brown.
2/231	As 2/230 all done in gold.	2/255	As 2/135 in russet brown.
2/232	Cane and dentelle border, dark blue and silver grey panels.	2/256	Pink border, hanging gold sprigs.
		2/257	As 2/256 in celeste 2 coats.
2/233	Gilded x and 4 dotted scrolled border, panels of birds and flies in colour by I Dovey.	2/258	Jones pattern, white and gold, Fraser Glasgow.
		2/259	As 2/253 in silver grey on Argyle shape.
2/234	Silver grey shaded border, russet ground with flower sprigs 1 in bottom of cup and saucer.	2/260	As 2/253 in Victoria green on Argyle.
2/235	Dark blue outside cane, C scrolls in gold.	2/261	Victoria green leaves, cane scrolls, cane and green sprig centre, Malvern shape.
2/236	Russet ground, cane flower heads, silver grey shaded leaves, swirling star centre.	2/262	As 261 in dark blue and cane.
		2/263	Victoria green shade leaf edge, Malvern.
2/237	As 2/236 ground in dark blue, cane leaves, no cane flowers.	2/264	As 2/263 shaded in silver grey.
2/238	Malvern, celeste 2 coats ground, dentelles inside, views in centre.	2/265	Antwerp blue printed hawthorn rim outside, ribbon shaded silvery grey.
2/239	As 2/208 in dark blue.	2/266	As 2/265 ribbon printed in bronze instead of Antwerp blue on Argyle.
2/240	Dessert as 2/216 in dark blue, cane leaves, no cane flower and no sprig in centre.		
2/241	Dark blue leaves, cane shaded panels, russeted ground, 6-star centre but not in cup.	2/267	As 2/265 Ribbon in red centre and silver grey shaded.
		2/268	As 2/239 maroon 2 coats instead of dark blue, Argyle.
2/242	Russet ground, cane and silver grey shaded leaf and C scrolls.	2/269	Blue green, blue shaded ribbon and sprig, Argyle.
2/243	Leaf scrolls and ++ in gold, cane flower heads, Dresden Parrot on stump of tree in the centre by S Dovey.	2/270	As 2/226 dark blue leaf and cane.
		2/271	As 2/270 Green leaf and cane.
		2/272	As 2/226 in red.
		2/273	As 2/226 in blue.
2/244	Is 500 done outside Argyle shape with lines inside cup and gold edge.	2/274	As 2/95 on Argyle, 2 panels in cup and 3 in saucer.

2/275   Argyle Victoria green on biscuit, gilded reserve flower heads, green spots.

2/276   As 2/275 in dark blue.

2/277   Elaborately gilded modelling, 4-star centre.

2/278   Red ground border, gilt trailing sprig.

2/279   As 2/278 in pink, this is all colour, no gold.

2/280   As 2/270 in chrome green.

2/281   Greeny blue, red and gold beetle-like shape round rim.

2/282   Gold, blue and thin red lines, white edge.

2/283   Gold, green and thin red lines, white edge.

2/284   Enamelled blue edge, hanging arch shapes printed in Antwerp blue below silver grey ground.

2/285   As 2/284 printed in Antwerp blue, gold edge and bits.

2/286   As 2/284 printed in Antwerp blue gold bits, blue edge.

2/287   As 2/286 printed in Antwerp blue, gold edge, fine gold line outside.

2/288   As 2/286 printed in bronze, gold bits, red ground and gold edge.

2/289   As 2/288 green ground instead of red.

2/290   As 2/288 pink ground instead of red.

2/291   As 2/288 in bronze and pink ground, pink edge.

2/292   As 2/288, red ground, every other arch gilded.

2/293   As 2/288 on Malvern, printed in bronze.

2/294   As 2/293 printed in Antwerp blue, silver grey ground.

2/295   As 2/293 printed in bronze, maroon ground.

2/296   As 2/293 printed in bronze, green ground.

2/297   As 2/278 in pink, no gold, ground a little distance from edge.

2/298   As 2/297 in green.

2/299   Blue ground, C scroll and dot gold edge, dentelles centre.

2/300   Pink ground, C scroll gilding, gold edge.

2/301   Spiky twigs and trellis in gold, gold edge.

2/302   Vermicelli in gold.

2/303   Gilded border with leaf scrolls, barbed wire and dots.

2/304   Gold wavy edge, gilded panels with sprigs, star centre.

2/305   Rich white and gold, Glasgow shape.

2/306   Same gilding as 1601x white and gold, no green or cane leaf.

2/307   As 2/229 on Argyle.

2/308   As 2/278 on Argyle, done outside.

2/309   As 2/238 but dark blue ground and cane edge.

2/310   As 2/295 on Argyle done outside, line inside.

2/311   As 2/303 but inside border to cups as 2/118.

2/312   As 2/293 printed in bronze, Queen's brown, Malvern shape.

2/313   As 2/293 painted in silver grey, pink ground, Argyle.

2/314   Pink ground, printed in silver grey, gold bits, as done for Brian-Newcastle.

2/315   Printed in bronze, Maroon ground, as above.

2/316   Printed Saxon border in silver grey and blue green ground.

2/317   As 2/316 printed in bronze, green ground and gold, French.

2/318   As 2/295 printed in Antwerp blue, silver grey, Argyle.

2/319   As 2/296 printed in bronze, chrome green ground.

2/320   Gilded leaf scrolls and hanging twigs.

2/321   Cane and dark blue ground, leaf scrolls left white, 6-star centre, no star in cup. (This on Exhibition shape, see 2/470.)